Ties
That Bind

Ties
That Bind

A Social Contracts
Approach to Business Ethics

Thomas Donaldson

Thomas W. Dunfee

Harvard Business School Press

Boston, Massachusetts

Library of Congress Cataloging-in-Publication Data
Donaldson, Thomas, 1945–
    Ties that bind: a social contracts approach to business ethics /
Thomas Donaldson and Thomas W. Dunfee
        p.   cm.
    Includes bibliographical references and index.
    ISBN 0-87584-727-7 (alk. paper)
    1. Business ethics. 2. Social contract. I. Dunfee, Thomas W.
II. Title.
HF5387.D65 1999   98-42222
174' .4—dc21   CIP

Contents

Preface   VII

1   Why Contracts?   1

2   The Social Contract for Business   25

3   Hypernorms: Universal Limits on Community Consent   49

4   Ethical Norms and Moral Free Space   83

5   Hypernorms Revealed: The Hypernorm
     of Necessary Social Efficiency   117

6   Moral Free Space Revealed   139

7   ISCT and Ethical Decision Making: Priorities, Proxies,
     and Patterns   175

8   When Ethics Travel: The Promise and Peril of Global
     Business Ethics   213

9   Social Contracts and Stakeholder Obligations   235

     Notes   263

     References   271

     Index   287

     About the Authors   305

Preface

Corporate leaders face ethical dilemmas everywhere, but nowhere is their challenge greater than on the global stage. A particularly vivid example was the call in the mid-1990s for Royal Dutch Shell to intercede in Nigeria to prevent the execution of the environmental activist and author Ken Saro-Wiwa. Shell procrastinated and ultimately decided to send a weak letter of protest. This action did not satisfy the critics who subjected Shell to boycotts and intense public criticism after Saro-Wiwa was hanged. The implication was that Shell was in a better position to exercise leverage against the military government of Nigeria than nation-states or the UN. Yet, it was only a few years ago that major global companies were criticized for dominating vulnerable governments for their own advantage: ITT in Chile, Exxon in Italy, Northrop in Japan. Now business critics suddenly want global corporations to take action. The dilemma was captured in the July 20, 1996, issue of the *Economist:* "Multinationals used to bully poor countries. Maybe they should start again."

But by whose standards should business be judged? What explains the changing expectations for business behavior? When should managers, for example, go along with the expectations they find in different cultures? Do corporations have any obligation to protect the human rights of those affected by their decisions? In this book, we propose the concept of a social contract to help unravel these issues.

In one sense, the social contract concept is as old as philosophical speculation. Surely, the "compact" with God spoken of in the Old Testament and the imaginary agreement among hypothetical members of the state in Plato's *Republic* (1968) are influential examples of social contracts in intellectual history. The social contract writings of Locke, Rousseau, and Hobbes were blueprints for social change in modern Europe. Today, the venerable contractarian device promises striking contributions to modern business issues. A growing wave of efforts in the 1980s and early 1990s applied contractarian thinking to a vast range of economic issues. During the same period, the sophistication and rigor of contractarian theoretical frameworks increased dramatically. This volume is dedicated to taking another important step in the evolution of contractarian thought about economic issues.

Our aim is to extend significantly the application of social contracts to business. In so doing we cut against the grain. Business ethics, we assert, is more a bundle of shared understandings than a set of fixed pronouncements. It exists as a rich and at times even internally inconsistent mosaic. Business ethics should be viewed more as a story in the process of being written than as a moral code like the Ten Commandments. It can and should, we argue, adjust over time—to evolving technology, and to the cultural or religious attitudes of particular economic communities.

At the same time, there exist principles so fundamental that they categorically command our allegiance. These include the principles of fairness, of respect for other people, and of the value of integrity. We grant these eagerly. But these principles turn out to be consistent with many possible business worlds. In business ethics, then, the challenge is for business communities to shape *their ethical worlds* in such a way that they are not only fair but relevant. The challenge is to shape their worlds so that they are faithful to timeless intuitions, but also are reflective of their members' more local values, including ones that are cultural or religious.

Aiding our effort in this book is the fact that the terminology of social contracts is to some extent already familiar to business managers. Research has shown that many managers already tend to think in terms of unwritten agreements and unspoken promises. It has shown (Reidenbach & Robin, 1990; Robertson & Ross, 1995) potential far-reaching receptivity to ethical standards grounded in contractarian concepts. Even so, the specific implications still need to be put into a logical structure. Managers confronted with urgent ethical dilemmas cannot be expected to pause in the middle of hectic schedules to reflect carefully on the detailed implications of the terms of a hypothetical social contract or to search for microsocial contract norms. Thus, we provide some "translator" concepts, suitable for hands-on application to day-to-day business problems whenever possible.

Acknowledgments

Ed Hartman provided extensive and insightful comments on the first draft of the manuscript, and to him we are much indebted. Greg Dees provided extremely helpful, cogent comments. Their influence is evident in numerous places in the manuscript. Beyond the elaborate comments of Greg and Ed, we were aided immensely by two anonymous HBSP reviewers and also by helpful suggestions made by Deborah Cohen, Bill Frederick, Mark Hanna, Don Mayer, Iwao Taka, and Danielle Warren. We, of course, bear the final responsibility for any shortcomings.

We would also like to acknowledge the outstanding research assistance of Melissa Choi, Ashley Damron, Jennifer Dunfee, and Jonathan Nunes. Lauretta Tomasco provided her usual highly competent, cheery assistance in assembling the final manuscript. Nikki Sabin of the Harvard Business School Press deftly kept our feet to the fire to insure that the book was finished.

We appreciate the useful comments of many colleagues, both the critics and the fellow travelers. Though too numerous to mention, you have made this a stimulating and entertaining journey!

In writing this book, we have on occasion used material from 3 earlier writings. Chapter 1 draws on material from Donaldson, T. 1998. Negotiated integrity: The social contracts of business. Paper presented at the Ethics of Contract and Other Promises Conference, Southern Methodist University, 25 February. We thank the editors of the *Academy of Management Review, American Business Law Journal*, the *Business Ethics Quarterly*, and *Economics and Philosophy* for their permission to use material from the following sources:

Donaldson, T., & Dunfee, T. W. 1994. Toward a unified conception of business ethics: Integrative social contracts theory. *Academy of Management Review*, 19(2): 252–284. Reprinted with permission of Academy of Management, P.O. Box 3020, Briarcliff Manor, NY 10510-8020. Reproduced by permission of the publisher via Copyright Clearance Center.

Dunfee, T. W. 1996. On the synergistic, interdependent, relationship of business to ethics and law. *American Business Law Journal*, 34(2): 317–326. Reprinted with permission of the *American Business Law Journal*.

Dunfee, T. W., & Donaldson, T. 1995. Contractarian business ethics: Current status and next steps. *Business Ethics Quarterly,* 5(2): 173–186.

Donaldson, T., & Dunfee, T. W. 1995. Integrative social contracts theory: A communitarian conception of economic ethics. *Economics and Philosophy,* 11(61): 85–112. © 1995 Cambridge University Press. Reprinted with the permission of Cambridge University Press.

Ties
That Bind

I

Why Contracts?

Multinationals are being dragged down by "a ghost in the system . . .
some sort of slight blurring that causes us to make subtle, but in the end
far-reaching, mistakes in assessing developments."

—Cor Herkstroter, Chairman, Royal Dutch Shell (*Economist* 1997: 65)

In downtown Dallas, Texas, stands a statue of two businessmen in
the act of shaking hands. The statue and the idea it expresses have
deep importance for ethics, and even greater significance for business
ethics. People shake hands. They give their word. No writing; no
lawyers. Their word is enough. Even this simple concept of the sanc-
tity of a handshake can ennoble business.

In this book we explore an important implication of such a handshake, one that reaches far beyond two individuals. For the same logic
that sanctifies a handshake between two individuals also sanctifies the
agreements in economic communities that are woven throughout the
business world. These are the informal but critical agreements—or
"social contracts"—that provide the warp and woof of economic life.
There are, we will suggest, agreements that exist within industries,
national economies, trade groups, and corporations; further, we will
argue that these implicit "contracts" are critical for understanding
business ethics. It is not accidental that this notion of a contract, sym-
bolized by the handshake, is at once the paradigmatic notion of business and the key to unlocking many of the deeper problems of business ethics. In this chapter, we will sketch the case for employing
social contracts in business.

The Example of Shell Oil in the Mid-1990s

Let us begin by considering a case. In 1997 the *Economist* ran an article with the unusual title, "Shellman says sorry." The "Shellman"
referred to was Mr. Herkstroter, chairman of the Dutch half of Shell.
The article described how Herkstroter accepted responsibility for key

environmental mistakes, mistakes that had catapulted Shell into one of its worst public-relations nightmares in its history. The company's problems, it turned out, were ethical ones.

One of those ethical problems concerned Nigeria. The company was criticized for supporting a military government that had responded with rights-offending violence to criticisms about environmental policies. Shell had been pushing for a $3.6 billion gas-development project in the Nigerian delta. Some Nigerians, outraged by the possible environmental impact of the gas project, complained loudly. Several tribesmen were killed in the violence that followed. In response, the Nigerian government imprisoned many activists and threatened even worse punishments. After a questionable trial, the Nigerian government ended up hanging nine environmental activists from the Ogoni region, including author Ken Saro-Wiwa (*Economist*, 1995a). Critics asserted that Shell's strategy had helped to precipitate the trial, and that had the company made even a small effort, the executions would never have occurred.

Another problem for Shell concerned a large oil-buoy storage facility in the North Sea named the Brent Spar. In the summer of 1995, just as the company was about to sink the rig six thousand feet deep in the North Atlantic, activist groups intervened, complaining that oil and heavy metals would contaminate the environment. The Greenpeace organization, in particular, was determined to stop the operation, and its members tried to intercept the rig using small boats—to the horror of European television viewers and Shell's public-affairs professionals. Some of Greenpeace's tiny boats were almost sunk by aggressive Shell ships, and the entire David and Goliath spectacle was played out on the nightly news (*Economist*, 1995b). Shell quickly became the object of a gas boycott by millions of European consumers, and was denounced during violent demonstrations in Germany (Harveson & Corzine, 1997). The company finally yielded to the protests, and decided against sinking the rig in the North Atlantic. In 1978, three years after the original event, the Brent Spar remained moored in a Norwegian fjord, with Shell having spent millions of dollars developing alternative dumping plans (*Oil and Gas Journal*, 1997). But even at that time, the company had not yet decided which disposal plan to choose (Harveson & Corzine, 1997).

Shell's travails were ethical in nature, and harmful to its standing in both the business world and the eyes of the public. In 1997 the *Financial Times* identified Shell's ethical problems as the key reason for the company's dramatic drop in ranking in its annual survey of Europe's most respected companies. Even Shell's public-relations counteroffensive drew criticisms. Shell argued that its Nigerian oil plans benefited everyone in Nigeria, and further that because it was a private company it should have done just as it did, i.e., stay out of politics. In response, the *Economist* noted that as Nigeria's biggest producer of oil, Shell generated 50 percent of the government's revenues—revenues often embezzled by government officials and nearly always misspent. As the magazine pointed out, Shell could hardly pretend to have no political impact on Nigeria (*Economist*, 1995a). One good-sized U.S. city registered its protest by boycotting all of Shell's products (Edmond, 1997). Even God seemed to be rooting against Shell. The World Council of Churches accused Shell's Nigerian unit of polluting the Ogoni area and of inertia in the face of the government's brutality (Knott, 1997).[1]

How had Shell, a company renowned for its "principles" and Dutch/English integrity, gone bad? Had it lost its sense of right and wrong? Or did the explanation lie deeper—in the need for Shell's ethical awareness to grow with the evolution of global social problems?

We begin this book with the daunting and difficult questions surrounding Shell's predicament because we believe their answers lead to deeper issues—and down an intriguing road of exploration that finally terminates with social contracts. Answering these questions successfully, we believe, requires a different approach to business ethics, an approach that exposes the hidden but all-important understandings or "contracts" that bind industries, companies, and economic systems into moral communities. It is in these economic communities, and in the implicit understandings that provide their ethical glue, that the stuff of business ethics is found. The approach we take is also one that, ironically, references a yet deeper, and universal "contract" superseding all the individual ones. We call the social contract theory we describe in this book Integrative Social Contracts Theory, or ISCT.

Shell Oil: Exploring beneath the Surface

Shell's response to its troubles was monumental, and largely successful. Indeed, the Nigeria/Brent Spar episode proved to be a nearly unprecedented learning experience for the company. It is important to see what it was that Shell learned, and how its understanding was conditioned by a new awareness of the relevance of community-born ethics.

Shell turned upside down in the aftermath of the Nigeria/Brent Spar episodes. One of its actions was to organize roundtables in four-teen countries that brought together 159 Shell executives and 145 external participants including members of pressure groups, acade-mics, researchers, journalists, and other opinion formers (Limited, 1996: 3). It listened to the company's enemies as well as its friends. Through this process Shell articulated a commitment to health, safety, and the environment that recognized the goals of causing "no harm" to people and "protect[ing] the environment." These goals were implemented in striking ways, as the company

- required contractors to manage health, safety, and the environment (HSE) in line with this policy.

- required joint ventures under its operational control to apply this policy, and used its influence to promote it in its other ventures.

- included HSE performance in the appraisal of all staff and rewarded accordingly (Dutch/Shell, 1998).

Most important of all, Shell changed its famous underlying Princi-ples. In its revised statement of business principles published in 1997, Shell for the first time formally committed itself to supporting "fun-damental human rights in line with the legitimate role of business" (Harveson & Corzine, 1997).

Such dramatic actions clearly constituted a risk for Shell. "This opens a potential Pandora's box," says Mr. John Elkington, chairman of SustaiNability, a London-based consultancy. "If you tell some gov-ernments you're going to discuss human rights, you might not get a project at all" (Wagstyl & Corzine, 1997).

But the most interesting question to ask was not exactly what Shell had done, but *why* it had done it. Shell's initiatives in the wake of Nigeria and Brent Spar signaled, among other things, a fuller recogni-tion of the subtlety of ethics. Herkstroter, Shell's chairman, was quoted as saying that he believed that multinationals were being dragged down by what he calls "a ghost in the system . . . [by] some sort of slight blurring that causes us to make subtle, but in the end far-reaching, mistakes in assessing developments" (*Economist*, 1997).

Shell's actions signaled a new recognition of the importance of soci-ety's changing moral expectations around the globe. A Shell report noted:

- "Demographics— . . . Migration is on the increase. For example 20 million immigrants have arrived in the USA in the last 30 years. Large proportions of these have been Hispanic or Asian."

- "Social structures—new nationalist sentiment has emerged and sometimes erupted, undermining old political structures. Religious fundamentalism is a further threat to the status quo."

- "Sustainability of resources—No-one now takes for granted that, when scarcity strikes, more resources will automatically be found or produced. . . . [T]he pressure not to waste has grown rapidly in the last 20 years" (Limited, 1996: 6).

Shell's report concluded: "Expectations [of people around the world] have changed and are changing. Expectations of government (more cynical and diminishing), just as much as expectations of multinational enterprises (more cynical and more demanding), are shifting" (Limited, 1996: 6).

Opaque Glass: The Impetus for Social Contracts

For Shell the Nigeria and Brent Spar episodes put issues of changing societal expectations in sharp relief. They forced Shell, for example, to recognize that Europeans had shifted their ethical attitudes toward the environment. Indeed, the incidents forced Shell to recognize that people everywhere around the world, and not only in Europe, had come to place a heightened value on the conservation of natural resources. From the vantage point of this new, evolving ethical perspective of the environment, multinationals had nontrivial responsibilities. The episodes further forced Shell to recognize that some countries, Nigeria for example, had distinctly *non*-European ethical expectations for companies. As long as Shell could maintain a monolithic conception of its own ethics, and could, as a part of that monolithic conception, draw a sharp distinction between private economic activity on the one hand and public/governmental activity on the other, it could downplay its responsibilities in Nigeria. Private, for-profit companies like Shell should not be concerned about human rights or the environment because they were not *public* entities with *public* responsibilities—or so Shell's conception went. But once Shell began to understand that people in Nigeria and, indeed, citizens of other emerging economies expected large multinationals to play a public role, it was forced to reconcile its own conception of responsibilities with theirs. The evolving ethical attitudes of emerging economies, Shell came to see, had to be factored into Shell's own interpretation of its global ethical responsibilities. In general, then, the episodes had the effect of forcing Shell to recognize that unless it confronted global and regional changes in attitudes, it could not draw a discernible line between ethical and unethical behavior for itself.

In the language that we will be using in this book, Brent Spar and Nigeria may be said to have forced Shell to recognize the importance of the "social contracts" that framed its business activities. By the late 1990s, Shell had come to view the implicit agreements or "extant social contracts" that evolved in Europe, Nigeria, and elsewhere as critical components of its business context. Shell increasingly monitored these changing communal understandings, and they played a growing role in the company's planning and actions. As mentioned earlier, Shell developed systems during the late 1990s to collect data and input from many sources, including even activist environmental and political organizations, in order to be able to utilize that information in its planning. From the vantage point of social contracts, Shell's efforts made good sense.

The phenomenon of a large company such as Shell coming to factor social contracts into its ethical decision making may seem ironic. After all, ethics has been a subject that people have likened to stone; ethics must be rock-hard, they assume, or "situational" ethics may intrude. "Situational" or "conditional" ethics, in turn, popular wisdom has it, lead to the worst sort of ethical rationalization. Someone who is honest when it is convenient to be honest, and dishonest when it is not, is said to be morally bankrupt.

The approach of social contracts that we plan to defend does not overturn this popular wisdom. Our approach confirms that the social contracts that arise from specific cultural and geographic contexts have legitimacy—but only within *limits*. It acknowledges the boundaries of certain transcultural truths, for example, transcultural concepts such as the "human rights" referenced in Shell's revised Principles. The social contract approach we will adopt holds that any social contract existing outside these boundaries must be deemed an illegitimate one. In this sense, all particular or "microsocial" contracts, whether they exist at the national, industry, or corporate level, must conform to a hypothetical "macrosocial" contract that lays down objective moral boundaries for any social contracting.

But our approach does assert that morality is conditional or situational, at least in the sense that two conflicting conceptions of ethics can sometimes both be valid, and also in the sense that community agreements about ethics often matter. Two economic systems need not have precisely the same conception of the ethics of insider trading, for example—their views about what is wrong with insider trading may differ, yet both may be legitimate. And an economic actor such as Shell that attempts to discern its ethical responsibilities without recognizing the social contracts in the communities it impacts can fall prey to moral blindness.

As social contracts change, so too do the challenges for business. It is difficult to deny that the ethical game in business is played by different rules, and harbors different penalties and benefits, than it did decades ago. Broad shifts of moral consensus have impacted many fronts. In subtle but farther reaching shifts, managers and members of the general public have gradually redefined their view of the underlying responsibilities of large corporations. The view has shifted from attitudes half a century ago that limited the responsibilities of companies largely to that of producing goods and services at reasonable prices, to a view today where corporations are held responsible for a variety of fairness and quality-of-life issues. In companies throughout the world, gender issues, racial issues, and questions of the clash or compatibility between work and family, are now assumed to be the proper province of corporate management. Many managers now think twice before firing talented women or minorities. Managers themselves have adjusted their view of the proper objectives of corporations. Since Brenner and Molander's update of Baumhart's seminal survey of the ethical opinions of 1961 *Harvard Business Review* readers appeared in the late 1970s (Brenner & Molander, 1977), the percentage of corporate managers who consider the proper function of the corporation to lie beyond merely maximizing return on investment for share owners has remained well above 60 percent. Whether this shift is in the right direction, and whether it is mindful of the narrow objectives of most for-profit corporations, remains hotly debated. But the existence and size of the shift cannot be doubted.

Some shifts in social contracts are driven by the advent of new knowledge and awareness. One hundred years ago, few cared about the moral implications of the manufacture of cigarettes. Today, the tobacco industry and the devil are seen as fellow conspirators. Public ethical opinion, which until recently confined itself to the morality of production and marketing of cigarettes, now extends one layer deeper to the morality of investment. In turn, public opinion targets not only tobacco manufacturers, but also tobacco investors. Furthermore, hundreds of investment funds have been criticized for merely owning stock in companies that engage in a range of ethically suspect activities, including manufacturing cigarettes, sourcing products from overseas suppliers using child labor, netting dolphins in catching tuna, killing whales, mistreating animals in experiments, and neglecting the environment. On Wall Street, the confusion has also spawned new product lines. So-called social investment funds, ones that apply various screens on their investment portfolios, have become numerous, and now control hundreds of billions of dollars of private money (Lydenberg, 1996).

Shell, then, with its troubles in the 1990s, stands as an example of a much broader challenge to the existing methods of approaching ethical issues in business. It is a challenge that confronts scholars as well as practitioners. Both practitioners and scholars have often neglected to examine the impact of varying and changing community standards on moral practice. Both have often failed to grasp the significance of company-specific, industry-specific, or culture-specific standards. And both have sometimes overlooked the fact that moral clarity can only exist when settled convictions about right and wrong are internalized by business communities.

As the foregoing discussion suggests, the challenge of a social contracts approach to business ethics is to find a theory that accepts basic moral precepts, such as "Don't lie," "Be fair," and "Respect the environment," even as it refuses to pretend that these broad-brushed concepts provide full moral clarity. The challenge is to articulate an approach that holds fundamental truths to be relevant even as it accounts for legitimate differences in business communities and historical periods. Our inability to do so to date is surprising insofar as we have known for decades that the standards of business ethics change. In for-profit corporations, norms of disclosure and competitive practice vary according to industry and strategic context (Robertson & Nicholson, 1996: 1095–1104). Ethical standards of organizational leadership are known to vary dramatically from organization to organization (Posner & Schmidt, 1996).

One response has been simply to abandon the search for a satisfactory ethical theory altogether. Regrettably, this is the choice made by scores of business ethics researchers; a significant component of the business ethics literature fails to identify its foundations in ethical theory. We find this wrongheaded. Without some theoretical compass, business ethics too often reflects either a particular author's intuitive response or political bias. Without a compass, the analysis of individual case studies often is used as a tacit substitute for general theory, and false inferences are drawn and applied. More than once, business ethics has deserved the criticism sometimes made in common-law contexts that "hard cases make bad law." Principles and solutions that arise from the intuitions of individuals, and that are not tested by theoretical concepts with recognized merit, frequently confuse more than they enlighten.

Why, then, has a workable theory been so elusive?

Two Problems and a Solution

Problem 1: A Conflict of Methodology in the Field of Business Ethics

From one vantage point, the search for theory has been frustrated because the field of business ethics has been mired in dual methodologies. The confusion results from the sharp dichotomy in research methods used to analyze business ethics. One group of researchers approaches business ethics through empirical or behavioral ideas, i.e., through concepts that describe and explain factual states of affairs, such as managerial motivation, organizational accountability structures, and relationships between ethical behavior and financial performance. In other words, this camp focuses on the "is" of economic affairs. The other camp focuses on normative concepts, i.e., ideas that, while not necessarily grounded in existing business practices and structures, are what ethicists call "prescriptive." They guide us to what we should do. In this vein, most philosophers remind us that no amount of empirical accuracy, including an infinite array of facts, can ever by itself add up to an "ought" (Sorley, 1904/1969). To suppose that one can deduce an "ought" from an "is," or, what amounts to the same thing, that one can deduce a normative ethical conclusion from empirical research, is to commit a logical mistake some dub the "naturalistic fallacy" (Moore, 1903/1951: 10–14).

These two approaches to business ethics, which we will call the "empirical" and the "normative," have produced two powerful streams of business research. Over the last fifteen years, researchers with philosophical training have introduced purely normative, nonempirical methods to the study of business ethics, just as they introduced them earlier to the fields of legal and medical ethics. In this way, the philosophical tradition of ethical theory has contributed rigor to ongoing discussions of business ethics (Barry, 1982; Bowie,

1988; Donaldson, 1982; Freeman & Gilbert, 1988; French, 1979; Gauthier, 1986; Ladd, 1970; May, 1987; Nickel, 1974; Sen, 1985; Shue, 1981).

Meanwhile, using the alternative perspective, business school researchers with training in empirical methods have applied their techniques (often adapted from existing approaches in marketing, finance, and elsewhere) to study important issues in corporate and organizational ethics (Akaah & Riordan, 1989; Cochran & Wood, 1984; Fritzsche & Becker, 1984; Hunt, Wood & Chonko, 1989; Kabanoff, Waldersee & Cohen, 1995; Trevino & Youngblood, 1990; see particularly Randall & Gibson, 1990, and sources cited therein for an extensive overview of this literature). This research has been extended by the development of frameworks suggesting relationships among key behavior variables and interconnections between the two divergent streams of research (Ferrell & Gresham, 1985; Hunt & Vitell, 1986; Jones, 1991; Trevino, 1986). These frameworks focus on predicting or understanding ethical behavior, and they have generally either incorporated broad statements of ethical theories, such as utilitarianism, rights, and justice (Ferrell & Gresham, 1985), or relied upon concepts from moral psychology (Jones, 1991; Trevino, 1986).

But while each side of the methodological standoff sometimes recognizes conclusions from the other side, attempts to integrate the two have been rare. This has resulted in a methodological chasm difficult to cross. Two exceptions are the recent works of William Frederick and Thomas Jones. Both attempt to establish broad lines of connection between normative and empirical theory. Frederick's book, *Values, Nature and Culture in the American Corporation* (1995), is one of the first truly "integrative" theories of business ethics. It is "integrative," moreover, in the full sense defined by Linda Trevino and Gary Weaver (1994), who have accurately identified three distinct types of normative/empirical approaches to ethics.[2] In their terms, Frederick's theory is more than a merely "parallel" theory that fashions an ad hoc series of connections between the two streams of normative and empirical inquiry. And it is more than a "symbiotic" theory, which allows a merely pragmatic rather than theoretical merger of the normative and empirical. Instead, it is an attempt at a truly "integrative" theory that fuses the empirical into the normative (Trevino & Weaver, 1994). Frederick attempts the integration by noting that values do not stand apart from us, or we from them. All values are securely anchored within nature. He argues that three fundamental "clusters" of values exist, entitled respectively the "econo-

mizing," the "aggrandizement of power," and the "ecologizing" clusters. If these three clusters are incompatible with each other, and if
this incompatibility explains fundamental tensions in business and
society, as Frederick asserts, then this is big news for business ethics
researchers.[3]

But no matter how powerful an analytic tool Frederick's theory
turns out to be, some wonder whether he has succeeded in fully integrating the normative and the empirical (Donaldson, 1994). To claim
that values *emerge out of* biological processes is not the same as saying that values are to be fully *explained by* biological processes. Reasons are not always causes. For example, mathematical reasoning in
one sense is caused by the biological processes of brain development.
But it goes without saying that understanding the Pythagorean Theo-
rem, or how calculus works, is not tantamount to understanding biology or brains. As philosophers of science note, the logic of many
explanation types is simply noncausal.[4] Indeed, in one important
sense, the claim that values derive causally from nature is noncontroversial—from where else could they come, one might ask, but from
nature? This is not to detract from Frederick's theory; it is merely to
put it in its proper context.

Thomas Jones's framework, like Frederick's, has some important
parallels with the integrative approach introduced in this book. His
emphasis on the context of ethical decision making and on the notion
that "human beings may respond differentially to moral issues in a
way that is systematically related to characteristics of the issue itself"
(1991: 372) is consistent with our own claim that normative and
empirical factors can influence one another. In addition, his incorporation of the factor of social consensus, with its emphasis on implied
social agreement, is implicitly contractarian. Nonetheless, his approach remains primarily empirical in that it seeks to understand the
causal interaction of norms and issue-factors, and falls short of being
truly "integrative" in the Trevino/Weaver sense.

Hence, with a no man's land separating the two camps of normative and empirical research, the search for a workable, comprehensive
theory of business ethics has been stymied. In spite of such significant
attempts to reconcile the disparate viewpoints, the two worlds of
empirical and normative research in business ethics remain at a re-
spectful distance from one another.

This is not to deny that important work has occurred. Investiga-
tions of specific issues, such as corporate governance (Blair, 1995) or
management's reaction to internal stakeholders (Polonsky, 1996),

have often revealed details important for making ethical decisions. Analyses of trends and patterns of social and moral norms have frequently offered insights about evolving attitudes (Preston & Windsor, 1991). And broad summaries of concepts and theories about business ethics have often synthesized shared understandings among philosophers (Wood, 1991).

Integrative Social Contracts Theory, as we will explain, is an explicit attempt to integrate the two rival camps of methodology meaningfully. To be sure, ISCT is foremost a normative theory. Its principal tenets, i.e., the terms of the macrosocial contract, the priority rules, and its general emphasis on communal consent, are all prescriptive or action-guiding norms. Nonetheless, this very normative structure is meant to constitute a kind of container for empirical or behavioral principles. It relies more than any other contemporary theory in business ethics on the "is" of economic affairs; it is in the "container" of ISCT that one discovers the rules and implicit understandings that exist in the day-to-day world of modern business.

Problem 2: The View from Nowhere

No single theory has emerged that is fully capable of providing guidance about the gamut of challenging business ethics matters that fill business ethics casebooks and confront practicing business people. For want of a usable theory, many academics, including nonphilosophers (Buchholz & Rosenthal, 1998; Hosmer, 1994), have turned to the pivotal traditions of ethical theory—in other words, to the broad normative theories of consequentialism, virtue ethics, Kantian deontology, and pragmatism. Consequentialism has been among the most used, especially in application to problems of professional ethics. Consequential approaches define both what is good and what constitutes right action in terms of the consequences of actions. To the extent that a person's or corporation's actions succeed in achieving what the consequential theory defines as "good," the action itself is morally praiseworthy. So, for example, the consequential theory of utilitarianism advanced by Jeremy Bentham (1789), John Stuart Mill (1965), and others is a theory that defines right action in terms of what contributes to the greatest happiness of the greatest number.

An early example of the application of consequentialism to business ethics was the use of an "end-point" analysis by Pastin and Hooker in their controversial article attacking the ethical basis of the

U.S. Foreign Corrupt Practices Act (1980). Pastin and Hooker argued that while undesirable, certain forms of bribery had good consequences in terms of saving jobs, satisfying the interests of shareholders, etc., and for that reason were morally permissible. Later, Ronald Green (1991) used consequential moral reasoning in an attempt to demonstrate that the excuse "everyone's doing it" may actually serve as a valid justification for business conduct—at least under specific, consequentially defined, conditions. An extensive literature in business ethics has arisen that involves empirical researchers' examining whether corporate ethics might be justified consequentially through achievement of higher profit levels (see, for example, Aupperle et al., 1985; Jones, 1995).[5]

Other basic ethical approaches have also been employed in business ethics. Robert Solomon has adapted Aristotle's teleological theory of ethics to business (Solomon, 1992); Buchholz has adapted the doctrine of pragmatism (Buchholz & Rosenthal, 1998); and Evan and Freeman have employed Kantian deontology (Evan & Freeman, 1988). Many writings have even employed multiple ethical theories in evaluating particular business practices (Brummer, 1991; Buchholz, R., 1989; Hosmer, 1994; Pastin & Hooker, 1980), or incorporate both consequential and rights-based factors in lists of principles or questions to be applied by business decision makers (DeGeorge, 1993, chap. 3; Nash, 1981). In an early response to the tendency to apply multiple viewpoints, Cavanagh, Moberg, and Velasquez (1981) proposed an elaborate decision model for sorting out theoretical ethical approaches.

Yet, none of these philosophically inspired attempts has been fully satisfactory. What has gone wrong? Why has no one been able to use these singly or in combination, to establish a single, generally accepted paradigm in business ethics?

We believe the difficulty of such approaches lies largely in their imprecision. As sometimes happens when grand, broadly drawn theories are applied to specific issues, the results are blurry. Put differently, the pivotal traditions of ethical theory, when applied in undiluted form to real-world problems, have offered a "view from nowhere."[6] They have been incapable of locating the complex, particular problems of corporations, industries, economic systems, marketing strategies, etc., in a way that would provide an institutional "somewhere."

The phrase "from nowhere" is not entirely pejorative. Indeed, one of the most important things ethical theory can do is to provide a "view from nowhere," meaning a view that is universal, dispassionate, and impartial. When John Rawls tells his remarkable story about justice (Rawls, 1971) he purposely puts the original contractors, those who must choose the principles of justice, behind a "veil of ignorance" that blinds them to all particular facts about themselves. It prevents them from knowing anything about who they are, i.e., how rich they are, how healthy, how old, or how religious. They are blind to whether they are black or white, live in splendor or squalor, are joiners or loners, are Republicans or Democrats. It is a view from "nowhere"—one bereft of personal knowledge—and designed with a clever purpose. For to the extent that contractors knew their particular circumstances, they might be biased by them, and might in turn select a principle of justice that would be unfair to others. To the extent that someone in the original position knew that he was a rich owner of property, he might be inclined to choose a principle that made the right to private property absolutely sacrosanct and inviolable. What guarantees the universality and impartiality of ethics is that it speaks for all of us, blending our voices—it is not the voice of a specific ethical stance, and so it can be said that its point of view is "nowhere."

But while the view from nowhere is essential to ethics, it cannot exist alone. As the German philosopher Kant notes, even the abstract truth of the Golden Rule (including his own version of the Golden Rule, the Categorical Imperative) must be conditioned by particular facts (Kant, 1785/1959; 1788/1956). In applying the Golden Rule, for example, I must possess facts about how I "would have others do unto me," about how my actions will affect you, and so on.

The "view from nowhere" runs even deeper in the world of business since it is inescapably "artifactual," or, in other words, inescapably dependent upon convention and agreement for its shape and character. As we have explained elsewhere (Donaldson & Dunfee, 1994, 1995; Dunfee & Donaldson, 1995) and will discuss in greater detail in chapter 2, business is different from other key social institutions such as the family in being almost entirely the product of human design. This "artifactual" character of business means that the rules and structure of business can vary dramatically from culture to culture, from industry to industry, and from company to company. The world of business is rich with institutions. It is, as it were, institutionally "thick" in a way that many other human institutions are not. This raises Herculean problems for the institutionally "thin" theories of ethics.

This, more than anything, is what Shell Oil failed to appreciate fully. By simply taking its handful of principles, and by holding this array up in front of their eyes as if it were a moral lens, and by looking at all the world through this single lens, Shell availed itself of a "view from nowhere." Herkstotter's comment mentioned earlier is haunting: the company's weakness was "a ghost in the system . . . some sort of blurring that causes us to make subtle, but in the end far-reaching, mistakes" (*Economist,* 1997). Shell's view from nowhere was indeed blurry. As acknowledged by the company, it missed the changing social contract among Europeans about the relevance of the environment; it missed the national expectation in Nigeria that a company with Shell's power possessed certain social and political obligations; and it missed the fact that the entire world community had moved farther in the direction of believing that for-profit multinational corporations have identifiable responsibilities for protecting human rights. Shell's ethical awareness needed to grow with the evolution of global problems.

Consider another example, this time not a case study, but a social institution. The social and legal institution that possesses the most profound significance for business is that of private property. Without the institution of property and its accompanying concepts and legal procedures, "business" as such would not exist. But as legal theorist Stephen Carter (1992) has noted, the institution of property can be subject to local institutions and local customs, making its ethical interpretation more elusive.[7] "There is nothing unusual in calling upon the courts to ascertain industry practices," writes Carter. "The investigation of custom has long been central to adjudicating disputes between private parties." Doing so, he continues, "is virtually a staple of contract law" (1992: 130). Different industries often work out different ethical norms for handling property issues, norms that Carter calls "local property rules." They do so for many reasons, including considerations of tradition and efficiency. As an example, Carter refers to the norms that have evolved among cattle ranchers in Shasta County, California. These ranchers, he reports, keep to a very strong norm that "absent the most egregious violations of the evolved local property rules, it is inappropriate to seek state enforcement of one's rights. . . . Ranchers whose cattle do damage are expected to make amends, usually in kind rather than in cash, and most small damages are left to lie where they fall" (1992: 133). Arbitrating moral and even legal disputes among Shasta County cattle ranchers cannot proceed independently from these local property norms. Legal theorist

Richard Epstein (1992) provides another example. He discusses the well-known case of *International News Service* v. *Associated Press* (248 U.S. 215 [1918]) in which the International News Service (INS) was prevented from gathering news about World War I directly, and copied news releases from the Associated Press Service, which was a competitor. Epstein argues that in deciding against INS, the Supreme Court could only have been correct if it took into account the broadcasting industry's "local norms" on property rights in the news. Had the industry norms been different, the outcome could, and should, have been different.

Perhaps the most intractable aspect of the "artifactual" problem in business ethics is cultural variety. Economic institutions, even more than most other human institutions, are subject to striking cultural diversity. Some cultures emphasize property-rights dimensions of intellectual property, while others emphasize cooperative behavior and societal sharing of innovations (Swinyard, Rinne, & Kau, 1990). Some tightly constrain the use of firm-derived (inside) information in securities markets, while others show considerable indifference to the phenomenon. How are these differing responses to be reconciled? Is a society that de-emphasizes property rights in favor of cooperative sharing immoral? Or vice versa? Is there only a single approach to the use of inside information in securities transactions that satisfies the normative standards of business ethics? That is, does (or should) business ethics theory mandate a particular form of restriction on insider trading? Should Singapore be required to base its approach to intellectual property on utilitarian grounds? And by what rationale should a Muslim culture be subjected to a comprehensive system of Kantian-based economic ethics? If the response is that theories of universal ethics such as utilitarianism or Kantianism serve only to identify the core values that apply to a small set of behaviors within a given culture, then what constitutes the source and justification of many of the detailed, day-to-day ethical standards for business activities around the world?

A Solution: Social Contracts

Contractarian approaches using methodology derived from classical political philosophy have evolved as a significant tool for approaching such fundamental problems. This book is an attempt to articulate a detailed version of that approach. At the heart of the social contract effort is a simple assumption, namely, that we can understand better the obligations of key social institutions, such as business or government, by attempting to understand what is entailed in a fair agreement or "contract" between those institutions and society, and also in the implicit contracts that exist among the different communities and institutions within society. The normative authority of any social contract derives from the assumption that humans, acting rationally, consent—or at least would consent hypothetically—to the terms of a particular agreement affecting the society or community of which they are a member. In this manner contractarian theories utilize the device of consent, albeit it is often *hypothetical* consent, to justify principles, policies, and structures.

As Scheppele and others note, no monolithic version of social contract exists; rather, it has been employed throughout history for a variety of theoretical and practical purposes. The French Huguenots used the social contract in the pursuit of religious liberty; Locke used it in defending property rights from the king; and Rawls used it to define the principles of distributive justice. Scheppele writes, "We do not assume that there is just one contractarian method. There are many, and a consideration of contractarianism as a general theoretical approach involves a consideration of the differences among these various methods and the choices that must be made in their design" (Scheppele & Waldron, 1991: 195).

Further, contractarian approaches can be designed to take existing institutions, such as the corporation, into consideration, and in this way provide the essential context for making ethical judgments about economic behavior. Social contract reasoning is an obvious candidate to use in analyzing business ethics issues because it moves away from a bare "view from nowhere" stance to one that reflects the "thickness" of business practices and institutions. Local property rules such as those adopted by the Shasta County California Cattle Ranchers, or recognized norms of behavior among participants in the news service industry such as Associated Press or INS, can be construed as implicit agreements or social contracts. Similarly, the implicit and explicit agreements that define the responsibilities of CEOs and other managers to share owners can be construed as social contracts helping to define managerial responsibility. With social contracts, one is no longer limited to seeking ethical guidance from highly generalized statements such as, "Corporate CEOs should act in a way that reflects integrity and high moral character." Their ethical responsibilities can be interpreted, rather, through the implicit agreements or social contracts that channel the lifeblood of their activities: their relationships with their shareholders, customers, employees, and the state.

The History of Social Contract Theories in Business

A variety of attempts have been made to apply social contract reasoning to business. In 1982, Donaldson sought to construct the outlines of a social contract for business capable of providing concrete insights into the nature of obligations for corporations. Following the classical tradition of using a hypothetical agreement as a device for parsing specific rights and responsibilities, he imagined the terms of an agreement between business firms (all productive cooperative enterprises) and society (individual members of a given society in the aggregate). Other attempts to connect the social contract concept to business and economic events emerged during the 1980s. In 1982, Norman Bowie offered a brief description of the social contract between business and society in his book *Business Ethics*. In his 1986 book, *Morals by Agreement,* David Gauthier utilized concepts of economic rationality to advance the notion of a hypothetical "agreement" among rational, self-interested agents that formed the basis for a collective morality. In 1988, Michael Keeley developed a progressive theory of organizations using social contract concepts in his book *A Social Contract Theory of Organizations*. Keeley utilized the contract metaphor in a nontraditional way, viewing the firm as a series of contractlike agreements about social rules.

In 1989, Donaldson extended a modified version of his social contract model to the global level. Using again the imaginary social contract as a heuristic device, he relied upon reason and intuition to identify terms in the contract that establish a minimal floor of responsibility for global corporations (Donaldson, 1989).

Contractarian approaches are now used to evaluate a host of issues. The legal theorist Kim Scheppele (1993: 151) has recently supported restrictions on insider trading through a contractarian analysis that she stresses is capable of providing "concrete guidance in working out how to think about the ethics of insider trading." She argues that consent must be "based on more detailed and context-dependent knowledge of specific features of American life and of particular individuals." Her results are specific rather than abstract. After analysis, she justifies restrictions on insider trading based upon a contractually derived desire to provide equal access to financial markets. Similarly, the economist Robert Frank (1993) has advanced a contractarian view of regulatory policy in emerging market economies. As Frank notes, "Recent decades have seen a resurgence of contractarian thinking about the nature and origins of the state" (1993: 258).

In 1991, Dunfee emphasized real or "extant" social contracts as constituting a significant source of ethical norms in business. He argued that when these real but usually informal social contracts are based upon free and informed consent, and when the norms they produce are consistent with the principles of broader ethical theories, they become prima facie obligatory. Shortly thereafter, the authors of the present book (Donaldson & Dunfee) began writing a series of articles dedicated to integrating the broad, traditional approach of the social contract with "extant" social contracts. We have called our approach Integrative Social Contracts Theory, or ISCT (Donaldson & Dunfee, 1994, 1995; Dunfee & Donaldson, 1995). The present book is an attempt to give full expression to the concept of ISCT.

What Is ISCT? Pluralism versus Relativism

To use terminology common to philosophers, ISCT is "pluralism," not "relativism." It allows for tolerance without amoralism by combining two previously unconnected traditions of contract thinking. As the foregoing discussion implies, social contracts can take two distinct forms:

- The hypothetical or "macro" contract, reflecting hypothetical agreement among rational members of a community.

- The "extant" or "micro" contract, reflecting an actual agreement within a community.

The first or "macro" contract refers to broad, hypothetical agreements among rational people. Such contracts are designed to establish objective background standards for social interaction. For example, John Locke's requirement that government respect the rights of people, or Rawls's specification of the two principles of justice, derive from "macro" or hypothetical styles of contracting. The second, or "extant," contract refers to nonhypothetical, actual (although typically informal) agreements existing within and among industries, national economic systems, corporations, trade associations, and so on. For example, the ethical principles accepted by accountants or lawyers reflect "micro" or "extant" social contracts.

Integrative Social Contracts Theory is "integrative" in the sense that it combines these micro and macro forms of social contract. In doing so it attempts to capture the strengths of each, even as it misses respective weaknesses. The traditional weakness of macro contracts is their vagueness. Like deontology or consequentialism, they are a form of traditional ethical theory that sometimes provides a blurry, if essentially correct, picture. Consider John Locke's famous social contract. It is well and good to say with Locke that governments should respect the right of citizens to property. But just *how* should governments respect it? Does it follow that they should forbid any "taking" of property as unjust? Or only that they should compensate any "taking"? And, by the way, just what constitutes "taking"? These and other questions expose the limits of macro-style social contracts. They often omit necessary detail. By integrating micro or extant contracts into ISCT, a more fine-grained ethical analysis becomes possible. Micro contracts, in short, fill in what macro contracts leave out.

The acknowledged weakness of the extant contract, on the other hand, is that such contracts can be morally out of bounds. For example, an implicit contract among the members of a housing neighborhood that specifies that members not sell a house to any African American could be accepted by all the members of the neighborhood, but would be morally wrong.

The advantages of combining the two should now be obvious. By insisting that business ethics take full account of the extant agreements within companies, industries, and other economic communities, the blurring usually associated with traditional ethical theory is avoided. And by insisting that any extant contracts cohere with the moral limits established by a broad macro or hypothetical contract, relativism is avoided.

It will help to pause a moment and reflect upon the last remark. For despite the fact that utilizing a traditional macrosocial contract should avoid relativism, some theorists have continued to criticize early versions of ISCT as "relativistic." What is meant by "relativism," and what relation does it have to ISCT? The relativist view is grounded in the assumption that a person or culture *believing* an act is morally correct, helps *make* it morally correct—or at least to make it correct for *that* person or *that* culture. In its pure form, relativism would allow any individual or community to define ethically correct behavior in any way they wished. No matter how inhumane, no matter how bizarre, their ethics would be on a par with everyone else's.

Relativism's argument is tempting, especially when one realizes that people often fall prey to an arrogant universalism or absolutism. Why should you be able to impose your views on me? And why should one person's or one country's view of ethics apply to all other persons or countries? These are important questions that relativism poses starkly. Needless to say, the smug French, Japanese, or American cultural chauvinist who believes her flag stands for Eternal Goodness is sometimes surprised even by the very question of relativism. It is not accidental that ultranationalists are frequently people who have spent little time in other cultures. Ethical sensitivity often involves a growing respect for the mores, dress, political systems, religion, and even culinary tastes of cultures other than our own. Tolerance is an important value.

The very logic of ISCT entails tolerance. Tolerance is an extension of the emphasis on consent and choice. Notice that the right of choice on the part of individuals is an assumption underlying all contractarian approaches, including ISCT. Without consent, without the right of people to choose whether to agree to a contract or not, there can be no contract. ISCT even extends this assumption to include a right of choice for *communities*. Business communities can, within limits, choose the ethical norms that guide them. Under ISCT, business communities cannot claim that *their* set of ethical norms is necessarily universal; they must exercise tolerance of some approaches from different communities.

But one may ask, If ISCT implicitly endorses tolerance, then doesn't it amount to a form of relativism? It does not amount to relativism for two reasons. First of all, as explained earlier (and as we will explain in detail in later chapters) not all microsocial contracts are legitimate. Some are out of bounds ethically, namely, those that violate conditions laid down by the macrosocial contract. Second, it is important to see that the very challenge posed by relativism has nothing to do with tolerance. Insofar as relativism asks members of Judeo-Christian culture to respect the moral freedom of others by not coercing members, say, of a Confucian culture to capitulate to their values, then it similarly dictates that members of Confucian culture should refrain from doing the same in reverse. In this sense, tolerance is a global value, not a relative one, essential to the assumptions of ISCT and inconsistent with relativism. Relativism simply denies that there are values such as tolerance, freedom of choice, or justice that can be universalized, and would proclaim the relativity of all values to either

individuals or to individual cultures. As relativism sees it, if one individual, or one culture, accepts tolerance, so be it. That *is* the correct
moral attitude for that person or culture. But if another individual, or
another culture happens to reject tolerance, that too is fine. From the
vantage point of relativism, no value is broader than the person or
culture that propounds it.

While the debate over universalism and relativism often assumes a
simple, binary form—Are you a relativist or are you an absolutist?—
the underlying issues are much deeper. In fact, very few, if any,
respected traditional moral philosophers subscribe to a doctrine of
pure relativism. Not only is radical relativism inconsistent with the
basic assumptions upon which ISCT is based, but the results may be
simply too bizarre and repugnant to accept. To believe that no ethical
view held by an individual or culture is better than any other view is
equivalent to believing child rapists are as worthy as child educators.

Similarly, few people around the world would qualify as extreme
universalists, i.e., "absolutists" in the sense that they believe there is a
single, clearly articulated, blueprint of morality that specifies the
moral details of everyday life for everyone. With the exception of the
most conservative of fundamentalist religious believers, most persons
(including many fundamentalists) agree that any linguistic formulation of moral truth, regardless of its source, is subject to some form of
human *interpretation*. Further, although many fundamentalists may
believe in a detailed morality, some do not extend their conviction to
a belief that everyone should be bound by their own religious
doctrines. For these reasons, the universalism/relativism controversy
should be seen less as a struggle between polar opposites than as an
ongoing discussion about the range of permissible viewpoints across a
wide continuum of possible positions. The continuum begins with
extreme relativism and ends with absolutism.

ISCT fits squarely in the middle of this continuum, as demonstrated
in Figure 1-1. It avoids absolutism or extreme universalism by making
room for tolerance and a respect for community identity, that is to
say, space for communities to tailor norms to their participants' economic and cultural aspirations. It similarly avoids relativism by rejecting the notion that any community-held norm is automatically as
good as any alternative norm.

ISCT is correctly identified as a pluralism. It is pluralistic in three
ways. First and most obvious, it is pluralistic in its acceptance of
many community interpretations of business ethics. Second, it is pluralistic in its acceptance of many kinds of moral theories. There may

be a tendency to see the various ethical theories as competitive, and to suppose that one must either be a utilitarian, or a virtue ethics theorist, or a deontologist, etc. This view is losing ground in philosophy (Becker, 1992), and indeed we believe contractarian approaches to be consistent with a number of alternative ethical theories. The possibility of significant ethical pluralism has received increasing attention in recent years.[8] In the present book we presume a pluralistic viewpoint in the sense that we regard the truth of ISCT to be independent from the truth of any particular traditional ethical theory.

ISCT is offered as a pluralistic theory in a third sense. We reject the notion that ethical theories must be designed only for practitioners or

---

Figure 1-1   ISCT within the Continuum of Relativism/Universalism

Extreme relativism	No ethical view, regardless of source or basis, is better than any other view.
Cultural relativism	No ethical view held by one culture is better than any other view held by another culture.
Pluralism (ISCT)	There exists a broad range of ethical viewpoints that may be chosen by communities and cultures. The possibility exists that conflicting ethical positions in different cultures are equally valid. There are, however, circumstances in which the viewpoint of a particular culture will be invalid due either to a universally binding moral precept or to the priority of the view of another culture or community.
Modified universalism	There exists a set of precepts expressible in many different ethical languages that reflects universally binding moral precepts and that captures many issues of global ethical significance. These precepts rule out the possibility of two conflicting ethical positions in different cultures being equally valid.
Extreme universalism (absolutism)	There exists a single set of precepts expressed only in a single ethical language that reflects universally binding moral precepts and that captures all issues of global ethical significance. These precepts rule out the possibility of two conflicting ethical positions in different cultures being equally valid.

only for theorists. In this book, we present ISCT as a theory that should be *used* as well as footnoted. Interestingly, managers do often use the terminology of social contract in describing, for example, relationships between their firm and the local community. Employees also frequently speak of the "implied agreements" that surround policies and procedures, including ones affecting downsizing, corporate pensions, and due process. Corporate pensioners may, for example, express belief in a social contract obligation on the part of the firm to take steps to guarantee that their retirement remains secure. Similarly, politicians sometimes make use of contractarian language when describing business-government relationships.

In this book, then, we seek to advance the interconnection between the micro and the macro, between the extant and the ideal, by presenting a comprehensive social contract theory for business. Deriving from roots in classical social contract theory, the view we will propose recognizes ethical obligations based upon two levels of consent: first, to a theoretical macrosocial contract appealing to all rational contractors; and second, to the terms of specific, real microsocial contracts applying to members of numerous localized communities. Through this process, we seek to put the "is" and the "ought" in symbiotic harmony, which, interestingly enough, requires the cooperation of both empirical and normative research in rendering ultimate value judgments.

As mentioned earlier, the "view from nowhere" associated with traditional ethical theory is insufficient for resolving complex problems of business ethics. The unanchored "nowhere" viewpoint requires mooring by the implicit agreements that populate the institutionally "thick" environment of business, i.e., by social contracts. Nonetheless, the impartiality expressed by traditional ethical theory is critically important for any form of ethical analysis. The "view from nowhere," consequently, must be supplemented, not abandoned.

We began this chapter with the image of two businesspersons shaking hands, an image that symbolizes the role of voluntary commitment in the business world. As we have seen, the concept of voluntary commitment can be extended to the broader issues of business ethics through the notion of microsocial and macrosocial contracts. By integrating these distinct notions of social contract, business ethics may be provided with a foundation that is both pluralistic and prescriptive. The remainder of the book articulates the structure of that foundation.

2

The Social Contract for Business

Social contract has been a powerful image for the support
of democratic forms of governance. In effect, a mythical agreement is used
to give legitimacy to a very real set of laws and institutions.

—Axelrod (1986: 1106)

A firm that allows its product to become contaminated with salmonella can kill dozens and sicken thousands. Another that decides to make a risky investment in developing a cure for a Third World disease can greatly enhance the health and quality of life for millions. A third that sells components for nuclear weapons to a rogue nation may endanger hundreds of millions. Business ethics, the focus of this book, is a subject of monumental significance. Business activity as a whole clearly improves the lives of people by providing needed goods and services. Yet, clearly, some ethical framework is a necessary condition for business. Even with its power to uplift, business can also corrupt and damage.

Business by its very nature is a group activity. At the core of most successful business relationships are foundational values such as trustworthiness and promise keeping. Deception and theft of property impose significant costs on business. All forms of economic organization require a minimal threshold of ethical behavior to support an environment conducive to productive business operations.

In this chapter we summarize ISCT, and we explore how the concept of a social contract can help to illuminate both the thresholds and the business synergies for ethics.

The Foundations of a Social Contract for Business Ethics

Our primary task is to unravel the potential of social contracts as a foundation for an adequate ethical framework for economic activity. We begin by noting that at the core of all contractarian approaches is the acceptance of and respect for human autonomy. As Aristotle notes, all ethical behavior begins with choice. Furthermore, consent, a

form of choice, constitutes a theoretical pillar of mainstream economic theories. Through social contract theory we will explore the
role that consent and autonomy play in ethical relationships in economic life. Among other things, we will examine the extent to which
economic actors may, either individually or in groups, collectively
frame their own morality.

We utilize the approach of the classic contractarians such as Locke
or Hobbes, but we add an important point. We inquire as to the type
of agreement, based upon the consent of the participants, that could
provide a framework of morality for today's business world. In the
traditional manner, we begin with a thought experiment that envisions the terms of a contract providing a foundation for economic
ethics acceptable to a diverse set of imaginary contractors (some
greed-driven egoists, some deeply religious altruists, most probably
in-between) who represent the varied attitudes of the modern world.
We assume that these contractors are rational, i.e., not afflicted by
inconsistency or logical confusion, and that they are knowledgeable,
i.e., they know the range of facts accepted at the time as being true.
We do not assume, as Rawls does (1971: 367), that these hypothetical
contractors are ignorant of all facts concerning themselves. They may
or may not know that they are Christian, Muslim, of a risk-adverse or
risk-prone personality, etc. We assume only in this regard that they do
not know of what economic communities they are members. For
example, they do not know that they work for XYZ corporation,
participate in country N's economic system, pay dues in worker union
K, or ply their trade in profession P or industry Q. These facts about
their economic membership are hidden from them. In a similar way,
their level of personal wealth is obscured. They are ignorant of
whether they possess a massive fortune, or nothing at all. In this
thought experiment, one might envision all of rational humanity
capable of voluntary choice and afflicted with the partial amnesia just
described, gathering together for a global convention to construct a
fundamental framework for ethical behavior in economic activities.

We do not assume, as again Rawls would, that the contractors are
ignorant of their economic and political *preferences*. An individual
may know her preferences—that she prefers wine to beer, employment in a worker-owned firm to employment in an investor-owned
firm, a libertarian to a socialist form of government.

The question then becomes what terms, if any, would be acceptable
to these contractors?

We must add the proviso that even though individual contractors may know their personal economic and political preferences, *we* who undertake the social contract thought experiment do not know those preferences. To put the matter differently, we are confronted with an *undetermined* mix of contractor preferences. Hence, in order to answer the question of what terms would be acceptable to these contractors, we must find the terms that would be acceptable to a large number of configurations of contractors' preferences.

Finally, we assume that the contractors do not come to the table entirely bereft of moral principles. They at least bring with them the underlying senses of right and wrong with which they have grown up. They bring with them these settled understandings of deep moral values, which we will call "hypernorms." Because the contractors are unaware of other economic preferences and memberships, they lack detailed knowledge of their economic morality. Yet even though they lack such detailed knowledge, they know the basic values to which they subscribe. Some may profess philosophical utilitarianism. Some may profess philosophical Kantianism. Others may adhere to ethical principles articulated in their preferred religion (in Judaism or Christianity this might be the Ten Commandments; in Buddhism it might be the principles of the "Dhamapada"). And some may subscribe to the specific principles that have been handed down to them historically through their family, their village, or their culture.

When these hypothetical yet rational global contractors confront the fact that it would be impossible to obtain an intellectual consensus concerning adoption of a single morality as the framework for global economic ethics, how will they go about finding a basis for agreement? First, we assume that many are driven by an innate moral sense (Wilson, 1993), which leads them to seek and to recognize elements of a foundational morality. That is, most humans are "hardwired" to be ethical (Wright, 1994). Second, we focus upon *economic* ethics. In economic matters there are special considerations that must be of concern to rational, knowledgeable contractors. For example, rational contractors realize the vital importance of having a framework of morality as a foundation for economic interaction. Without a core common morality, we would have no more than the economic analogue of a Hobbesian state of nature (Velasquez, 1992). Economic life would be, using Hobbes's language, "nasty and brutish," if not also "short." Such chaotic economic conditions have prevailed from time to time in nations that lacked the social and political background institutions necessary to sustain an ethical framework. In such a state, promises are not kept. Property is not respected. Violence is used to obtain economic advantage. Capital markets either are distorted, or fail altogether owing to a fundamental lack of trust.

We assert that rational contractors would accept a limited set of core assumptions in framing their search for a common economic ethics, where "economic ethics" refers to the principles establishing the boundaries of proper behavior in the context of the production and exchange of goods and services.

These assumptions are as follows:

- All humans are constrained by bounded moral rationality.

- The nature of ethical behavior in economic systems and communities helps determine the quality and efficiency of economic interactions. Higher-quality and more efficient economic interactions are preferable to lower-quality and less efficient economic interactions.

- Ceteris paribus, economic activity that is consistent with the cultural, philosophical, or religious attitudes of economic actors is preferable to economic activity that is not.

In virtue of the first two of these propositions, individual contractors would desire the option to join and to exit economic communities as a means of leveraging their ability to achieve the benefits of either greater efficiency or greater compatibility with preferred philosophical, community, or religious norms. The significance of these principles will be discussed briefly in the sections that follow.

Bounded Moral Rationality

The argument that economic agents are constrained by bounded rationality is coming to have increasing acceptance even among economists (Conlisk, 1996). Bounded *economic* rationality derives from the recognition that human cognition is subject to serious physical and psychological limits. There is substantial evidence that individuals make systematic errors in reasoning.[1] Decisions are often required in the face of insufficient information or time constraints that prevent one from making necessary calculations. The heuristics chosen to deal with these constraints often contain biases that lead to incorrect decisions. For many of the same reasons, we argue that moral agents are similarly constrained by bounded *moral* rationality. This phenomenon has two major components as follows:

1. Individual moral agents are constrained in their ability to discover and process morally relevant facts necessary to implement their preferred ethical theories.

2. Ethical theorists are constrained in their ability to devise a calculus of morality that coheres well with settled moral opinions.

Bounded morality is reflected in the common difficulty involved in using existing ethical theories to resolve difficult ethical dilemmas. Should Shell have used economic, or even political, leverage against the military government of Nigeria to try to prevent the execution of the environmental activist and author Ken Saro-Wiwa? Were U.S. firms correct in cutting all ties to apartheid South Africa? Was it wrong in the 1990s for Al "Chainsaw" Dunlap, the U.S. corporate downsizing specialist, to create shareholder wealth by laying off thousands of workers at underperforming companies? In many cases the difficulties extend to the level of application, so that reasonable individuals armed with the same facts and who accept the same ethical theory may achieve different results in applying the theory. For example, even two utilitarians may come to incompatible conclusions concerning the same dilemma due to a different interpretation of what counts as "pleasure." Two Kantians may likewise diverge in their analysis due to different assumptions about what is or is not "universalizable," i.e., the question of which maxims should govern a world in which all people show deep respect for the value of others. Those who think that applying one of the traditional ethical theories from the literature in Western philosophy will yield simple, clear-cut answers to each of these questions have probably not had the pleasure of attempting it.

In its broadest sense, "bounded moral rationality" includes a host of acknowledged limitations, for example the problem of incommensurability associated with utilitarianism (How do I know that my pleasures and pains are commensurable with your pleasures and pains?). We mean here, however, to use the concept in a more restricted sense. First, we mean for it to refer to straightforward difficulties that humans encounter in processing and interpreting ethical data. Humans are finite creatures, and the ability of any given human to process data is limited. Consider a contemporary ethical issue debated in many developed countries: namely, the ethics of corporate downsizing. To assess the morality of a particular act of downsizing, whether in general or in a specific instance, one must reference a maze of complex facts. This is true even if one believes oneself to be reasonably clear about the normative or ethical concepts at stake. It is also true whether one is a committed Rawlsian, believing that systemic inequalities are unjust unless they work to the advantage of everyone, including the least well off, or if one is a Hayakian or Friedmanite believing that liberty is the linchpin of market morality. One needs to have a detailed grasp of the consequences of downsizing for the stockholders of the firm as well as for the managers and employees. One must have some view as to the long-term social consequences of accumulated patterns of downsizing, and of the tendencies toward increased or decreased efficiency of corporations under downsized conditions. All of this is fiendishly difficult for finite minds to accomplish with any confidence. This pattern of difficulty, indicative of the "boundedness" of moral rationality, is similar to Herbert Simon's concept of the same name. Human beings have finite intellectual resources and will inevitably be forced to "satisfice" in both economic and moral decision making.

In the same vein, the resources required to gather information for a given moral decision are limited. Reflection and data gathering are often costly in terms of time and energy, and these resources are finite. Still further, just as certain psychological factors may make it difficult to come to a rational decision concerning economic choices (Conlisk, 1996), resulting in phenomena such as the "winners' curse" (Thaler, 1992), psychological hurdles may impede ethical decision making. As a consequence, moral agents may end up using an inappropriate or defective decision heuristics as a means of attempting to cope with a required decision. For example, David Messick has shown that *when* moral information is provided to a moral agent, i.e., the timing of the receipt of information, can skew one's moral judgment about the fairness of a particular action (Messick & Bazerman, 1996).

But rational moral agents confront another kind of limit, different from that popularized by Simon. Their moral rationality is bounded by the limited ability of moral theory to account for commonsense moral convictions and preferences. Hadari (1988: 655) argues that "no known ethos has managed to be entirely coherent." Contemporary discussions reveal instances of slippage between what common sense agrees is morally correct and what moral theory dictates. For example, common sense agrees that family members are to be preferred over strangers; and if a total stranger were drowning alongside one's spouse, and only one could be saved, common sense dictates saving one's spouse. But significant familial partiality is difficult to reconcile with traditional moral theory (Donaldson, 1990). (See also Symposium on Impartiality and Ethical Theory, 1991.) Certainly no one has argued that moral theory should be tested entirely by reference to settled moral conviction; indeed, it is because we often want to do the reverse, i.e., to test common conviction by theory, that theories are developed. Yet most moral theorists find it hard to imagine that a correct theory would fly in the face of some of the most universally held, firmly believed, moral convictions.

One disturbing result of what we are calling bounded moral rationality is moral uncertainty. For insofar as the correctness of each moral decision must be referenced to an infinite array of facts, or subject to theories that clash with key moral convictions, we are doomed to confront moral risk. Life is more confusing than we might hope. While we applaud the efforts of scholars such as Hardin (1988) and Baron (1990) who seek techniques for improving moral decision making, we believe that they remain a long way from solving the problem of bounded moral rationality.

This brings us to a final major point about the significance of bounded moral rationality. We believe that it is crucial to notice that moral life in economic affairs is not only bounded, but also *strongly* bounded. It is this final aspect of the boundedness of moral rationality in economic life that makes business ethics even less determinant from the standpoint of general moral theory than ethics in, say, family or political life. Economic systems are products of artifice, not nature, and their structures can and do vary immensely. Such systems (which include the laws, practices, and value systems that inform economic practices) are, in a word, *artifacts*. People create them. People make them what they are, and people might have chosen to make them differently.

An analogy will help. Because they are artifacts, economic systems share important characteristics with games. Just as people can change the rules of games or invent entirely new games, so too can they change the rules of economic practice, or invent new practices. The evolution of the corporation and of market economics from 1800 to the present is striking testimony to the plasticity of the corporate form and of capitalism. The definitions of economic practices are stipulated rather than given by nature.

Yet this amazing plasticity creates problems for the moral analysis of economic systems. For, in the same way that it would be impossible to create a general theory of the ethics of games without knowing in advance *which* game was under consideration, so too it is impossible to create a general theory of the ethics of economics without knowing at least the general shape of the economic system under consideration. The ethics of basketball, or of soccer or squash, must be contoured somewhat to the rules of these particular games. Similarly, the ethics of client entertainment, negotiation, and employee compensation must be contoured somewhat to the rules of particular economic systems in which they occur.

In an analogous way, knowing all the moral theory in the world does not equip one to specify in advance the moral norms of business ethics, much less the norms for the specific contexts of gift giving, negotiation, and employee compensation. In each, the ethical norms must be contoured to the rules of the specific economic practices and the notions of fairness of the participants. This is not to deny that some extremely general moral prescriptions hold for all economic practices and, for that matter, for all economic systems. For example, refraining from flagrant dishonesty, torture, and intentional killing are required in all human activities. Nor is it to deny that economic systems, unlike games of pick-up basketball, have dramatic implications for people who are not directly a part of the rule-formation process.

We do, however, deny that one can know in advance what the correct rules of business ethics are for a specific system without having detailed information about the system and its participants. We deny, for example, the possibility of knowing in advance whether ethics requires that a high company official from an airline visit the surviving relatives of an airplane crash and present them with money (as Japanese airline officials have traditionally done), in contrast to, say, merely offering sympathy and minor assistance. To know what ethics requires here we must know both what local custom encourages and also something about the system of compensation in the economic system. In the United States, we possess a well-developed adversarial system for delivering compensation to victims. It is cumbersome and expensive, but relatively reliable. In Japan and elsewhere the legal system for delivering compensation is less developed and less reliable. Thus, against the background of such cultural habits, it would be reasonable to place greater moral burdens on the shoulders of Japanese corporate officials for voluntarily compensating and helping the families of victims, than on those of U.S. corporate officials.

Business itself is rife with complex systems to which moral judgments must be contoured. In order to evaluate the downsizing strategies followed by Al Dunlap (1996), one needs to understand a great deal about the structure of capital markets, the institutional context for layoffs and terminations of particular types of employees, the types of support provided for job retraining and transition in the public sector, and the structure of the surrounding job market and government assistance programs. One cannot render an adequate moral judgment on the basis of the practice alone (e.g., that plant closing is unethical per se, and that laying off large numbers of employees is always unethical). This very requirement of a full understanding of the context of decisions adds significant uncertainty and complexity to moral decision making in economic contexts.

We now see why moral theorists have found it so difficult to devise a single moral theory capable of clearly resolving most common ethical dilemmas in business. Any moral calculus used in business must be applicable to an incredibly wide variety of contexts that arise from radically different economic systems. Just as it is impossible to create a general theory of economics without knowing the institutions, history, and culture of the people to whom it will apply, so too one cannot devise a general theory of economic ethics without understanding the types of organizations, people, and transactions to which it will apply. One can only imagine Immanuel Kant's response if he walked into the modern equivalent of a drawing room and was asked, "Professor Kant, how does the Categorical Imperative apply to hostile takeovers, or to software piracy?" Without a solid familiarity with the institutional shape of modern business, including its institutional arrangements for intellectual property, the Sage of Konigsberg would be, uncharacteristically, at a moral loss.

Ethical Behavior and Efficiency

Rational contractors will understand that successful economic communities and systems require a foundation of ethical behavior.[2] At a minimum, business done efficiently often requires a certain level of trustworthiness. The evolution of a mutual fund industry is greatly handicapped in a culture—as in the Russia of the 1990s—in which you cannot trust another party to handle your funds honestly and where the background institutions are insufficient to provide legal remedies against fraud and misappropriation. Further, in order for capital markets to operate efficiently, many transactions must be done on the basis of oral promises buttressed by fundamental honesty.

When a mutual fund manager places an order for 10,000 shares of stock in a society where trust is emphasized, it is expected that both sides will honor the transaction, even when the price of the stock makes a sudden dramatic move unanticipated by the parties. Neither side will lie as to what actually occurred—"you must have heard wrong, the order was for 1,000 shares, not 10,000." In an economy based upon a strong foundation of ethical behavior, overall transaction costs should be reduced so that simpler forms of interaction are possible. Transactions in such an economy can often be secured by trust instead of through expensive legal strictures.

The same basic relationship between ethics and efficiency also holds true at the level of the firm. Few would disagree that there is a relationship between the level of ethical behavior on the part of a firm's employees and the ability of the firm to achieve its objectives. Higher levels of ethical behavior should reduce opportunism and shirking while at the same time instilling greater consumer and stakeholder confidence in the firm. This may lead to greater consumer demand and reduced regulatory costs. Further, the direct costs of opportunism to the firm (preventable employee absences and carelessness, internal theft, even sabotage) are reduced. A higher level of ethical behavior within a firm may constitute a significant comparative advantage vis-à-vis firms that have much higher costs due to the unethical behavior of their employees and managers. The costs to the less ethical firm would include the direct costs of opportunism, lost customer and stakeholder confidence, and increased regulatory costs.

Personal Precepts

Rational contractors will believe that, both for themselves and for others, it is good for economic behavior to be consistent with cultural, philosophical, or religious attitudes. Many individuals have personal cultural, philosophical, or religious beliefs that they seek to fulfill in interactions with others. We shall refer to these desires, preferences, and attitudes that involve cultural, philosophical, or religious beliefs inter alia as "personal precepts."[3] Personal precepts may be based on religious, ethical, or sociopolitical convictions, or on something else. They may include observance of religious dietary laws or a religiously motivated refusal to accept any form of medical assistance. They may involve a belief that it is wrong to discriminate on the basis of gender or sexual preference. They may be business specific, for example, the precept that it is wrong to pose as a journalist in order to obtain information from a competitor, or that it is wrong to employ attack ads directly focused at a competitor and the competitor's product.

Muslim managers may wish to participate in systems of economic ethics compatible with the teachings of Mohammed (Esposito, 1988: 116–202); European and American managers may wish to participate in systems of economic ethics giving due respect to individual liberty; and Japanese managers may prefer systems showing respect for the value of the collective (San, 1987). Individual corporations may also have value preferences. IBM in the late twentieth century prided itself on a buttoned-down, well-controlled culture, even as Hewlett-Packard thrived on creative chaos.

Individuals constantly make decisions influenced by their personal precepts, which are part of their larger set of utilities. We have all known people whose personal precepts are so powerful they virtually always dominate a decision. Relatively few in number, such individuals act in strictly principled ways, and seem inflexible because they rarely, if ever, are influenced by nonpersonal precepts. Seemingly an admirable characteristic—it is a compliment to be called a person of principle—a dominating personal-precepts preference may be problematic, as in the case of a Christian Scientist who refuses to accept medical assistance for her critically ill yet curable child. Others, probably a vast majority, hold weaker personal precepts, so that other types of preferences often win out. The form that these tradeoffs take signals the strength of the personal precepts. Megan decides whether or not her desire for eating hamburgers at a given moment should dominate her beliefs about animal welfare. Bill decides whether his desire for a Nike soccer ball outweighs his concern that underage workers in Pakistan may have made the balls. Susan ignores her belief that it is wrong to promise an unrealistic delivery date to a customer when faced with an urgent need to make a given sale. Individuals apply whatever form of reasoning they choose, regardless of whether it conforms to some external definition of logic, or appears consistent to an objective observer. John may condemn as a lie the act of posing as a journalist to get information from a competitor, but may think it perfectly proper for a corporate marketing researcher to pose as a journalist to insure independent opinions concerning the firm's products.

Rational contractors would desire the freedom to specify more precisely the norms of economic interaction as a response to the opaque world provided by strongly bounded moral rationality. They would wish to maintain their freedom as groups or communities to make specific interpretations of what "bounded" moral rationality requires in economic transactions. They would want to do so for the reasons just demonstrated, i.e., in order to be able to seek for themselves greater efficiency and a higher level of compatibility with their personal precepts. In some instances this freedom of interpretation would be connected to their desire to specify ethical norms that facilitate better business; in others it would be intended to maintain their cultural distinctiveness or to reflect their religious or cultural values.

In other words, bounded moral rationality leaves a significant amount of moral opaqueness confronting the contractors. However small or large, a discretionary area of morality lies in their view. Later we shall call this discretionary area "moral free space," but for now we wish only to note that rational contractors will reserve the right to exercise a certain amount of moral freedom within this area—to fill in what is left unclear—in order to make their world more efficient and compatible with their underlying personal precepts.

Both these considerations—first, the desire to enhance efficiency by reducing uncertainty, and second, the need to maintain freedom of cultural, philosophical, and/or religious interpretation—imply that contractors will choose terms of the macrosocial contract that allow the generation of specific community-level moral norms regulating economic activity. In effect, the contractors in the macro contract will adopt a principle allowing the existence of community-specific micro contracts that serve to reduce the moral opaqueness left by the bounded nature of moral rationality. Thus, the term "microsocial contracts" represents agreements or shared understandings about the moral norms relevant to specific economic interactions. By allowing communities or other groups to define at least some moral norms for themselves, and allowing individuals to choose the economic communities of which they are members, the macro contractors affirm the possibility of microsocial contracts.

The Social Contract for Business Ethics

As we indicated previously, one useful way in which to envision the macrosocial contract is to imagine that all of humanity—endowed with rationality and knowledge and subject to the conditions described earlier—convene to establish a moral agreement. At this convention, again, all would be aware of their own economic and political preferences. This is important because they would thereby realize the necessity of establishing a system in which they have the best chance of achieving their own goals. Within the broad context of the macrosocial contract, each hypothetical global contractor would have an equal input of consent. This necessarily follows from recognition of the liberty and autonomy of each contractor. That is, in deciding the terms of the agreement, each person would have an equivalent vote. We assume great diversity across the global contractors. But no single hypothetical contractor would have a greater claim or interest than any other.

What, then, would be the nature of an agreement sufficient to overcome bounded morality and provide a moral framework for economic activity while reflecting the diverse personal precepts of the contractors? In the first place, as we argued at length earlier in this book, it would be impossible for global humanity to agree upon a particular "thick" (Walzer, 1992a) morality that would spell out in detail the boundaries of ethical behavior in economic relationships. The establishment of an ex ante detailed code for ethical behavior would necessarily compromise cherished preferences on the part of large groups of people. If an agreement concerning a large set of ethical principles or a particular dominating calculus is ruled out, then the only remaining solution is to agree upon a process or broad framework by which moral rules will be established under appropriate circumstances.

Knowing that moral rationality is bounded, and hoping (1) *to enhance efficiency by reducing uncertainty*, and (2) *to live in an economic environment compatible with their underlying cultural, ideological, and religious interpretations*, the contractors participating in the macrosocial contract would adopt an approach in which individuals have the freedom to choose the economic groups with which they affiliate. They would realize that they must rely—at least partially—upon community-specific microsocial contracts for establishing contextually appropriate rules of economic ethics. The term "microsocial contract" is used to emphasize that an important component of economic morality must emerge from agreements or shared understandings about personal precepts within a group or community. Indeed, unwritten agreements and unspoken promises among groups that must interact successfully in order to achieve both individual and mutual goals are the core framework for economic ethics. This important principle is captured in the expression "social contracts." Integrative Social Contracts Theory (ISCT), the terms of which we now spell out in some detail, constitutes the formal structure for a framework of business ethics as social contracts.

Moral Free Space

The freedom of individuals to form or join communities and to act jointly to establish moral rules applicable to the members of the community, a freedom that, as we have seen, macro contractors would endorse, may be described as "moral free space." The moral rules freely adopted by a community would reflect that community's particular goals, environments, resources, experiences, and so on. These rules would specify boundaries for economic behavior while reflecting the moral preferences of the members of the community. The rules would support the community's objectives, which might run from maximum wealth generation to insuring a fair distribution of wealth and income and guaranteeing a minimum quality of life for every member of the community.

Moral free space is a primary element of ISCT because it allows individuals within groups to specify particular moral norms as a means of enabling the satisfaction of personal precepts and economic efficiency. Moral free space implies that communities will have significant leeway in the manner in which they choose to generate their own moral rules. It does not imply, however, a moral free-for-all. The moral norms generated within a community must be acceptable to a clear majority of the community in order to be consistent with the macro contractors' desire to preserve, within practicable limits, the autonomy of individuals. Thus, the norms must be authenticated by the uncoerced consent of the majority.

The simplest way to insure this is to specify that in order to be binding, a moral norm generated by a community must be supported by the attitudes of a clear majority of the community, even as it is reflected in their behavior. To put it differently, the norm must be what we will call "authentic."[3] The norms could be generated in any of a wide variety of ways. After all, moral free space implies that communities should have significant leeway in the manner in which they choose to generate their own moral rules. In some communities, norms may emerge and change through formal processes of debate and decision making. Levi Strauss went through multiple levels of decision making in deciding to begin withdrawal from sourcing products in China. In other business communities, norms may be formed in a distinctly informal way, evolving out of interactions among members of the community. The accepted boundaries of gift giving and entertainment may be well established within a given industry when certain types of entertainment and gifts exchanged between salespeople and prospective customers become a generally accepted status quo.

The ultimate test of authenticity for a particular norm, however, would be whether it is accepted by a clear majority of the community as standing for an ethical principle. Note that an individual community member might disagree with a particular norm and might even take steps to try to get the norm changed, but still could hold the attitude that the norm constitutes an appropriate standard because of the manner in which it is generated. Consider, for example, the generation of economic norms within the Roman Catholic Church. A few Catholics may regard the vow of poverty taken by priests as extreme or unnecessary. Yet these same dissenters may nonetheless respect the economic norm as binding upon priests because it has been generated in accordance with the proper procedures of the Roman Catholic Church. The consent of these "accepting dissenters" would count toward establishing that principle as an authentic moral norm even though they might prefer a different standard. Their agreement with the norm-generation process within the community and their acceptance of the outcome constitutes consent to the microsocial contract.

So long as one is a member of a community, one has an ethical obligation to abide by the extant authentic norms that are recognized as proper in the attitudes and behaviors of a clear majority of the membership. The global contractors, open to cultural and economic diversity, would find it necessary to employ a broad and flexible definition of "community." Communities may be formed in any of a wide range of ways. Essentially, they evolve out of the marketplace as individuals interact and form various types of relationships, some formal and some informal. A broad definition of the concept of community must necessarily be employed. A community is a self-defined,[4] self-circumscribed group of people who interact in the context of shared tasks, values, or goals and who are capable of establishing norms of ethical behavior for themselves. Examples of a few of the vast array of economic communities capable of generating moral norms within their moral free space are given in Table 2-1.

The table makes evident the wide variety of communities that qualify as microsocial within ISCT. They vary in size from international organizations to small groups of a few people within an organization. They may be formally constituted, or they may evolve out of informal social or economic interactions. Political communities and organizations that operate at the global level are also microsocial communities. Thus, to the extent that a large set of global actors satisfy the ISCT definition of communities—e.g., the international oil industry—they constitute a microsocial community. The same is true of nation-states. The legal and cultural dimensions of a nation-state may have a significant impact on the generation of authentic norms within its physical and legal boundaries. It may itself contain millions of smaller communities capable of generating their own authentic norms.

One may join or become a member of a community in a wide vari-

---

Table 2-1 ISCT Microsocial Communities with Moral Free Space

Categories of Community	Examples
Political/economic entities	European Community United States New Jersey
Industries (informal)	Chemical manufacturers Software producers Travel agents
Corporations	Canon Microsoft United Way of America
Subunits of organizations (formal)	General Counsel's office Human Resources department
Informal communities within organizations	Networked female managers Networked African-American managers Managers who regularly golf together
Partnerships	Coopers & Lybrand Goldman, Sachs
Professional associations	Caux Round Table American Bar Association National Association of Realtors
Transactional communities	Those engaged in an auction All engaged in trading NYSE securities
Trade associations	International Chamber of Commerce Chemical Manufacturers Association Better Business Bureaus Cincinnati Board of Realtors

ety of ways. Membership in a community can derive from an express contractual commitment, as in the case of entering into an employment contract with a term of years, or it may just involve participating in a group and being acknowledged by others as a member. Some communities may be temporary, as in the case of a team of professionals working on a particular acquisition, and some communities may undergo a steady change in membership. A familiar example is that of an auction. Anyone who participates in an auction becomes a member of the auction community with an obligation to follow its generally understood norms. Ethical norms of auctions may include requirements concerning disclosures of agency relationships, honesty in reporting financial evidence of capacity to back up bids, and not interfering with the efforts of others to bid. One who participates temporarily in an auction, and thereby makes instrumental use of it, becomes obligated to abide by its legitimate norms—at least during the time period relevant to her participation. Those who make up the auction community are entitled to act within their moral free space to establish rules that constitute a condition of participation in the group. Without violating hypernorms, the existing members of a community may establish formal conditions of membership binding on all future potential members as long as those conditions meet the test of authentic norms.

Thus, the first clause of the macrosocial contract is:

1. Local economic communities possess moral free space in which they may generate ethical norms for their members through microsocial contracts.

Exit and Voice

Rational, knowledgeable contractors will construe consent as an ongoing phenomenon, reflective of the personal freedom of the individual contractors. Hence, the consent to microsocial contracts will be regarded as open-ended, which in turn gives rise to a continuing ability and right to revoke consent.[5] This right of revocation equates with the right to *exit* a community. A community member may be bound by clear majoritarian norms with which she personally disagrees, but she has the option of exiting the community.[6] One may exit from an economic community that has norms one finds objectionable. A morally disgruntled corporate employee who objects to norms pertaining to the use of foreign suppliers accused of human-rights violations may quit and seek employment elsewhere. A member of an industry trade association may resign in response to a change in authentic norms effectively allowing the advertising of tobacco products or liquor to young teens. A lawyer may resign from the American Bar Association in response to authentic norms within that organization that support choice concerning abortion.[7] In all of these cases, individuals are acting in response to the morality of the community by severing their membership, thereby absolving themselves of community-based obligations to conform to the objectionable morality.

Exit is often a dramatic option, and it may entail substantial costs. Changing jobs typically involves nontrivial transaction costs, and it may not be possible to find an equivalent job. If one resigns from a state bar association in protest against norms pertaining to confidentiality (e.g., norms applied in such a way that one cannot disclose that a corporate employer once sold the ingredients for a nerve gas to Hussein's Iraq), the resulting inability to practice law may make it difficult or impossible to earn a living. Morality is not costless, nor should it be. In our assumptions about the nature of economic morality, we hold that individuals price such choices and factor their moral desires against other dimensions of a decision.

Another option, entailing a different range of costs, involves the moral analogue to civil disobedience. As we will discuss in the next section and again in chapters 3 and 5, norms generated in moral free space must be tested against universal standards, or "hypernorms," in order to become ethically obligatory. Reasonably believing that an authentic norm of an organization violates a hypernorm, a morally disgruntled employee could deny the legitimacy of the norm through a refusal to follow it. If indeed the norm violates a hypernorm, conforming to it is not ethically obligatory, and the dissenting employee is within her rights in refusing to follow the norm. In addition, by holding a dissenting attitude and acting inconsistently with the norm, the employee's action weakens the case for the authenticity of the norm itself. If a sufficient number of the members of the community come to hold an attitude similar to that of the dissenter, the norm will lose its status as authentic.

Consider, for example, a manufacturer directly operating unsafe plants employing eleven-year-old children in developing countries. An employee in the home country who refuses to carry out job functions that contribute to the operation of those plants may well act consistently with the assumptions of ISCT. Similarly, a manager of a particular corporation that has an authentic norm requiring all managers to contribute personal funds to a political action committee might view that norm as inconsistent with a hypernorm supporting uncoerced political participation in democratic societies. The manager may refuse to contribute to the PAC and in doing so remain completely consistent with the principles of ISCT.

Yet members of microsocial contracts have more options available to them than merely the right to civil disobedience. Short of moral refusal lies the right of voice. The right of voice is the right of members of a community to speak out for or against existing and developing norms. The macrosocial contractors would want such an option for parties of microsocial contracts in order to insure that the evolution of norms within the contract satisfies the condition of consent. Even when members consent to relatively autocratic norm-generating mechanisms in their economic communities, the need for voice exists in order to insure that these mechanisms deliver the kinds of outcomes that are broadly acceptable to members. One is not compelled to exercise voice as part of the norm-generating process, nor is a norm necessarily defective if it is generated according to a procedure acceptable to the community, even if the procedure did not entail the exercise of voice. It is only necessary that voice remain an option. The right to exercise it must be available if circumstances require. Economic communities in which political coercion is used to stifle voice, as has been alleged to be the case for certain types of organizations in the 1990s within mainland China, are de facto incapable of generating authentic norms. To the extent that exit and voice are impermissibly repressed, they are also de jure incapable of generating binding ethical norms under ISCT.

Thus, the second clause of the macrosocial contract is:

2. Norm-generating microsocial contracts must be grounded in consent, buttressed by the rights of individual members to exercise voice and exit.

Hypernorms

Understanding that it is impossible to create ex ante a thick universal morality regulating economic ethics, the global macrosocial contractors would rely on moral free space for the generation of the essential ethical foundation for economic activities. But they would not necessarily deny the existence of a thin universal morality, nor of principles so fundamental that, by definition, they serve to evaluate lower-order norms. Defined in this way and reaching to the root of what is ethical for humanity, precepts we choose to call "hypernorms" should be discernible in a convergence of religious, political, and philosophical thought, or at least it is a reasonable hope that we should discern such a convergence. The concept of a hypernorm is used to establish the boundaries of moral free space, and individual hypernorms would limit the imposition of ethical obligations within a given microsocial community. We call such principles "hypernorms" because they represent norms by which all others are to be judged. The search for hypernorms is basically a search to validate statements such as Taylor's (1989: 64) that "many accept as their highest good . . . a notion of universal justice and/or benevolence," and Walzer's (1992a: 9) that "perhaps the end product of this effort will be a set of standards to which all societies can be held—negative injunctions, most likely, rules against murder, deceit, torture, oppression and tyranny."

The global contractors would not allow microsocial contracts (even with unanimous local consent) that condoned practices unethical wherever they occur, such as exploitative child labor, corporal punishment for employees, or barbarously unsafe working conditions. We call authentic norms compatible with hypernorms "legitimate" norms. The difficult questions concerning the specific nature of hypernorms and how they may be identified will be discussed in chapters 3 and 5.

Thus, the third clause of the macrosocial contract is:

3. In order to become obligatory (legitimate), a microsocial contract norm must be compatible with hypernorms.

Conflicts among Norms

The global contractors would anticipate the certainty that legitimate community-generated norms would sometimes conflict with one another. Recognizing both their bounded rationality and the frequency of conflicts occurring among norms in various economic communities, they would want a means to arbitrate and resolve such conflicts. Note that the problem only arises when two legitimate norms come into conflict, which is to say that each of two competing norms satisfies the test of an authentic microsocial contract norm and each is compatible with hypernorms. Otherwise, if one of a set of competing norms violates a hypernorm, it is eliminated from consideration for priority. For example, if a German company were asked by Iraq during the 1990s to sell equipment for the production of biological weapons, the conflict between its home community's abhorrence of biological weapons and Iraq's tolerance of them[8] is easily resolved if it can be established that biological weapons violate a hypernorm proscribing the indiscriminate killing of the innocent.

The issue is far more difficult when the conflict occurs between two legitimate norms. For example, in India some companies for years guaranteed employees that they would provide a job for at least one of the employee's children. The practice appears to be an authentic norm—it is extremely popular among the workers of companies that adopt the policy and is also accepted among members of the surrounding community. The practice does not obviously conflict with any hypernorm;[9] nonetheless, it would be regarded as nepotism in many Western countries. Would it be permissible, then, for a Western company with a subsidiary in Jamshedpur, India, to replicate the job guarantees of the Indian Tata company?

Clearly, the global contractors would require that any set of priority rules designed for arbitrating such conflicts remain consistent with the terms of the macrosocial contract. As is the case with hypernorms, the global contractors would not be capable of specifying the complete list of priority rules, ex ante, within the framework of the macrosocial contract. Instead, it is necessary to rely on the general proviso that any rules applied be consistent with the other terms of the macrosocial contract; in this way, at least in theory, an elaborate set of rules could emerge. Priority rules, for example, might emerge as follows. Because the macrosocial contract emphasizes the freedom of individual communities to develop ethical norms, it follows that preference should be given to norms that do not adversely restrict the freedom of other economic communities to create and support their own norms. Further, when legitimate norms have an impact solely within their community of origin, they should, ceteris paribus, be allowed to stand, even when they are inconsistent with the norms of other communities. Consider the case of an Indonesian manager participating in a real estate auction within Australia. To the extent that the moral rules pertaining to public auctions are different in Australia from Indonesia, the Indonesian manager should follow the Australian auction norms so long as doing so has consequences primarily confined to Australia.

Thus, the fourth and final term of the macrosocial contract would read as follows:

4. In cases of conflicts among norms satisfying macrosocial contract terms 1–3, priority must be established through the application of rules consistent with the spirit and letter of the macrosocial contract.

Summary of the Macrosocial Contract

In summary, then, we argue that rational global contractors, aware of many of their personal circumstances and also of the constraints of bounded moral rationality, and desiring to provide a moral framework capable of supporting economic activity and of maintaining freedom of cultural, philosophical, and religious interpretation, would agree to the following *de minimis* macrosocial contract setting the terms for economic ethics:

THE GLOBAL ISCT MACROSOCIAL CONTRACT
FOR ECONOMIC ETHICS

1. Local economic communities have moral free space in which they may generate ethical norms for their members through microsocial contracts.

2. Norm-generating microsocial contracts must be grounded in consent, buttressed by the rights of individual members to exercise voice and exit.

3. In order to become obligatory (legitimate), a microsocial contract norm must be compatible with hypernorms.

4. In cases of conflicts among norms satisfying macrosocial contract terms 1–3, priority must be established through the application of rules consistent with the spirit and letter of the macrosocial contract.

Certain key definitions are used throughout this book in discussing the implications of the ISCT macrosocial contract. An "authentic norm" is one that is generated within a community's moral free space and that satisfies the requirements of terms 1 and 2 of the macrosocial contract. As will be discussed at length in chapter 4, authentic norms are based upon the attitudes and behaviors of the members of their source communities. A "legitimate norm" is an authentic norm that passes the hypernorm screen (term 3). A norm has to be established as legitimate before it may become binding for members of the norm-generating community. "Priority rules" describe the principles consistent with the requirements of term 4, which are used to resolve conflicts among competing legitimate norms.

We offer ISCT in this book as a means to highlight the ethical relevance of existing norms in industries, corporations, and other economic communities, even as it must limit the acceptable range of such norms. The theory promises in this way to reach beyond the generality of, say, Kantian deontology or "virtue" ethics to allow a more detailed normative assessment of particular ethical problems in business. ISCT is heavily contextual and thereby establishes an agenda for empirical research as a means for establishing authentic ethical norms in industries, corporations, alliances, and regional economic systems. Its application obviously requires close scrutiny of existing ethical attitudes and practices in institutions as dissimilar as the European Community, Levi Strauss, the international rubber market, and Muslim banking. In so doing the theory adds greater specificity to the search for principles of business ethics.

ISCT is designed to recognize the substantial diversity present in economic communities. It accommodates the widely held intuition that somewhat different ethical precepts are appropriate for different industries, companies, and professions. The ethics of professional doctors need not be precisely the same as the ethics of journalists. Nor do the gift and entertainment practices within a Japanese keiretsu need to conform to the practices for government contracting within the United States. In accommodating diversity, ISCT is open to variety in individual and cultural values and preferences. It recognizes the relevance of transcultural moral understanding, even as it refuses to impose a broad conception of the "Good" upon dissenters.

3

Hypernorms: Universal Limits
on Community Consent

All law is universal; but there are some things
about which it is not possible to speak
correctly in universal terms.

—Aristotle (*Nicomachean Ethics,* 1137b13)

Moral cosmopolitans and pluralists have engaged for decades in a multifront war spanning the academic and the practical realms. As the battle has raged, philosophers and political scientists have taken particular, and often highly complex, positions. But their battle has implications for far more than academics. It affects the practical realms of foreign policy and business practice. Pluralists usually reject the idea that there can be any such thing as a human "essence." Their emphasis, instead, is on diversity, especially cultural diversity. From the viewpoint of the cosmopolitans, (or "universalists," as they are sometimes called[1]), the pluralist's position is tantamount to rudderless leadership, a kind of political amoralism that leaves global business leaders and politicians helpless. On the other side of the battle, the cosmopolitans defend the shared or universal character of the human experience. They are purveyors of a one-size-fits-all suit of clothes, which everyone should seek. To the pluralists, the cosmopolitans' emphasis on shared humanity often appears a sleight of hand: a Procrustean approach with no room for diversity or dissent.

The Role of Hypernorms in ISCT

ISCT avoids the extremes of either position by recognizing the dynamic relationships among the authentic ethical norms of diverse communities, bounded in turn by universal principles. The latter principles are called "hypernorms" in ISCT. As discussed in chapter 2, hypernorms are recognized by the macrosocial contractors as key limits on moral free space, and are essential to establishing consent in microsocial norms while recognizing precepts and values common to most people. Hypernorms constitute principles so fundamental that, by definition, they serve as "second-order" norms by which lower-order norms are to be judged. Defined in this way and reflecting the deepest sources of human ethical experience, hypernorms are discoverable, we have reason to hope, in a convergence of religious, political, and philosophical thought.

Because hypernorms play a primary role in limiting moral free space, a key question from the vantage point of ISCT is this: To what principle or principles would macro contractors consent in order to reflect their belief that moral free space should not be unlimited? Since such principles are designed to impose limiting conditions on *all* micro contracts, they cannot be derived from a single micro contract, but must emanate from a source that speaks with univocal authority for all micro contracts. Such a source would need to constitute a second-order moral perspective, which is to say that it would need to be a perspective from which all first-order, or micro, perspectives could be evaluated. The contemporary philosopher Charles Taylor's (1989) idea of a "hypergood" is precisely such a second-order perspective and is the conceptual analogue to our notion of a "hypernorm." Hypernorms are second-order moral concepts because they represent norms sufficiently fundamental to serve as a source of evaluation and criticism of community-generated norms.

Hypernorms also have an analogue in international law in the several-decades-old doctrine of *jus cogens*, described by D'Amato as the "supernorm against which all ordinary norms of international law are mere 97-pound weaklings" (1990: 1). Parker and Neylon (1989) have extended the concept by arguing that the substantive reach of *jus cogens* extends to the entire body of human-rights norms and may even be considered to preempt customary law. Thus, the concept of a second-order peremptory standard is familiar in both philosophy and law, and as we will demonstrate later in this chapter, in many other fields as well, including business.

In ISCT, hypernorms are identified and validated by the macro contractors. These far-reaching norms, moreover, are credited with independent status: indeed, most hypernorms are considered as presumptive and axiomatic elements of the theory.[2] Individual contractors are presumed to share at least a few, key, generic moral attitudes—and these attitudes are interpreted to entail the apprehension of hypernorms. However, the *source* or *sources* of most such attitudes are left unspecified by ISCT (exceptions will be discussed later). This is not meant to rule out the possibility, as Rowan's insightful commentary on ISCT suggests (1997), that all hypernorms might someday find justification within a form of macrosocial contract argument. Indeed, many philosophers believe that *all* moral norms are rooted within a social contract justification. It is only to say that, for the time being, we make no such claims.

Hypernorms may be broken into three distinct categories depending upon their source and their role within ISCT. First, there are *procedural* hypernorms that specify the rights of exit and voice essential to support microsocial contractual consent. These two hypernorms are specified in the original macrosocial contract, and are analogous to other concepts common in philosophical literature. For example, we envision the right of voice as encompassing yet extending beyond Habermas's recognition of substantive rules of argumentation. For Habermas, rules of argumentation constitute fundamental prerequisites for important forms of human communication. They may include rules such as those suggested by Alexy: "every subject with the competence to speak and act is allowed to take part in a discourse"; "everyone is allowed to question any assertion whatsoever"; and "everyone is allowed to express his attitudes, desires, and needs" (Habermas, 1990: 89). The right of exit, for its part, prohibits coercive restrictions on egress from microsocial communities. Although much of the concern is with physical coercion, extreme forms of economic coercion may also run afoul of the right-of-exit hypernorm. As discussed in chapters 4 and 6, voice and exit are vital to support consent within the microsocial contracts and thereby validate standards of behavior generated within the moral free space of communities. We underscore the importance of these principles by identifying them as formal terms of the macrosocial contract.

Second, there are *structural* hypernorms that are necessary for political and social organization. For example, the right to property, although it is defined differently by different societies, is supported by an economic hypernorm that obliges members of society to honor institutions that promote justice and economic welfare—within, of course, the bounds of other hypernorms. (We discuss a comprehensive "efficiency" hypernorm—one connected to the right to property—in greater detail in chapter 5.) In a market system, for example, in order to have a viable economic community, members must not only have the right to use personal and real property, but also must be able to exercise the right to transfer ownership rights to others (even Marxist economies allow certain forms of personal property). Or, consider the right to fair treatment under the law. Again, while different societies may define such a right differently, with some societies even eschewing formal judicial mechanisms, any society that lacks institutions for promoting judicial fairness has denied its citizens an important structural social benefit.

As a practical matter, structural hypernorms must be instantiated in background political and legal institutions that are capable of recognizing, for example, property rights and the right to fair treatment under the law. Structural hypernorms are implicit in the purpose of the macrosocial contract. In particular the macrosocial contractors are assumed to desire the efficient production of goods and services in a manner consistent with their core values. In chapter 5 we discuss at some length the underpinnings of a structural hypernorm essential to the efficient generation of both social justice and economic welfare.

The final and vitally important category of hypernorms is *substantive* hypernorms, which specify fundamental conceptions of the right and the good. (See Table 3-1 for categories of hypernorms.) In this book we are especially concerned with those substantive hypernorms that apply to economic activity. Whereas procedural and structural hypernorms are specified or implicit within the macrosocial contract, substantive hypernorms are to be found on the outside. They are, in effect, *exogenous*. Some may argue that one must specify the source of hypernorms in order to have a fully satisfactory approach to business ethics (Mayer, 1994). We disagree. Whatever the final answer to the question of whether hypernorms have sources in nature as immutable verities, or instead reflect the common humanity of global citizens as similar solutions are found to shared problems across the world, that answer is not critical to their value within ISCT. Instead, their existence is specified and recognized within the macrosocial contract, enabling decision makers to engage in a search for relevant hypernorms within given contexts. The importance of the concept and its role within ISCT is sufficient to allow for some ambiguity in their specification and identification. As Sisella Bok remarks:

> [C]ross-cultural cooperation will continue to lag far behind existing needs unless it can draw upon fundamental values that have traditionally promoted the cohesion and survival of communities under stress. Agreement regarding their justification is unlikely; but we can no longer afford not to press the long-standing dialectic regarding "universal values" beyond today's conventional certainties about the self-evidence or nonexistence of such values (1992: 12).

Table 3-1 Categories of Hypernorms

Type	Definition	Justification in ISCT	Source	Sample Hypernorms	Examples of Recognition in the Literature of Ethics
Structural	Principles that establish and support essential background institutions in society	Specification by macrosocial contractors	Microsocial contracts (at the level of economic systems)	The duty to develop and fulfill obligations in connection with social structures that are efficient in achieving necessary social goods	Adam Smith
Procedural	Conditions essential to support consent in microsocial contracts	Specification by macrosocial contractors	Macrosocial contract	Rights of voice and exit essential to support microsocial consent	Jurgens Habermas
Substantive	Fundamental concepts of the right and the good	Recognition by macrosocial contractors	Convergence of human experience and intellectual thought	Promise keeping, respect for human dignity	Michael Walzer, Chikuro Hiroike, legal doctrine of *jus cogens*

The Nature and Sources of Substantive Hypernorms

The concept of a structural hypernorm will be discussed at length in chapter 5, as we discuss the example of the "efficiency" hypernorm in some detail. The procedural hypernorms protecting voice and exit were discussed in chapter 2 and will be elaborated upon in chapter 6 as we discuss their implications for moral free space. In this section, we explore the concept of substantive hypernorms by discussing their basic nature and by providing examples of principles that people and institutions have presumed to be hypernorms. We emphasize again that the specification of a definitive listing of hypernorms is not necessary to the understanding and application of ISCT. ISCT does not envision a decision maker applying the grand statute of hypernorms to a decision in the same manner that a judge might apply the U.S. Internal Revenue Code to a tax question. As we noted in the earlier discussion of relativism, the claim to have found a final list, expressible in a particular natural language and definitive for all moral situations, constitutes a form of moral absolutism. We offer no such list of hypernorms, even though some commentators have encouraged us to do so. Instead, we explain why offering such a list would be a mistake, and, in line with Rowan's suggestion (1997: 109), we will suggest "epistemic ground(s) for the discovery of hypernorms."

In this matter, our normative inquiry shares one similarity with empirical inquiry. Empirical science has not, to date, succeeded in achieving a single language of explanation for describing the physical world. We must, rather, content ourselves with a variety of sets of concepts that best explain their relevant aspects of the physical world. The languages of chemical composition, of magnetic fields, and of functional biological entities must coexist, at least in our present state of knowledge. They cannot be integrated perfectly. For certain purposes, and for certain communities of empirical inquirers, some principles are preferable to others. For example, the differing concepts of biology on the one hand and chemistry on the other may help explain a given event in the human brain. The two languages will converge in predicting certain basic events, even as they diverge with respect to others. Almost always, they will diverge regarding the details. Nonetheless, it would be wrong to say that the brain "really" is a biological entity rather than a chemical one. In one instance, and from the vantage point of a particular scientist with a certain range of experiences, the language of biology may be best. In another instance, and for another scientist, the language of chemistry may prove more helpful.

The same is true in the moral realm. For certain purposes an Asian business community may find that the language of human rights—notably a moral language that is almost exclusively Western in its history and origin—is best for expressing a fundamental moral insight. The Asian business community may even opt to express their conviction in the English language. For other purposes, they may prefer a different formulation, say one expressed in the Chinese language and using Confucian concepts. Because each community must sometimes use moral concepts drawn from *its* traditions and experiences in order to express its views most clearly, and because it also must sometimes use its own natural language rather than a foreign language for clearest expression, it would be a mistake to offer a definitive list of hypernorms. Most communities must, as a matter of moral necessity, find and articulate their own hypernorms, using the concepts and linguistic terms that are right for them.

Before undertaking the task of providing a sufficient demarcation of hypernorms, a brief word is necessary to explain why substantive hypernorms are required as a supplement to procedural and structural hypernorms and also why the concept is realistic. Reasonable commentators such as Hartman (1996b) have argued that the search for any sort of preemptory ethical standard or theory is likely to spiral into an ad infinitum search for a nonexistent holy grail of morality. Further, Hartman is concerned that such a search may detract from a pragmatic approach to resolving ethical disputes, and he ultimately concludes, "I do not think that they [Donaldson and Dunfee] need hypernorms at any level to make their most important points" (114). Some scholars have expressed concern that any resulting list of hypernorms will not be sufficiently thick to provide adequate protection for what they consider vitally important interests or values (Mayer & Cava, 1995), while others have suggested essential modifications of the hypernorm concept, e.g., Mayer (1994), Nelson (1996), Rynning (1996), Taka (1996b).

In response we note along with other philosophers, including Habermas, that certain minimal moral conditions must be presumed even for meaningful discourse. These include the rules of engagement for the effective discursive interaction that people in a free society must have in order to arrive at shared moral conceptions. In this way, Habermas, for example, establishes a kind of minimal morality of intercommunication that precedes the search for a more substantive, or "thicker," morality. Hence, the very notion of morality presumes, according to him, background rules of engagement necessary to facilitate the free and open search for hypernorms.

Such a minimal morality, in which only discourse-protecting hyper-norms would be recognized, is too thin for the purpose of making hard choices in business. In themselves, conversational rules provide no basis for establishing the principles of common humanity served by institutions of social justice and welfare. This is the basis of Walzer's (1994: 12) criticism of Habermas. If we can agree only that we desire justice and welfare, and on the rules of conversation to follow in perusing conceptions of justice and welfare, we are left with close to normative nihilism.[3] We lack a rudder with which to steer.

A richer conception of hypernorms is gained through Rawls's recent justification of his "political conception of justice." While he limits the scope of his own conception to specific societies, Rawls (1993) argues that one advantage of his articulation of a political conception of justice is that, if the principles of the conception were accepted by contending cultures, "they could serve as the basis for adjudicating conflicts among them." In the same manner, an important role for hypernorms in international business is to serve as a reference point for arbitrating disputes. If all economic participants, for example, can agree with the International Labor Organization's position that "child labor" is not to be tolerated, this can be the basis for discussions that forge agreements about what counts as "child labor."

Rawls wisely limits his own claim of overlap to so-called reasonable doctrines, i.e., a doctrine that is "theoretically consistent and comprehensive, practically potent (an exercise of practical reason), and belongs to, or draws upon, a tradition of thought and doctrine" (1993: 59). He argues that within such a scope "we can hope [a conception of justice] can gain the support of an overlapping consensus of reasonable religious, philosophical, and moral doctrines in a society regulated by it" (1993: 12, 144–145).

While we do not intend to settle the question of which particular hypernorms are valid in this book, we nonetheless again reject the view that hypernorms are limited only to procedural principles as asserted by Habermas (1990). Our project, instead, fits within the scope of what Walzer (1994) has called "moral minimalism." "Minimalism is not foundational," writes Walzer. "[I]t is not the case that different groups of people discover that they are all committed to the same set of ultimate values." Rather, moral minimalism "consists in principles and rules that are reiterated in different times and places, and that are seen to be similar even though they are expressed in different idioms and reflect different histories and different versions of the world" (1994: 18). When U.S. television viewers in 1989 saw marchers in Prague waving signs saying "truth" and "justice," they knew, however obliquely, what the marchers meant, even though they did not share all of the marchers' ideas. Among the supporters of the Prague demonstrations, notes Walzer, there were even Christian fundamentalists, for whom secular "truth" and "justice" are not the most important things (1994: 19).

There is as of yet no Esperanto of global ethics that speaks with univocal meaning to all. Rather, ethics is inevitably expressed in ways that are "thick" with culture, tradition, and institutional significance. Thus limited, the claim for the existence of hypernorms becomes the claim for a significant area of overlap among local cultures. Like Rawls's political conception of justice, our notion of hypernorms is such that, were hypernorms accepted by contending cultures, they could serve as the basis for adjudicating conflicts among them. And as with Rawls's political conception of justice, our notion of hypernorms need not mean that all moral conceptions in a society fit neatly under a master set of values (to which alternative conceptions are subordinate). Rather, as Rawls would say, they may be only principles compatible with the major value systems supported within a population.

Because hypernorms are by definition *capable* of gaining an overlapping consensus of reasonable religious, philosophical, and moral doctrines, then *if* they exist, we should hope to discover a real-world convergence of religious, philosophical, and cultural beliefs. The existence of such a convergence is compatible with the middle area of the relativism continuum presented in chapter 1; and the existence of such a middle area implies the possibility of a broad convergence of basic values *even if* it were to turn out that agreement upon a common language and a common set of propositions (of the sort that Extreme Universalism envisions) is impossible.

However unlikely, it is logically possible (we can imagine without logical contradiction) that no such convergence would occur, or that convergence would occur around illegitimate norms. In 1943 it was logically possible that Hitler's Nazi regime would become triumphant and the world would converge around a set of twisted, anti-Semitic, moral norms. Such an outcome may have been highly improbable, but it surely possessed a nonzero probability of occurring. And yet *if* such a convergence around illegitimate norms had occurred, it would not make anti-Semitism less ethically repugnant. Anti-Semitism would have remained an ethically repugnant doctrine from an objective moral perspective; the majority of people around the world would simply have failed to recognize its moral ugliness. Unjustified persecution remains unjustified persecution, whether or not people recognize it as such.

Yet, on the assumption that billions of people possess at least moderate moral rationality, we have good reason to hope that threads of moral convergence should be discoverable in behavior patterns around the world. When Hitler's Germany adopted anti-Semitism, a significant portion of the remainder of the world kept its head. And even *had* the world taken up anti-Semitism as a global majoritarian doctrine, common threads of agreement on many other moral matters would likely have remained. Indiscriminate lying, murder, theft, and large-scale bribery would likely have maintained their strongly negative moral image. Moreover, we remember that even in Hitler's Germany, numerous members of the intelligentsia resisted the wave of hate, and spoke out against the anti-Semitism being preached. Indeed, many of these scholars and writers were forced to flee for fear of persecution.

Similarly, if hypernorms exist, then we have reason to hope to find threads of convergence around many, if not most, fundamental ethical principles. Moreover, we can at least hope that those people around the world who have studied the history of ethics and of ethical thought will have views that converge around certain basic moral attitudes. If hypernorms exist and relativism is false, then those people with reputations for either moral insight or skills, for example, moral exemplars from specific communities as well as respected philosophers and theologians, can be expected to express views that, when analyzed, converge in the same general direction. Here again, the expectation cannot be a 100 percent probability, since it is logically possible that hypernorms exist despite chaotic disagreement among moral savants around the globe. There is nothing logically self-contradictory about imagining a world in which moral savants disagreed completely. But because moral savants are by definition capable of reflecting something deeper than mere taste, and because they should be exemplars of moral rationality, we should expect to see their views, like those of the communities they guide, converging in a common direction.

Unfortunately, the impression left to outsiders of the history of moral philosophy is of turmoil and conflict. Those observers without the will or time to read intellectual history are often left with a relativistic impression of a battleground of opposing ideas. The same mistaken impression emerges of religious traditions. Both sets of impressions contain bits of truth, but are wide from the mark. It is true, for example, that John Rawls's famous difference principle (where those in society who are worst off deserve special attention when structuring social systems) differs from Aristotle's notion of "liberality" (the virtue of giving). It is also true that the Hindu conception "action-less action" (where one acts not for the fruit of action, but for a higher sense of "self") is different from the Muslim concept of "Zagat" (charity to the poor). But there is more to unite these broad conceptions of ethics than to separate them.

While granting that a convergence of ethical views is likely, we do not take a position about whether hypernorms have a purely rational basis as Kant argues (Kant, 1788/1956), or a partially empirical and historical basis as Hegel argues (Hegel, 1807), nor do we think resolving such a venerable and fundamental epistemological question is necessary to identify hypernorms in spite of the commentators that have urged us to try to do so.[4] Instead, we propose to use the existence of the convergence of religious, cultural, and philosophical beliefs around certain core principles as an important *clue* to the identification of hypernorms. We proceed in this manner because, again, even if hypernorms are certified solely through the light of reason, we should expect to encounter patterns of the acceptance of hypernorms among people around the world. Hence, patterns of religious, cultural, and philosophical belief can serve as a clue, even if not as complete validation, for the identification of hypernorms.

There is considerable evidence documenting common moral principles and even methods of moral reasoning across diverse cultures (Kohlberg, 1968). We will discuss this literature later in this chapter. Although hypernorms are universals, they will of necessity be identified and interpreted from the vantage point of a particular decision within a particular cultural environment. We believe that many of the core hypernorms are generally known and that it is important to encourage business decision makers to stop and think about the existence of relevant fundamental moral principles. Understanding hypernorms is not as difficult a task as some have suggested.

As explained in chapter 2, a vitally important presumption to consider in applying ISCT to an ethical decision is whether or not a hypernorm exists relevant to the decision. Once it is clear that a decision involves ethical issues, those making a decision must make an ex ante determination whether there are hypernorms prohibiting, affirming, or circumscribing potential courses of action. Those rendering ex post judgments concerning decisions already made must focus on the action taken. Both judgments entail looking for evidence of relevant hypernorms. If two or more of the following types of evidence confirm widespread recognition of an ethical principle, the decision maker should operate on the basis of a rebuttable presumption that it constitutes a hypernorm. The more types of evidence in support of a hypernorm, the stronger the presumption.

Evidence in support of a principle having hypernorm status:

1. Widespread consensus that the principle is universal.

2. Component of well-known global industry standards.

3. Supported by prominent nongovernmental organizations such as the International Labour Organization or Transparency International.

4. Supported by regional government organizations such as the European Community, the OECD, or the Organization of American States.

5. Consistently referred to as a global ethical standard by international media.

6. Known to be consistent with precepts of major religions.

7. Supported by global business organizations such as the International Chamber of Commerce or the Caux Round Table.

8. Known to be consistent with precepts of major philosophies.

9. Generally supported by a relevant international community of professionals, e.g., accountants or environmental engineers.

10. Known to be consistent with findings concerning universal human values.

11. Supported by the laws of many different countries.

Once having gone through these steps and having identified a presumptive hypernorm, the decision maker needs to consider whether evidence exists to overcome the presumption. If two or more of the following are found, then the presumption may be rebutted. However, the more types of evidence that support the presumption in favor of hypernorm status, the more types of evidence necessary to override the presumption.

Evidence countering the hypernorm presumption:

1. Evidence from the presumptive list to the contrary, e.g., that the putative hypernorm principle does not represent a universal value.

2. Evidence from the presumptive list in support of hypernorm status for a mutually exclusive principle.

3. A decision context such that applying the presumptive hypernorm would result in the violation of a widely recognized human right.

Identifying Hypernorms

We now consider a few examples to demonstrate the process of identifying hypernorms.

■

International Bribery

A manager for an airplane manufacturer makes/is considering a payment of $5 million to go personally to the Minister of Defense of a developing country to "win" a contract for jet fighters.

It is not necessary to identify the full range of hypernorms applicable to all forms of bribery. The question instead is whether a hypernorm applies to this particularly egregious form of the practice. Transparency International, the OECD, the OAS, the Caux Principles, laws in numerous countries (Noonan, 1984), leaders of major accounting firms (Tarantino, 1997), major religions (Nichols, 1997), and major philosophies all support a presumption that this practice violates a hypernorm. Although one might believe that there is widespread acceptance of making payments of this type to gain jobs and enhance profits, that would not be sufficient to overcome the presumptive hypernorm.

■

Gender Discrimination

A global express delivery firm owns its own fleet of vans and trucks and regularly employs women drivers in its worldwide operations. The firm conducts operations in Saudi Arabia, which has customary norms prohibiting women from driving based upon interpretations of Islamic sources. The firm's managers are deciding/have decided whether to assign a woman to drive a van.

Again, it is not necessary to parse out the full range of hypernorms pertaining to gender discrimination. Prohibitions of this selective type of gender discrimination can be found in standards of the

United Nations, the ILO, the laws of many countries, major philosophies and religions (see A. Mayer, 1991; D. Mayer & Cava, 1995). The evidence appears to meet the standard establishing a presumption. On the other hand, the Saudi norm is based upon a religious interpretation; but this understanding is not shared by the vast majority of other Muslim countries (A. Mayer, 1991). Again, the hypernorm is established.

■

Market Research

A marketing research firm gathers information about clients' products by asking questions of randomly selected consumers. The consumers are told that the caller is conducting an independent consumer survey. The firm's employees do not reveal that they are conducting the research for a particular company because of evidence that it would bias the results.

Here, the question is whether there is a hypernorm that would apply to this case. Although truth telling in general is supported by many religions, philosophies, and laws, as well as in statements of proper business behavior made by many types of organizations, none of these are specific enough to apply to the question of whether one need volunteer information in this type of interaction. It would appear that no hypernorm applies to this practice.

■

Workplace Safety

A global chemical firm operates a plant in Korea. At all of its plants around the world it requires workers to wear helmets when overhead cranes are operating in the vicinity. The Korean workers do not like the helmets, and they have walked off the job twice to protest having to wear them. A manager for the chemical firm is deciding/has decided to waive the helmet requirement.

Again, we believe that a presumptive hypernorm requiring feasible workplace safety practices essential to protect against serious physical injury is easy to recognize in this circumstance based upon global industry practice, ILO standards, major religious and philosophical precepts, and so on. Although local norms do not require helmets and the workers themselves prefer comfort over safety, these objections do not appear sufficiently strong to overcome the presumption.

We have attempted to provide straightforward examples of identifying hypernorms in order to demonstrate how, in many cases, the process is relatively easy and noncontroversial.

We now turn to more detailed concerns about searches for substantive hypernorms. On first glance, the phenomenon of cultural diversity seems to fly in the face of substantive hypernorms. Vast moral divergences have been documented among cultures and nations, including fundamental differences in approaches to business ethics. As some claim, "[t]here does not appear to be a single list of content areas—even defined abstractly as harm, right, and justice—that can capture the moral world of all peoples" (Haidt, Koller, & Dias, 1993: 625). These findings extend to the cognitive domain and the "predictions of cultural psychology, which states that psychological processes such as moral judgment may work differently in different populations" (Haidt, Koller, & Dias, 1993: 625). In an analysis of managerial behavior covering the United States and fourteen other countries in Europe, the Middle East, and Asia, Peterson and others (1993) reveal dramatic differences among managerial values and the ways in which managers are recruited, selected, and evaluated. A widely reported, massive study of global managers conducted by the *Harvard Business Review* (Kanter, 1991) found that managers' views were determined more by cultural affinity than geographic affinity. Robertson and Schlegelmilch (1992) found that even between two relatively similar nations, the United States and the United Kingdom, corporate ethics practices and managers' perceptions of the importance of various ethical issues vary significantly. For example, for U.S. companies, major ethical issues of concern are drugs, alcohol, and employee theft. In the U.K., environmental pollution and quality control are considered the most pressing ethical issues. Even the basic strategies to communicate ethics vary. Robertson and Schlegelmilch (1992) discovered that U.S. companies, in contrast to those in the U.K., are more inclined to disseminate codes of ethics to all employees. In a related domain, Hillman and Keim (1995) analyze wide variance in approaches to the business-government interface around the world.

Although there is considerable theoretical and empirical research supporting the divergence thesis, that is only part of the story. At the same time there is substantial research identifying significant areas of convergence, even where, on first impression, one might only see divergence. As research proceeds on the topic of the similarities and differences among business ethics around the globe, the convergence thesis remains strong and vital in its competition with the divergence thesis. That is to say, the thesis that the business ethics accepted and practiced around the globe tend to converge around certain principles, rather than showing either random relationships or diverging, is being supported by recent studies across a number of literatures. Within the business and society literature, Wartick (1995) explicitly defends the convergence thesis in "Organizational Cultures in Transnational Companies: An Empirical Analysis of Shared Managerial Values," and a score of additional studies lends support to it. Wartick tests the convergence thesis with his own empirical study focused on individual values, but his findings dovetail with a series of previous empirical findings in that literature.

Business theorist William Frederick (1991) has identified a set of normative corporate guidelines that he derives from an analysis of convergence among six intergovernmental compacts (including, e.g., the OECD Guidelines for Multinational Enterprises, the Helsinki Final Act, and the ILO Tripartite Declaration of Principles Concerning Multinational Enterprises and Social Policy). An example of a relatively specific universal principle posed by Frederick as a result of his research is his assertion that MNCs should adopt adequate health and safety standards for employees and grant them the right to know about job-related health hazards.

Within the social psychology literature there are numerous studies focusing on identifying universal values and common cognitive processes. One of the most challenging research tasks is identifying a valid method for comparing individuals across cultures. One study (Bond, 1988) shows promise for constructing a universal values instrument. The study compared responses from students in twenty-one cultures to the Chinese Value Survey that purports to represent values fundamental to Chinese culture as determined by Chinese scholars. Main effects for culture were found in scores for social integration versus cultural inwardness and reputation versus social morality. The results were then compared with an earlier study using the Rokeach Value Survey for nine of the cultures. A pooling procedure was used to weed out "associations unique to particular cultures (emics), leaving a residue of relations common across all. This shared structure constitutes a universal grid of values instrumental in making empirically grounded statements about cultural differences at the level of individuals" (Bond, 1988: 1014). The "pan-cultural dimensions of value" surely reflect common elements of human socialization. For example, the Bond study found sex effects across many different cultures, which he suggested must "reflect universal differences in socialization practices distinguishing the sexes" (1014).

Social psychologists Schwartz and Bilsky (1987) have proposed a theory based upon motivational domains derived from a set of universal human requirements. They describe it as "a theory of a universal psychological structure of human values" (1990: 878). To test the theory, they conducted an empirical study (1990) on respondents in Australia, Finland, Hong Kong, Spain, and the United States (coupled with an early study in Germany and Israel) and found substantial similarity in the respondents' value priorities (with a limited exception in Hong Kong). They found strong evidence of universality in both the content and the structure of the motivational domains of the individuals studied. The key issue remains, of course, whether the findings would be replicated if extended to even more diverse cultures.

In the field of international relations, Nadelmann (1990) has identified powerful global norms that prohibit the engagement of either nations or individuals in certain activities. He asserts that "(a)cts such as piracy, slavery, trafficking in women and children for purposes of prostitution, and trafficking in controlled psychoactive substances are all prohibited." Significantly, he attributes many of these prohibitions to "moral and emotional factors related to neither political nor economic advantage but instead involving religious beliefs, humanitarian sentiments, faith in universalism, compassion, conscience" and other similar factors (1990: 479).

Legal scholar Phillip Nichols (1997) has concluded that the exchange of public assets for private gain by public officials who accept bribes is condemned by explicit language in the holy writings of Buddhism, Christianity, Confucianism, Hinduism, Islam, Judaism, and Sikhism. Nichols points out that not only are such actions legally prohibited in every country, even those thought to be the most corrupt, they are also inconsistent with Kantian, utilitarian, and rights-based ethical theory and were explicitly condemned by Adam Smith and Karl Marx. Noonan (1984) provides a similar analysis concerning the widespread legal condemnation of bribery.

As Nichols demonstrates, it is possible to extend the analysis beyond particular academic fields to encompass religious and philosophical writings. In a much earlier attempt, Chikuro Hiroike, founder of the Institute of Moralogy in Japan, considered the writings of the "great sages" who had lived exemplary lives (e.g., Socrates, Christ, Confucius) to derive principles of what he called a Supreme Morality (Taka & Dunfee, 1997).

One of the more striking pieces of evidence in favor of a convergence of basic values came in 1993 when representatives of all of the major world religions met in Chicago. The representatives' combined interfaith declaration, entitled *Towards a Global Ethic* (Council for a Parliament of the World's Religions, 1993), was the result of a two-year consultation among more than two hundred scholars and theologians representing the world's communities of faith. Leaders from all the world's major faiths signed the declaration, containing scores of substantive points of agreement about ethical principles. Interestingly enough, one of the major principles endorsed by the group was that every principle expressed in their Global Ethic "can be affirmed by all persons with ethical convictions, whether religiously grounded or not" (1993: 3). In addition to the formal agreements of religious communities, one can examine nonreligious agreements such as the United Nations' *Universal Declaration of Human Rights* (1948), in which virtually all nations of the world affirmed a set of basic rights, or the many other international documents that embrace rights principles. Similarly, there are economic agreements among nations that express moral norms. At the most specific level of detail are principles adopted by firms, industries, and organizations of senior business leaders. One of the most relevant of such groups is the Caux Round Table (CRT), an organization of senior managers from major global corporations. The CRT was formed in 1986 by senior executives from Europe, Japan, and North America to address global issues affected by the performance and conduct of international business. The CRT has developed an aspirational statement of Principles for Business designed to express a world standard against which business behavior can be measured. To reflect the multicultural nature of the group, the principles are based upon a combination of Eastern and Western ideals: *kyosei*, a Japanese concept emphasizing living and working together for the common good; and human dignity, a Western concept emphasizing the sacredness or value of each person as an end and not merely as a means to the fulfillment of others' purposes.

The Caux Principles encompass both general and specific standards. Consider the following excerpts from the Principles (1994):

Principle 2. The Economic and Social Impact of Business: Toward Innovation, Justice, and World Community.

Businesses established in foreign countries to develop, produce, or sell should also contribute to the social advance of those countries by creating productive employment and helping to raise the purchasing power of their citizens. Businesses also should contribute to human rights, education, welfare, and vitalization of the countries in which they operate.

Principle 3. Business Behavior: Beyond the Letter of Law Toward a Spirit of Trust.

While accepting the legitimacy of trade secrets, businesses should recognize that sincerity, candor, truthfulness, the keeping of promises, and transparency contribute not only to their own credibility and stability but also to the smoothness and efficiency of business transactions, particularly on the international level.

Section 3. Stakeholder Principles.

CUSTOMERS

We believe in treating all customers with dignity. . . . We therefore have a responsibility to treat our customers fairly in all aspects of our business transactions, including a high level of service and remedies for their dissatisfaction. . . . [We must] respect the integrity of the culture of our customers.

We believe that a multidisciplinary, cross-cultural process must be invoked to identify substantive hypernorms, as reflected in the scope of proxies we use to establish presumptive hypernorms. We note, with great encouragement, the increasing number of individuals who have been engaged in a search for universal values, beliefs, and cognitive processes. Coming from diverse intellectual and professional fields and from many cultures, some of which we have identified above, these individuals may be loosely grouped together as convergence scholars. Any growing convergence in the findings of the convergence scholars should be a sure beacon that helps to illuminate specific substantive hypernorms.

Foundations for Substantive Hypernorms

Many fundamental principles and concepts may be identified as foundations for hypernorms in given decision contexts. They may pertain to specific business practices, or they may be more broadly cast, as in the case of environmental issues and human rights. An example of the latter is Walzer's concept of "self-determination," which refers to the right of a people to take some control of their own destiny. Despite the existence of difficult issues, such as those involving Jews and Palestinians in the Middle East, most people would affirm the right of a people, in some form and to some degree, to influence the outcome of their own destiny. "Self-determination is abstracted from all of its reiterations, including our own," writes Walzer. "When ancient Jews and Gauls defended their freedom against the Romans, the arguments they made were hardly democratic; nor were they cast in the language of rights. But we have little difficulty recognizing the principle even in alien idioms" (Walzer, 1994: 68). This principle supports the basic concept of moral free space, discussed in the next chapter, but also may serve as a foundation for informed consent about chemical hazards.

Many lists of transcultural ethical norms include bona fide human rights. The set of ten fundamental international rights constructed by Donaldson (1989) will undoubtedly point toward important substantive and procedural hypernorms:

1. The right to freedom of physical movement

2. The right to ownership of property

3. The right to freedom from torture

4. The right to a fair trial

5. The right to nondiscriminatory treatment

6. The right to physical security

7. The right to freedom of speech and association

8. The right to minimal education

9. The right to political participation

10. The right to subsistence

We present these and other sources in Table 3-2, "Sources for Presumptive Hypernorms," and Table 3-3, "Sample of Foundations for Presumptive Hypernorms." The lists are meant neither to be exhaustive nor conclusive. They are meant to display a sample of sources and norms applicable to transcommunity contexts. Both tables organize information under two major headings, "Philosophical" and "Collective Agreement." The "philosophical" category in-

Table 3-2   Sources for Presumptive Hypernorms

Philosophical	Collective Agreement
Hans Kung (Kung, 1991) *Twentieth-century theologian*	Universal Declaration of Human Rights, United Nations (1948)
John Kline (Kline, 1994) *International relations theorist*	Council for a Parliament of the World's Religions (Towards a global ethic, 1993)
Richard DeGeorge (DeGeorge, 1993) *Contemporary philosopher, specializing in international business ethics*	Institute of Moralogy (1987)
John Rawls (Rawls, 1971) *Contemporary philosopher*	Chemical Manufacturers Association
Amartya Sen (Sen, 1992) *Contemporary economist*	Moral principles derived from international trade and business relationships—interpreted by William Frederick (Frederick, 1991: 166–167)
Immanuel Kant (Kant, 1785/1959) *Nineteenth-century German philosopher*	Moral principles derived from international law—interpreted by Terence Nardin (Nardin, 1983)
W. D. Ross (1930) *Early twentieth-century philosopher*	Global 2000 Report from Millennium Institute (Barney, 1993)
John Locke (1690/1948) *Eighteenth-century philosopher*	Caux Round Table (1994)
Henry Shue (1980) *Contemporary political scientist*	
Confucius (1948) *Ancient Chinese philosopher*	

cludes individual philosophers and theologians with reputations for ethical knowledge, e.g., John Rawls or Hans Kung. The "collective agreement" category includes agreements reached by different communities about common norms, e.g., the *UN Universal Declaration of Human Rights.* The second table, "Sample of Foundations for Presumptive Hypernorms," also includes five subcategories, namely "general," "global arrangements," "environment," "social," and "economic."

Table 3-3   Sample of Foundations for Presumptive Hypernorms

	Philosophical	Collective Agreement
General	Act only on the basis of principles that you could will everyone to act upon. *Immanuel Kant (Kant, 1785/1959)* [Practice] "reciprocity": Do not do to others what you do not want done to yourself. *Confucius (Confucius, 1948)[a]*	What you do not wish to be done to yourself, do not do to others. Or in positive terms: What you wish done to yourself, do to others! *Council for a Parliament of the World's Religions (Towards a global ethic, 1993)*
	We share a sense of the sacredness of the individual person and his conscience. *Hans Kung (Kung, 1991)*	All human beings are born free and equal in dignity and rights. They are endowed with reason and conscience and should act towards one another in a spirit of brotherhood. *Article 1, Universal Declaration of Human Rights, United Nations (1948)*
	[We must come to] the realization of [the importance of] benevolence. *Institute of Moralogy (1987)*	Our different religious and cultural traditions must not prevent our common involvement in opposing all forms of inhumanity and working for greater humanness. *Council for a Parliament of the World's Religions (Towards a global ethic, 1993)*
	[People should have] maximal liberty comparable with a like liberty for everyone else. *John Rawls (Rawls, 1971)*	A Fundamental Demand: Every Human Being Must Be Treated Humanely. *Council for a Parliament of the World's Religions (Towards a global ethic, 1993)*

[a] In the section "Analects," Book XV: 23. Quoted in Stewart & Donleavy (1995: 18). The article offers an interesting comparison of the Aristotelian and Confucian doctrines of virtue, asserting that the center of the Confucian ethic lay in the ideal of the "superior person" or *junzi*, and showing how the virtues of the *junzi* paralleled the virtues expressed in Aristotle's Golden Mean. For discussions of how Confucius affirmed the Golden Rule (although in a negative rather than positive formulation), see Allinson (1985, 1990).

Table 3-3, continued

	Philosophical	Collective Agreement
General (continued)		MNCs should respect the rights of all persons to life, liberty, security of person, and privacy. *Moral principles derived from international trade and business relationships—interpreted by William Frederick (Frederick, 1991: 166–167)*
	It is prima facie right to keep a promise, and prima facie wrong to lie. *W. D. Ross (1930)*	[Nations have a fundamental moral obligation, expressed in international law] to observe treaties. *Moral principles derived from international law—interpreted by Terence Nardin (Nardin, 1983)*
Global Arrangements	[People should strengthen] . . . international law and the rule of law . . . to restore the global political confidence that will permit action. *Global 2000 revisited (Barney, 1993)*	The principle of legal equality among states, the right to national self-defense, the duties to observe treaties and to respect human rights, the concepts of state sovereignty and non-intervention, and the duty to cooperate in the peaceful settlement of disputes. *Moral principles derived from international law—interpreted by Terence Nardin (Nardin, 1983)*
	[People should] . . . find and employ alternatives to war, violence, and militarism in resolving differences among nations and peoples. *Global 2000 revisited (Barney, 1993)*	We commit ourselves to a global ethic [of] peace-fostering . . . ways of life. *Council for a Parliament of the World's Religions (Towards a global ethic, 1993)*
	We must all work for the cause of "perpetual peace." *Immanuel Kant (Kant, 1785/1959)*	We all have a responsibility for a better global order. *Council for a Parliament of the World's Religions (Towards a global ethic, 1993)*

Table 3-3, continued

	Philosophical	Collective Agreement
Global Arrangements (continued)	Multinationals should cooperate with the local government in developing and enforcing just background institutions. *Richard DeGeorge (DeGeorge, 1993)*	[People should] . . . participate with government and others in creating responsible laws, regulations and standards to safeguard the community, workplace, and environment. *Chemical Manufacturers Association*
	Firms should . . . consider their impact on a range of stake-holders, i.e. parties involved with and affected by the corporation's actions. *John Kline (Kline, 1994)*	Everyone has the right to take part in the government of his country, directly or through freely chosen representatives. *Article 21, Universal Declaration of Human Rights, United Nations (1948)*
Environment	If a multinational builds a hazardous plant, it has the obligation to make sure that it is safe and that it is run safely. *Richard DeGeorge (DeGeorge, 1993)*	MNCs should control specific operations that contribute to pollution of air, water, and soils. *Moral principles derived from international trade and business relationships—interpreted by William Frederick (Frederick, 1991: 166–167)*
Social	[People should establish] . . . social and institutional conditions that actively resist corruption and favoritism by making opportunities for upward social mobility dependent on personal contribution rather than on class, cultural, or religious background or on race or gender. *Global 2000 revisited (Barney, 1993)*	Every human being without distinction of age, sex, race, skin color, physical or mental ability, language, religion, political view, or national or social origin possesses an unalienable and untouchable dignity. *Council for a Parliament of the World's Religions (Towards a global ethic, 1993)*
	[Social arrangements should be evaluated in terms of their ability to promote] a person's capability to achieve functionings that he or she has reason to value. *Amartya Sen (Sen, 1992: 4)*	All are equal before the law and are entitled without any discrimination to equal protection of the law. *Article 7, Universal Declaration of Human Rights, United Nations (1948)*

Table 3-3, continued

	Philosophical	Collective Agreement
Social (continued)		We condemn sexual exploitation and sexual discrimination as one of the worst forms of human degradation. *Council for a Parliament of the World's Religions (Towards a global ethic, 1993)*
Economic	[All persons have a basic right to] minimal economic security, [entailing a right to] unpolluted air, unpolluted water, adequate food, adequate clothing, adequate shelter, and minimal preventative public health care. *Henry Shue (1980: 20–23)* Multinationals should contribute by their activity to the host country's development. *Richard DeGeorge (DeGeorge, 1993)* Inequalities fostered by social institutions are tolerable only so long as they work to the advantage of everyone, including the worst off. *John Rawls (Rawls, 1971)* The right to own property is a direct extension of the right to own one's body. *John Locke (1690/1948)*	In the developed countries, a distinction must be made between necessary and limitless consumption, between socially beneficial and non-beneficial uses of property. *Council for a Parliament of the World's Religions (Towards a global ethic, 1993)* Everyone has the right to a standard of living adequate for the health and well-being of himself and of his family. *Universal Declaration of Human Rights, United Nations (1948)* If the plight of the poorest billions of humans on this planet, particularly women and children, is to be improved, the world economy must be structured more justly. *Council for a Parliament of the World's Religions (Towards a global ethic, 1993)* Everyone has the right to own property alone as well as in association with others, and no one shall be arbitrarily deprived of his property. *Article 17, Universal Declaration of Human Rights, United Nations (1948)*

Views about Hypernorms

Since the appearance of the articles that first articulated the ISCT concept (Donaldson & Dunfee, 1994, 1995; Dunfee & Donaldson, 1995), commentators have discussed hypernorms and, in some instances, have offered suggestions about their substance and form. In this section, we comment briefly on these writings.

Steinmann and Scherer, Frederick, and D. Mayer, among others, have all argued for more clarity on the fundamental epistemological nature of hypernorms. Bill Frederick (1995) has argued that hypernorms should be clearly understood to encompass values emerging from nature. Frederick states that "it is difficult to imagine principles more 'fundamental to human existence' than the nature-based values of economizing, technologizing, and ecologizing"(1995: 273). Ironically, the examples that we give in this chapter and in chapter 5 of substantive and structural hypernorms are consistent with, indeed sometimes nearly identical to, Frederick's lists of nature-based values. His disappointment is that we fail to take a definitive position supporting a naturalistic foundation for hypernorms. Interestingly enough, we have been encouraged to take the opposite position and to conclude that hypernorms are based, not on nature, but solely in reason (Mayer, 1994).

We remain agnostic on the ultimate source of hypernorms in spite of the well-intentioned encouragement from both sides of the argument to take a stand.[5] We hold to this position for multiple reasons. First, as we argued at length earlier, we do not believe that it is critical to our purpose of describing and justifying ISCT. Our criteria for substantive hypernorms are sufficiently open to capture hypernorms regardless of the epistemological source. Whether hypernorms are based in reason or in nature, they should be recognizable in a convergence of intellectual thought and should be proclaimed global norms. Our definition of hypernorms, reflected in the delineation of three separate categories, is quite flexible. This elastic definition is sufficiently resilient to capture both traditions.

Mayer and Cava (1995) argue that whether or not one finds a hypernorm of a certain kind depends upon whether one utilizes a naturalistic or rationalistic approach. They consider the example of gender equality in work settings, and assert that it is easy to discover a hypernorm supporting gender equality if one takes an approach of rationalism in ethics (although they add that other approaches, e.g., rights analysis, would more easily produce the same result). On the other hand, they suggest that if hypernorms are sought in an empirical convergence of global opinion, then no hypernorm of gender equality can be shown to exist. They assert that in any analysis of hypernorms, the outcome will be determined by epistemological factors. Mayer and Cava conclude that "the reality of a global hypernorm favoring gender equality in work settings is doubtful, since many countries appear to reject gender non-discrimination in work settings" (1995: 267).

In their analysis, Mayer and Cava also express dismay that a clearcut hypernorm fails to resolve international gender discrimination cases in a manner consistent with their intuitions. Husted (1996) expresses similar concern regarding the isolation of a hypernorm that condemns discrimination against HIV-infected persons.

We note that a clearer specification of the objectionable behavior at issue, e.g., gender or HIV-carrier discrimination, can often facilitate the identification of relevant hypernorms. For example, many instances of gender discrimination may also involve the denial of basic economic opportunity, and if so, another hypernorm, i.e., one dealing with a right to basic economic opportunity, may help to unravel the problem. To the extent that, on the basis of gender, a woman is being denied basic economic opportunity, it may be clear that her "different treatment" is unethical. On the other hand, some forms of different treatment, especially when encouraged by religious convictions and the attitudes of affected women, may not be unethical. Our point is that more precise definition of the issue, stemming from the process in which one first identifies the ethical decision and then seeks to identify relevant hypernorms, is more likely to produce results than a top-down analysis in which a simple, preexisting "definitive" list of hypernorms is used with deductive reasoning.

We believe that Mayer and Cava and Husted interpret our theory too narrowly. We did not exclude the possibility of the existence of other hypernorms by offering two relatively noncontroversial examples (Donaldson & Dunfee, 1994: 267). Nor would studying practices in "many countries" serve as a definitive test of hypernorms. The convergence we advocate goes much further and extends into deep patterns of belief, in global culture and in the views of respected moral, philosophical, and religious theorists. It is not limited to a narrow survey of legal practice among nation-states. As Dienhart (1995) notes, the search for hypernorms does not reduce to mechanics.

An additional question from Frederick's critique of hypernorms is fascinating: "If based in nature, then do hypernorms evolve?" The question of whether hypernorms change over time is closely tied to their epistemological basis. If not seen as evolving from nature, but from pure reason (as Kant would argue) or from God (as many religious theorists would argue), then it is difficult to interpret them changing at all. They are, rather, fixed by the nature of reason or the will of God. If viewed as deriving from an immutable and unchanging nature (as Spinoza would argue), then clearly they could not evolve. If, on the other hand, they are seen as deriving from an evolving natural process (as Marx or Tilhard De Jardin argued), then they clearly *may* change and evolve—albeit in a slow, glacial pattern. So, for example, if humanity and nature are seen as evolving in fundamental ways, then hypernorms do change over time in response to changing human needs and circumstances.

Hartman (1996b), who sees hypernorms as global authentic norms, believes that hypernorms do indeed evolve. He is therefore concerned with the process by which hypernorms are generated, and notes optimistically that "in due course bad hypernorms may change or disappear." It should be clear that the process of applying ISCT may result in variations in the hypernorms identified over time. That does not necessarily mean that the underlying set of hypernorms has changed. Instead, it may just reflect changes in the methodologies by which hypernorms are recognized.

Mayer (1994) expresses the concern that a convergence test for hypernorms may result in anomalies, such as a finding that there was no hypernorm against slavery in 1600, as he asserts.[6] Mayer further worries about an implication that there may not be a hypernorm against slavery in the year 2200. He offers as a solution a two-tier approach to hypernorms in which the "strongest" hypernorms would be based not only on shared practices and beliefs, but also on moral theory, widely celebrated and honored virtues, and values professed in morally mature societies.

Rynning (1996) joins Mayer in arguing for a broader definition of hypernorms. He advocates extending ISCT beyond a communitarian theory to incorporate liberal conceptions of ethics. He argues that "hypernorms could in addition be based on teleological ethical theories, where the good is defined prior to the right" (1996: 117). We note that there is nothing in our discussion of hypernorms that would exclude input from teleological theories. In fact, the convergence principle is explicitly open to inputs from all serious sources of intellectual thought. On the other hand, the convergence principle is not limited to one or two "certified" sources. Both Mayer and Rynning, we believe, interpret our prior, admittedly sparse, writings on hypernorms too narrowly.

Japanese scholars have provided useful insights into the role of hypernorms within the context of ISCT. Umezu (1995) has suggested an assembly of communities as a means for ascertaining and/or building moral consensus. Protected by Habermasian rules for communicative action, such an assembly would constitute an institutionalized moral consensus-building procedure. Although we applaud and encourage attempts to provide transparency for hypernorms, we remain concerned about introducing excessive formality into the process of identifying hypernorms. Taka (1996b) proposes amending ISCT for the Japanese experience by replacing hypernorms with the concept of a comprehensive norm. The latter are less than universal norms and may be perceived differently by one community than by another. Taka argues that this approach helps to overcome the problem of ambiguity in identifying hypernorms and would make ISCT more practical. We are concerned that such an approach effectively cuts loose the anchor holding the ISCT vessel against the tides of relativism. As Taka recognizes, the goals that he seeks to achieve can, in many cases, be met through the application of the priority rules where there is a general consensus among communities, or where the norm of a much larger community is held to dominate.

Nelson (1996) takes a similar tack, expressing concern that the broader the list of communities across which consensus is sought, the narrower any set of resulting hypernorms. She responds to this by looking to a more limited community for the source of hypernorms. In her application of ISCT to Richard Branson's defiance of French Sunday blue laws by opening his Virgin Megastore on the Champs Élysées on Sundays, Nelson looks to the national constitution to parse what is essentially a French hypernorm. To our view, instead of determining the existence of a hypernorm, which we think is unlikely to exist regarding the issues involved with this form of regulation, Nelson has instead identified a French authentic ethical norm. Thus the case seems more open to resolution by application of priority rules than reliance on hypernorms. Nelson also argues that there must be consideration of hypernorms "that pertain to profit," defining the proper emphasis on profit versus other objectives of the firm. We agree in part, but believe that such hypernorms are better grounded in the macrosocial contract as structural hypernorms (see chapter 5) than left to the search for substantive hypernorms.

Prevost (1997) raises the issue of the underlying need for ISCT insofar as substantive hypernorms are independently obligatory. Even granting that some alternative authority might be established for most or all substantive hypernorms, the role of ISCT in recognizing the significance of microsocial community norms and their relationship to universals remains salient. Ultimately, Prevost sides with those who prefer to minimize the role of hypernorms while emphasizing the role of microsocial contracts (Hartman, 1996a; Conry, 1995).

Steinmann and Scherer (1997) are among those who have suggested that hypernorms as we envision them may not actually exist. They cite Huntington and others to the effect that no "convergence of religious, cultural and philosophical orientations . . . actually exists at all" (1997: 22). And while this would not strictly rule out the existence of hypernorms (again, their existence is logically compatible with either a lack of convergence or with a global convergence around illegitimate norms), Steinmann and Scherer raise an important issue. Were no convergence discernible, then an important clue to the discovery of hypernorms would be lacking. Nonetheless, we find the arguments offered above on behalf of hypernorms compelling. Those who would deny their existence must show how the many detailed attempts identifying putative hypernorms or universals fail—something that Steinmann and Scherer have not, at least as of this writing, managed to do.

Most of those who have taken ISCT's concept of hypernorms or "second-order" principles seriously have utilized them to good effect, evidenced by the following examples: prohibiting bribery and extortion (Fritzsche et al., 1995; Puffer & McCarthy, 1997); protecting a right to safety (Strong & Ringer, 1997); and prohibiting slavery, piracy, genocide, and racism (Mayer, 1994). We note with interest that several writers have rejected the possibility of a hypernorm placing a blanket prohibition on environmental degradation, and instead have identified a hypernorm prohibiting environmental degradation only in cases where human well-being is directly and immediately threatened (Fritzsche et al., 1995; Mayer, 1994). This conclusion may be a consequence of considering the environmental question solely in terms of short-term impacts. We believe evidence supports a presumptive hypernorm prohibiting environmental actions directly harmful to humans, as was the case of business decisions leading to the mercury poisoning of a community water supply in Japan. But focus on the short term may cause one to miss evidence of a convergence toward concern about the long-term impacts of actions affecting the environment. There may well be an emerging hypernorm recognizing the importance of the environment to the ultimate survival and prosperity of humankind. Long ago William Blackstone (1974) argued cogently for a "right to a livable environment." In 1996, the Japanese Keidanren revised their Charter for Good Corporate Behavior to note that "the times require that corporate management actively incorporate nature conservation [and] preservation of the global environment . . . in their business strategies."

Hypernorms and Recognition

As Charles Taylor (1992) has noted, the general issue lying in the background of any search for hypernorms involves the two distinctive kinds of *recognition* required when considering global issues. When we give validity to widely respected transcultural norms, we in effect recognize the shared humanity that resides in each of us. When we assert the corresponding validity of moral free space (chapters 2, 4, and 6), we recognize the unique identity of particular peoples and cultures. As Taylor notes, the first is the universal recognition that is owed to any human, while the second is the recognition of one's own particular cultural or even individual identity (1992: 32). Susan Wolf acknowledges both forms of recognition—for example, she asserts that full public acceptance of each person as an equal citizen "may require two forms of respect: one, respect for the unique identities of each individual, regardless of gender, race or ethnicity; and two, respect for those activities, practices, and ways of viewing the world that are particularly valued by, or associated with, members of disadvantaged groups, including women, Asian-Americans, African Americans, Native Americans and a multitude of other groups in the United States." But both kinds of recognition have sometimes failed to find philosophical favor.

Most of the history of ethical theory in the Western world reveals a preoccupation with the former, "universalist" perspective, and a neglect of the latter, "unique identity" perspective. For example, the writings of Kant, Mill, Sidgwick, Rawls, and others speak hardly at all about the cultural affinities, gender or racial identities, and community memberships that inform so much of the commonsense interpretation of ethical issues. Such "particularist" identities are considered largely irrelevant in the face of the all-unifying identity of a person as a "human." Fortunately, this preoccupation with stripped-down ethical universalism has been coming under increasing scrutiny, and the work of philosophers such as Williams (1985) and MacIntyre (1981) have drawn praise for pointing out the danger of sterility in universalist moral interpretation. Culture-rich and community-rich contexts are coming to matter more and more for moral thought. Indeed, the turn taken by Etzioni and others to "communitarianism" (Etzioni, 1988) may be seen as a sympathetic extension of this very insistence to take community conceptions of the Good, and not merely universal precepts, as morally relevant. Clearly, ISCT, with its community-centered interpretation of economic ethics, fits comfortably into this new, evolving perspective.

Having identified the risk of sterility in universalism, we should remind ourselves that it is a mere trifle next to that of forgetting universalism altogether. Elevating family, community, ethnic, or national values over fundamental norms of respect and human decency is a well-trodden path to moral rationalization. To recognize one family's or one nation's moral identity is not inevitably a decisive consideration in tradeoffs with other values. Great art and literature frequently stress universalist over more immediate community concerns. The temptation to abandon human, universalist principles in the pursuit of family or community goals can lie at the root of moral tragedy. Characters from great literature often fight for family or community interests, blind to how they are trampling sacred human principles. Macbeth fought hard for his wife and family interests, just as Agamemnon did for his Mycenean community; but the resulting tragedies of their lives are told in ways that warn us of the dangers of placing family or community before universal principles. Again, most of us need little reminding of the privileged status of friends and family members; rather it is *strangers* we need reminding about.

In turn, much of the recent writing on multiculturalism expresses justified concern that respecting one's cultural identity, whether it be as a Christian, a Jew, a Muslim, a Native American, or whatever, may take precedence over respecting one's humanity and in this way deny some people proper respect, civil and political liberties, and decent life chances (Taylor, 1992). As Taylor writes, it may be that "women in patriarchist societies have been induced to adopt depreciatory images of themselves." They may have "internalized a picture of their own inferiority, so that even when some of the objective obstacles to their advancement fall away, they may be incapable of taking advantage of the new opportunities" (1992: 25). The plain truth is that ethics requires a balance between the universal and the particular, and when the balance is lost, the moral game is up.

In turn, ISCT endorses the ability to choose *from within* a partially communitarian perspective, but *without* sacrificing either the particular or the universal. It embraces a communitarianism that acknowledges that communities have a right to preserve their own identity—extending even to the choice of noncommunitarian arrangements—while recognizing that universal norms must limit such arrangements. Charles Taylor has remarked that "there must be something midway between the unauthentic and homogenizing demand for recognition for equal worth, on the one hand, and the self-immurement within ethnocentric standards, on the other. Cultures other than our own *do* exist, and we must learn to live together, indeed more and more, both on a world scale and co-mingled in each individual society" (1992: 72). In this sense ISCT is an attempt to find a middle course between ethical universality and cultural particularity. In the next chapter we discuss the communitarian perspective inherent in moral free space.

4

Ethical Norms and Moral Free Space

The stuff of a civilization consists largely of its substantive norms.

—Ellickson (1994: 184)

In this chapter we explore in detail the core ISCT concept of moral free space, define the key term "authentic ethical norms," discuss the role of communities and the process by which norms are generated, and suggest how to identify authentic norms when making business decisions.

Moral Free Space

Moral free space is the area bounded by hypernorms in which communities develop ethical norms representing a collective viewpoint concerning right behavior. Recognition of the existence of community moral free space is an important foundation of ISCT. Deal-breaking, and deal-making, aspects of business often depend upon ethical norms generated by business communities that have stakes in business transactions. This immutable fact is obvious to business practitioners. They readily recognize that standards for key business practices such as gift giving or entertainment vary significantly among communities—and that a "one-size-fits-all" template for business morality is an illusion. ISCT builds upon these rich, contextual standards in providing guidance for determining the boundaries of ethical behavior.

The term "moral free space" implies that it is right and proper for communities to self-define significant aspects of their business morality. As we saw in chapters 2 and 3, communities can, limited only by hypernorms and, in some instances, the superior norms of other communities, "fill in" the opacity left by bounded moral rationality in the pursuit of either greater efficiency or of certain cultural or religious understandings. These norms guide behavior and often help mitigate conflict. They may range from principles requiring disclosure of conflicts of interest by financial advisers to norms about dating coworkers. Activities involving cooperative behavior engaged in by large numbers of people often require the filling in of moral free space with ethical norms. Consensus about standards of behavior is typically a prerequisite for efficient and successful interactions.

Sometimes explicit contracts, laws, or written organizational rules are the source of essential ethical guidelines. Often, however, ethical rules develop informally through implicit agreements among groups of people. Such norms may evolve within a community, so that when strangers inside the community meet, they understand how the rule governs their interaction. Thus, complete strangers may readily understand that staggered or alternating entrance is the preferred form for traffic merging from two lanes into one, even though there has never been any discussion of the norm, nor any explicit promulgation of the norm by some authority. The business landscape is heavily laden with analogous unwritten ethical rules that guide behavior.

Community-specific norms, therefore, find their overall philosophical justification in the shape and rationale of the macrosocial contract. But why do specific ethical norms evolve? The first, most general reason relates to an inherent problem in the application of ethical rules. Devising ex ante a broad and comprehensive set of specific ethical rules that will be clear and satisfying in all future business relationships is a precarious undertaking. Many examples validate this prediction. The attempts to develop an ex ante Marxist morality as a guide for "just" economic activity in China and the Soviet Union failed utterly. In another vein, U.S. corporations have developed elaborate and extremely detailed ethical codes, sometimes spanning hundreds of pages, only to find that in many cases it is better to use shorter statements of values and credos and to provide a process, such as hot lines, to offer contextual real-time guidance. Thus, the phenomenon of bounded moral rationality frequently leads to reliance on norms that emerge only after a group's membership and objectives are determined and the context of the problem of unethical behavior is clear.

A second important factor supporting the evolution of informal norms is the enormous variety of moral preferences among individual community members and their communities. Firms, even within the same industry, may develop quite different values and traditions. The infamous litigation between Texaco and Pennzoil in the mid-1980s (*Los Angeles Times*, 1987) reflected the vast cultural gap between the two firms, particularly as to norms about negotiating. Pennzoil recognized obligations to honor promises deriving from informal agreements, while Texaco treated the terms of any deal as tentative until reaching a legally binding, formal contractual agreement. The case involved a negotiated acquisition by Pennzoil of Getty Oil, which had been announced by both parties and widely reported in the media. Nonetheless, after this publicity, Texaco made a successful bid for Getty. This conflict of ethical perspectives produced litigation alleging knowing tortious interference with the "contract" between Pennzoil and Getty. Pennzoil won a jury verdict of over $10.5 billion, which led to a bankruptcy filing on the part of Texaco and an ultimate settlement over $2 billion. The Texas jurors who stunned Texaco with its verdict apparently relied on their belief in ethical norms consistent with the claims of Pennzoil that Texaco had stepped way over the boundaries of proper behavior.

Third, corporations and other business organizations frequently reflect the religious or cultural attitudes of their employees or of the surrounding culture. Indeed, some firms evolve unique value cultures. A firm may describe itself, say, as an African-American, Jewish, or Christian firm and tout its orientation in its advertising.[1] The portrayal implies that the firm embodies desirable values regarded as positive attributes by potential clients and customers. Within the bounds of moral free space, these organizations act to select and nurture values that differ from those of many other organizations and that reflect their own preferences, ownership, and history. Across cultures, this contrast is even more dramatic. A bank in Saudi Arabia or Libya may be expected to express different values and norms in its behavior than one located in New York City or in Tokyo. Moral free space provides an ethical justification for this diversity.

Finally, the flexibility and openness of moral free space allows for the generation and modification of the ethical norms essential to enable organizations to accomplish their goals efficiently. For example, the principle of disclosure has different ramifications in the context of the sale of medicine than it does in marketing research. Full disclosure to subjects of the purpose and sponsorship of a particular marketing research study may compromise the study's quality and legitimacy. On the other hand, full and effective disclosure may be critical in order for consumers to avoid injury when taking prescription medicines. It should not be surprising when variant norms of ethical behavior emerge in the two industries.

The development of idiosyncratic norms in moral free space transcends social culture. Both authoritarian societies, such as the People's Republic of China (Wu, 1996), and highly socialized societies, such as

Japan (Taka, 1996a, 1996b[2]), allow for a surprising range of diversity in behavioral norms among their business communities. On the other hand, Japanese and Chinese organizations can be expected to differ significantly from their Western counterparts in the manner in which they utilize their moral free space.

Moral free space, then, (1) enables organizations to deal with the opaqueness that results from bounded moral rationality, (2) allows communities to reflect (within important limits such as hypernorms) their own chosen values and preferences, (3) provides for variances reflecting a world of enormous diversity, and (4) allows communities to develop ethical norms enabling efficient achievement of core goals. Having considered the nature and characteristics of moral free space, our next task is to discuss its key component, namely, authentic ethical norms.

Authentic Ethical Norms in Business

Authentic ethical norms represent the consensus of the individuals who constitute a given organization or group on the propriety of particular behaviors. The term "authentic" is used to indicate that the norm is genuine in a community, that it actually represents a community consensus concerning parameters of ethical behavior. Putative norms often turn out to be spurious upon closer examination. For example, the written "official" ethics standards for lawyers in a state may specify that corporate attorneys have a mandatory obligation to blow the whistle when they have believable evidence that their firm is violating criminal environmental standards. This seemingly worthy standard may be thought to represent the ethical norms of the community of lawyers formally expressing the standard. However, closer investigation may determine that most attorneys in the state believe the bar standard requires actions which, in their opinion, may constitute an inappropriate breach of confidentiality. Further, there may be evidence that virtually no lawyer in the state acts consistently with the standard. In such circumstances, the putative norm of corporate lawyer whistle-blowing would not be authentic.

Authentic ethical norms reflect the aggregate attitudes and behaviors of the members of an identifiable community. The concept of an ethical attitude is central to an understanding of moral free space within ISCT. We first discuss attitudes in reference to individuals. Individuals hold attitudes about what constitutes appropriate behavior in a given context. Attitudes are the product of personal values, experiences, and the environment in which one works and lives.[3] Often, they form over time as decisions are made and repeated. An individual beginning a new job may suddenly confront a novel problem, such as pressure from salespeople and colleagues to accept gifts or use frequent flier coupons in a manner inconsistent with company rules. The individual assesses whether or not the action is acceptable behavior and makes a decision as to how to act. The decision whether to accept the gift or to make personal use of coupons may recur. The evolving attitude may also be affected by influential others such as social friends or professional colleagues outside the firm, by the company's attempts to reinforce its rules, and by a myriad of other factors. Over time, an attitude crystalizes concerning the propriety of the action. Within organizations, employees support some putative rules while rejecting others. For example, individual employees might come to believe that the rules restricting accepting gifts from suppliers represent valid ethical obligations, while at the same time concluding that rules prohibiting personal use of frequent flier coupons generated from company travel are unjust. Employees might reject controversial rules regulating coupons by reference to general industry practices or prior practice within the firm.

Individual attitudes, thus defined, relate to the propriety of particular actions. They are more focused than general beliefs or values (be a good person, do not intentionally harm others, act to maximize utility). Because they are to some extent context specific, an individual may adopt attitudes that apply general values inconsistently. A salesman who holds the view that it is never appropriate to take something without permission from a neighbor's home may also hold the attitude that it is acceptable systematically to take supplies and equipment from her employer. Similarly, a unit manager may hold the view that it is important to be scrupulously honest in financial reporting within the firm, yet may think that it is legitimate to overstate deductions on income tax returns.

Ethical attitudes are malleable. They are constantly subject to the individual's reactions to experiences and changes in the environment. Abrupt attitudinal shifts may occur, for example, when an individual confronts an unfamiliar environment, such as a new job. Although ethical attitudes are associated with particular behaviors, it is assumed that individuals may, on occasion, act inconsistently with an ethical attitude. There are a number of factors that may produce actions at variance with attitudes. One may be coerced to act, as when employees who believe whistle-blowing to be ethically required forgo it after a threat from a superior. Or one may be deceived into taking an action inconsistent with one's ethical attitudes as, for example, when an employee concerned about the environmental impact of an assigned job relies upon false assurances.

A necessary condition for an authentic norm is that most individuals within the group hold attitudes consistent with it. Thus, an ethical norm for a particular community represents a certain form of the aggregate attitudes of community members in reference to the propriety of particular behavior. Group behaviors should ordinarily track closely with aggregate attitudes. A norm's authenticity depends both on the existence of behavior in accord with the norm and beliefs in accord with the norm.[4]

Many examples exist. For a long time there seemed to be an authentic norm in the United States holding that hard liquor firms should refrain from advertising their products on television. In 1996, amid some controversy, Seagram's started advertising on television, and soon other members of the industry followed their lead (*Wall Street Journal*, 1996). The norm had existed for nearly five decades, having been adopted as part of a voluntary Code of Good Practice of the Distilled Spirits Council of the United States in 1948. Presumably, firms in the industry agreed with the norm and followed it, although there was no industry enforcement mechanism or legal compulsion involved. Seagram explained their nonconforming actions by stating that the norm had become "obsolete." Seagram's contravention of the long-standing norm (with roots from 1936) was criticized by some members of the industry, and the three major television networks indicated that they would not accept advertising for hard liquor. Nonetheless, Seagram's actions may result in the evolution of a new norm within the industry.

The Internet constitutes an environment in which informal norms of appropriate behavior, or "Netiquette" (Shea, 1994), have rapidly appeared and changed as the uses and structures of the system have evolved. The Internet itself may enhance the development of authentic norms. Comments are posted publicly. Sometimes a posting party is publicly "flamed" with highly critical comments from several parties, and in some egregious cases, by tens of thousands. Communities are formed spontaneously, as in the case of people with common interests joining certain list servers, and they develop norms of proper, expected behavior. Two examples of Netiquette are "don't advertise on this list" and "don't give personal replies over this list." Consider the following statement of Usenet's norms given in a reference book for new Internet users.

> Almost no USENET groups allow ANY commercial messages. . . .
> Why not? Well, there are several reasons.
> First, because it's been mutually agreed to by everyone on the network. It's part of the deal. There's a general fear that if people were allowed to advertise the network would soon become nothing but advertisements. . . . [W]e will not let people bother others by trying to sell them things. It will always be VOLUNTARY whether anyone is exposed to such messages or not (Dern, 1994: 241).

Note how Dern's justification of the norm refers to an implicit mutual agreement among Internet users. Although his claim that "everyone" has agreed is surely hyperbole, it is plausible to assume that a substantial majority in many Internet communities agrees with the core idea behind the "do not advertise here" norm. On the other hand, there are lists in which advertising is acceptable; in fact, some are designed solely for the sale of goods and services. As is true in all areas, each community develops norms that reflect its own culture and goals.

Other typical Internet norms are that conversations should remain within certain topical limits (don't talk about opera on a sports list and vice versa) and that private email shouldn't be forwarded without the sender's permission, something that has become very easy to do with new technology. There are lists in which profanity or risqué comments are verboten, and other lists for which such language and topics are the raison d'être. Norms protecting privacy, allowing people to participate in an environment reflecting their own interests and values, and preserving the noncommercial nature of the Internet are clearly concerned with right behavior.

Finally, important norms exist across broad communities, such as nation-states or large business groups. No matter how large, however, any community is capable only of generating authentic ethical norms, not hypernorms. Hypernorms transcend communities, and by doing so create obligations for all communities. Authentic norms, in contrast, must be grounded in specific communities. Many norms having their source in large communities nonetheless reveal convergence with the norms of other large communities—a phenomenon, as argued earlier, that is suggestive of (although not proof of) the existence of a hypernorm. Consider, for example, the shared concern with trust.

Obligations related to trust, such as promise keeping, appear to be authentic norms throughout major business communities everywhere.

Attitudes plus Behaviors

The identification of authentic ethical norms is a critical source of business ethics in ISCT. It is critical to identify correctly *which* ethical norms are, in fact, genuine, particularly when the consequences of an error are dramatic. Tobacco company marketers may have thought that they had implicit support in community attitudes for low-key marketing attempts to induce mid-teens to start smoking. If they did so, and failed to read the moral tea leaves, they made a mistake that cost their shareholders substantial sums of money. Similarly, the Shell executives who planned to dispose the Brent Spar drilling station misread the authentic norms of the European community.

Why invoke consideration of *both* behavioral and attitudinal evidence in identifying authentic ethical norms? Shouldn't either alone constitute sufficient evidence of authentic norms? The answer is straightforward. Neither alone guarantees that a putative norm reflects a consensus among the membership of a community. Behavior may easily be coerced and may not represent the genuine attitudes of the community members. Thus, attitudes are added to behaviors to guard against the possibility of coercion. A strong case could be made for relying on attitudes alone, as long as it is possible to read accurately the attitudes of community members. Although identifying attitudes should be possible in circumstances in which one can use scientific methodologies, as a practical matter it is often necessary to rely upon presumptions and proxies. Such measures may, on occasion, result in a false reading of group attitudes. Thus, behaviors are added to attitudes to guard against the possibility of misreading a community consensus.

As Keeley (1988, 1995) has repeatedly warned, unethical behavior may be coerced within organizations. Some employees may use threats to compel their colleagues to comply with their practice of overbilling the firm for travel and entertainment expenses. In other cases, employees may be aggressively coerced to go along with or contribute to a sexist atmosphere rising to the level of "hostile environment" sexual harassment. Coercion may also occur in transactions between organizations. Bribes may be extorted through threats of physical violence or financial ruin. Even altruistic behavior may sometimes reflect compulsion rather than authentic norms: one may, for example, be subtly coerced to donate to the United Way or give blood by public disclosures and/or critical comments within an organization.

Because behavior is relatively easily coerced, evidence concerning behaviors in support of the identification of particular ethical norms should be discounted if there is any evidence of coercion. Behavioral evidence should be treated as valid prima facie, subject to evidence that the behavior has been coerced or is the result of deception or mistake. If the latter evidence is sufficient to discount the behavioral evidence, then attitudes alone may have to be the basis for recognition of authentic ethical norms.

Attitudes themselves, as opposed to the revelation of attitudes, are unlikely candidates for coercion. By definition, an attitude represents one's personal, private viewpoint concerning an ethical standard. Even though an attitude may be influenced by what may be characterized as inappropriate or coercive outside pressure, the attitude nonetheless represents the particular individual's orientation toward the practice. Tyler (1998) questions the propriety of playing upon a person's sense of justice to produce a false consciousness in support of outcomes in which the person is objectively disadvantaged. Although pejorative terms such as "brainwashing" or "reeducation" can be used to refer to such phenomenon, externally determining "correct" attitudes is highly problematic. Thus, for our purposes, the issue with attitudes is whether a genuine attitude has been identified, or whether researchers have been deceived, not whether a genuine attitude is the product of "coercion." To the extent the genuine attitudes are identifiable, they represent the foundation for community norms.

Coercion may indeed be a problem in one context involving attitudes. Certainly, it occasionally happens that individuals are coerced into misrepresenting their true attitudes. Filling out a questionnaire with one's name at the top may force an employee into concealing her true attitude. Having employees vote with a public show of hands in support of controversial workplace rules or processes produces an environment ripe for subtle intimidation. Secret ballots, guaranteed confidentiality, and other techniques may help to guard against these forms of coercion.

Beyond the danger of coercion, it is entirely plausible that individuals may seek to hide or misrepresent their true attitudes. Opportunists commonly try to convince others they are trustworthy. Messick

(1991: 321) has described the rational motives that may underlie "the tendency to endorse an ethical principle and to behave according to its opposite." If one can convince others of the genuineness of one's altruistic nature, one may draw the friendly attention of those who cooperate with and even reward altruists. Hence, one may try to pose as a believer in particular ethical principles. Some may even come to believe themselves that they hold the requisite moral attitude because a learned habit of self-deception may be a profitable characteristic (Messick: 322).

Those who believe that they are out of step may try to impart the false impression that they hold the attitudes they believe the community expects of them. Opportunism and social desirability bias may make it difficult to identify collective attitudes of a community with sufficient accuracy. For example, there may be many who actually hold an attitude inconsistent with a presumed norm against sexual harassment within a community. Because of social pressures and a desire to conform to what they perceive to be the norms of the community, they may signal socially desirable attitudes to outsiders. Such false signaling may result in outsiders' misreading authentic norms for that community. Proper survey techniques will often overcome the phenomenon of social desirability bias, but its existence greatly complicates the use of proxies and presumptions as a means of identifying authentic norms. The requirement of complying behavior as a necessary component of authentic norms serves as a check against possible misidentification.

An objection may be raised to the behavioral requirement for authentic norms on the grounds that it eliminates the norms of aspiration long considered part of the province of business ethics. For example, a putative norm that one should not engage in bribery in global transactions might meet the attitudinal test; but because competitive and political pressures produce substantial noncompliance, it would not rise to the level of an authentic norm.[5] The members of a particular corporation may hold the attitude that in a more perfect world, one should never engage in bribery, but that current conditions justify certain forms of payments. Attitudes that recognize an excuse or justification for certain forms of behavior in current circumstances are not really based on aspiration. Instead, a true aspiration-based attitude would be one to the effect that the world needs to change and members of our community should act now to try to bring about such a change. Attitudes of that type are fully compatible with the approach taken under ISCT. Statements and arguments concerning what should constitute proper behavior are part of the process by which attitudes and behaviors evolve among the membership of a community. Aspirational visions are part of the voice by which attitudes are changed and modified. Their role is not lessened in any way by the complying behavior requirement. When the conflict between aspirations and actual behavior is caused by coercion or significant deception, then the behavioral requirement should be discounted. This method of examination should also serve to sustain important norms based on aspirations.

As we have seen, there are a number of sound reasons why a behavioral test must be coupled with the attitudinal requirement. The social contracts approach is contextual. It assumes that many norms derive out of very specific contexts, and when they are acknowledged as right (wrong) behavior by a majority and are followed by most community members in future cases, they rise to the level of authentic norms. Attitudes often have some element of generality (bribes should not be paid to customs officials in China), whereas behavioral decisions are always entirely contextual in that they occur within a specific environment at a specific time. Attitudinal "norms" may be identified that are not ratified by community behavior. The practical implication of using attitudinal norms as ethical standards in such circumstances would be to condemn the majority of a community for acting unethically on the basis of the community's own norms. Such a conclusion may be sustainable in rare circumstances. But ordinarily there should be a particularly strong justification for adopting a standard at odds with the behavior of most members of the group. At the least, there would need to be a clear understanding of why the norm was not being followed (perhaps because of physical coercion within a repressive political community) in order to justify it on the basis of attitudes alone.[6] Adding a behavioral requirement increases the chances that a norm is genuine within a population.

There is also the possibility that the social desirability bias phenomenon may also apply at the level of the community as a whole. A majority within a group or community may think that it is desirable that the community be identified as following a particular ethical standard to gain positive public relations for the whole community. An organization may want to convey the impression that it is indeed concerned about environmental issues or equal opportunity. Most members of the organization express sentiments consistent with the standard, and they may in fact come to believe that they have adopted this attitude. Yet their behavior is not consistent with the attitude they profess. This type of "false attitude" should not be sufficient to sustain identification of an authentic ethical norm. Outsiders may suspect such false attitudes and therefore discount their reading of norms from the organization. This may have happened in regard to Shell and the Brent Spar incident.

In summary, in most cases, both attitudes and behavior must support an authentic norm. For example, a substantial majority of the members of a particular corporation may express the attitude that everyone in the firm has an (ethical) obligation to make at least a small donation to the United Way. This standard is publicized to reflect the charitable nature of the employees of the firm. Obligatory giving to the United Way would rise to the level of an authentic norm if it also were supported by consistent behavior on the part of a majority of the employees of the firm. But if due to economic circumstances, or some other reason, few employees actually give to the United Way, then an authentic norm does not exist. The aggregate attitude, by itself, should not be sufficient to establish an obligation for all members of the firm to contribute. It may be, as Richardson (1990) suggests, that a more narrow definition of the norm can be identified, e.g., that those who are financially above a certain level have an obligation to give. The more narrow statement may turn out to be an authentic norm supported by both attitudes and behavior.

Emergence and Evolution of Norms
within Moral Free Space

The process by which norms evolve varies among communities. The purpose, nature, and social environment of a community will greatly influence how norms are generated within a community. Particularly within organizations, factors such as the character of leaders, the backgrounds of employees, type of industry, and similar influences will be important. Even religious teachings and interpretations may be a dominant influence for an Islamic bank or a self-identified Christian corporation. McKee Corporation (manufacturers of Little Debbie's snack cakes) may reflect the attitudes of its Seventh-day Adventist founders even when it reaches a size of 2,700 employees. Or Ukrop's Super Markets in Richmond with 5,000 employees may have authentic norms that reflect the values of its Southern Baptist owners—maintaining the policy, for example, that it would be improper to sell liquor or be open on Sunday. Professional or industry norms may be a more important influence on the development of authentic norms within securities firms relating to such factors as the honoring of oral promises. Shared experiences and knowledge about technology and innovation may be influential in high-tech firms, whereas a love of the product may influence those who work for automobile manufacturers. Leaders of an organization may nurture authentic norms as in the case of McKee Foods or Ukrop's. Other authentic norms may evolve in a bottom-up manner as a result of common experiences and environmental influences within the organization. A key element is that, particularly within a clearly defined community such as a corporation, the members of the community understand the existence of a shared commitment to particular norms and can even specify them if requested.

Vidaver-Cohen (1993, 1995, forthcoming) has studied at length the phenomenon of workplace moral climate. She defines moral climate as "prevailing employee perception of organizational signals regarding norms for making decisions with a moral component" (forthcoming). The extensive literature on moral climate indicates that "organizational culture and climate are particularly influential determinants of moral conduct in the workplace" (1995: 318). Thus, moral climate is both the product of authentic ethical norms and a powerful intervening variable in the creation of new norms. Vidaver-Cohen (1993) has identified several of the key processes by which ethical climates, good and bad, develop (or emerge): leadership, organizational structure, policies, incentive systems, decision making, and informal systems. In a like manner, these should be expected to influence the development of authentic moral norms within the moral free space of organizations.

Outside sources may influence the development of norms. Law, particularly when it is perceived as legitimate by members of a community, may have a major impact on what is considered to be correct behavior. Thus, the U.S. Corporate Sentencing Guidelines may be expected to influence perceptions of appropriate structures and policies for assigning managerial responsibility pertaining to corporate social responsibility. Conventional wisdom holds that U.S. law has influenced changes in ethical norms pertaining to racial or gender-based discrimination and also as to the legitimacy of insider trading.

Routinized practices may evolve into authentic ethical norms over time as the conduct comes to be seen as the only right way to act. The sale of autos by negotiated price is seen as ethically legitimate,

whereas sale of nonprescription drugs is not. Real estate and paint-
ings may be sold by auction, while auctioning popular toys during the
holidays or umbrellas during a storm is seen as unfair and inappropriate (Kahneman et al., 1986).

Authorities who proffer "norms" as correct behavior may influence
the evolution of consistent authentic norms. DeGeorge (1993), for
example, has put forward seven general ethical norms designed to
enable multinationals to act with integrity. The first three are (1)
multinationals should do no intentional direct harm, (2) multinationals should produce more good than harm for the host country, and (3)
multinationals should contribute by their activity to the host country's development. DeGeorge then extends these norms with more
specific supplements—e.g., in transferring hazardous technology to
less-developed countries, multinationals are responsible for appropriately redesigning such technology so that it can be safely used in the
host country. DeGeorge is using the term "norm" differently than we
are. His norms are statements of correct behavior, which may be
inconsistent with the actions and beliefs of many people.

Yet norms proposed by authorities such as DeGeorge may influence
the development of attitudes and behaviors and thereby influence the
creation of ISCT authentic ethical norms. Intermediaries may be
important in the process by which expert norms become more generally accepted. For example, a resolution sponsored by the Interfaith
Center on Corporate Responsibility proposed to shareholders of J. P.
Morgan & Co. in 1998 asked that Morgan & Co. insure that its
operations contribute to the sustainable development of less-
developed countries. Reinforcement of DeGeorge's third norm by
intermediaries may eventually lead to its status as an authentic norm
in international banking.

The evolution and nature of norms have been the subject of substantial theoretical and empirical inquiry. Axelrod (1986) has suggested that the most powerful form of norm is a "metanorm," which
carries with it a subsidiary norm in which people are obligated to support the metanorm. Those who fail to support the metanorm are subject to stigmatization. For example, one who knows of child abuse
and fails to report the abuse may be stigmatized by the community
based solely on the failure to support the norm against child abuse.
Failure to correct the violation of a metanorm itself constitutes a
breach of community morality. Axelrod has suggested the following
list of mechanisms that appear relevant to the evolution of putative
norms into "authentic" norms under ISCT (see Table 4-1).

Table 4-1 Axelrod's Norm Support Mechanisms

Mechanism	Operation	Example
Metanorm reinforced by subsidiary norms	Stigma imposed on those who fail to punish or correct violation of a metanorm	Stigma of someone failing to report child abuse
Dominance	Stronger group uses power to coerce behavior of weaker group	Apartheid in South Africa
Internalization	Psychological self-enforcement, no incentive to defect	Believing Muslims who pray at designated time in set manner each day
Deterrence	Group stigmatizes, even where costly, to prevent future defections	Baseball umpires responding strongly to one being spat upon
Social proof	Actions of others as basis for one's own actions	Driving "with the flow of the traffic" to define speed limit
Membership	Formation of group defines what is expected of members	Organizational rules concerning gifts and entertainment
Law	Reinforces social norms by state-supported enforcement and also by legitimization	Seat-belt laws
Reputation	Reinforces a social norm by allowing additional inferences to be drawn about the kind of person the actor is	Wearing expensive clothes to the opera

Among Axelrod's mechanisms, internalization, social proof, membership, and reputation seem likely to be particularly important in the generation of norms within business firms. The relative influence of particular mechanisms varies among communities. Even the "harder" forms of influence, such as law and social deterrence, may not work in a given context. Laws banning all sales of alcohol or prohibiting the sale of certain products on Sunday have in the past failed to bring about corresponding changes in attitudes. A current example involves the awarding of scholarships based on need, e.g., through the federal Pell Grant program. The existence of the program "has affected parents' attitudes toward financial aid" (Stecklow, 1997: 1). Many parents misreport their income and assets when applying for financial aid for their children.[7] Legal attempts to establish a metanorm status have not succeeded, as many universities fail to report misrepresentations on financial aid applications to the government even though legally required to do so.

We have identified many influences on the development and evolution of authentic norms. The way in which authentic norms are generated may vary greatly among communities. We now turn to consider the communities themselves and their role in relation to authentic ethical norms.

Communities and Groups as the Source of Authentic Ethical Norms

Authentic norms derive from common attitudes and behaviors within a recognizable community or group. The importance of communities in the identification of ethical norms raises the question of whether there should be a strict, formal definition of the term "community."[8] We previously defined a community as "a self-defined, self-circumscribed group of people who interact in the context of shared tasks, values, or goals and who are capable of establishing norms of ethical behavior for themselves" (Donaldson & Dunfee, 1994: 273). This open-ended definition is intended to allow for great variety in the way in which people form relationships capable of generating authentic ethical norms. It recognizes that people may develop authentic norms within informal relationships, as, for example, in the context of a "shadow" or "informal" organization where information and even decision making flows outside formal organizational channels.

The corporation is probably the most significant type of community within the context of ISCT. Corporations usually have clear legal boundaries and a specified membership. Larger corporations tend to have ethics programs and managers devoted to resolving ethical problems both within the firm and in its interactions with others. It may be easier to identify and understand authentic norms associated with corporations, particularly as they are the most significant actors on the economic stage at the beginning of the new millennium. For these reasons, many of the examples and criteria that we use in this book involve corporations.

By their very nature, corporations contain systems designed to influence the attitudes of employees. Most formal corporate ethics programs have significant components directed toward employee training and communication. Informal brown-bag sessions, formal training classes, company newsletters, and ethics hot lines are all part of a vast arsenal of strategies used to influence employee attitudes. Assuming that firms must be efficient in this process in order to be successful in achieving their goals, it follows that formal organizational standards constitute prima facie authentic norms.

Firms work to create authentic norms. Additional norms originate among groups of employees. The result is the creation of millions of firm-level authentic norms within business corporations across the globe. The scope and nature of these norms vary greatly. Most organizations tend to have firmwide ethical norms considered applicable to all members of the organization. For larger corporations, the story is somewhat more complex. Corporations typically contain within themselves cohesive subcommunities. Among the many possibilities, subcommunities may be composed of departments, specialists, or task-related groups. They do not necessarily follow organizational lines. Norms may vary within an organization, even to the extent of subunits recognizing contradictory ethical norms. The public relations department of a drug company may have quite different norms from the scientists working in research and development. The general counsel's office in a corporation may have a cohesive set of ethical norms that differ in significant ways from those of the organization as a whole, and also from other units of the organization. Norms may evolve from common roles regardless of organizational form. Corporate lawyers assigned to divisions who operate outside of a general counsel's office may nonetheless develop common norms reflecting their similar role within the organization.

There are, however, many noncorporate communities that may also generate authentic norms critical to an understanding of business ethics. Some may be highly informal, even transient. Individuals may associate themselves with others and develop informal rules of behavior on the basis of very casual or incidental interactions. For example, a "common fate" identity may emerge whereby individuals having similar characteristics develop norms of mutual commitment.[9] Ethical norms arising out of such common fate identity may be very strong

(Messick & Bazerman, 1996). A corporation with a pervasive culture may create common opinions concerning proper behavior. People who recognize such norms, and who consider them obligatory among a defined set of others, constitute an ISCT community, even though they may not satisfy traditional criteria for recognizing communities. For example, based on shared values about research and teaching, ethical norms about the primacy of ideas and free inquiry may emerge among a community comprised of a diverse set of academics from disparate cultures, fields, and institutions. Authentic norms may evolve among people who tend to congregate at the water cooler for a morning coffee break. Ethical obligations can emerge among groups of people who would never have been thought of as a formal community prior to the creation of the norms. These examples emphasize the core element of the definition of an ISCT community: the capacity of an identifiable group of people to develop authentic norms.

The basic concept of community in ISCT recognizes that individuals interact in a limitless number of often spontaneous ways within the business world. The means of interaction and the output of the interaction are constantly changing, and may be particularly open-ended when business transactions occur across cultures. To try to identify ex ante the permissible characteristics of social-contract-capable communities is inconsistent with the assumptions underlying the very idea of moral free space. The most rational approach to the problem of bounded moral rationality recognizes that people will form into groups as they wish. Within most communities, both formal and informal, individuals act to devise local moralities essential to maintain the group and enable it to obtain its goals. This is true for Microsoft when its employees develop norms concerning work hours and protection of confidential information. It is also true for research scientists at Merck who develop a departmental norm that they want leeway to investigate Third World applications for potential new drugs, regardless of profitability.

Even though ISCT is open to informal community structures, the task of applying ISCT is made easier by the fact that the dominant institutions of the business world tend to be highly formal communities with defined boundaries. The identity of the employees of a major corporation, such as Merck, is readily ascertainable. This is true of most large corporations using a formal hiring process. Similarly, formality surrounds, even defines, becoming a member of a bar association, or a registered securities representative, or a certified financial

planner. All of these communities, in turn, have institutional structures and processes designed to generate preferred authentic norms
among their members. For example, all three of the professional communities mentioned above presumably have authentic norms defining
obligations of confidentiality applicable to their members while acting in a professional role.

In contrast to persistent, distinct communities such as corporations
and professional associations are the highly informal communities
that come into momentary existence around certain types of recurring
transactions. Membership in a transaction-based community tends to
be noncontinuous. One is only considered a member of the community during the time period in which the transaction is actually taking
place. The norms in these communities may only be applicable to the
single transaction that generates the "membership." Even so, the
norms from these ad hoc communities may be just as powerful and
influential as norms from more formal communities.

A good example of an informal, transaction-based community is
that of an auction. One may be recognized as a member of the auction community merely by participating. As discussed in chapter 2,
the instrumental use of the auction activity is sufficient to establish
membership through implicit consent. The membership in turn carries with it an obligation to abide by the ethical norms of that community, which may include a requirement that any agency relationships be disclosed, that intentions to seal a contract will be signaled
by certain gestures, that bidders have the financial wherewithal to pay
their bids, and so on.

An essential and defining characteristic of a community for the purpose of ISCT, then, is the ability of a given set of persons having some
form of association with one another to generate authentic norms.
One implication of this loose and flexible definition is that individuals
may simultaneously be members of lots of different communities.
Another is that a given ethical decision may implicate the norms of
several different communities. Chapter 7 will present options for sorting among competing, conflicting norms. The nature of the communities involved and their relationship to each other must necessarily be a
component of that process.

A final word is necessary about the nature of the communities in
which norms may be found. They may be separated into *horizontal*
and *vertical* categories based upon their relationship to each other.[10]
(There may also be relationships between communities that are nei-

ther vertical nor horizontal, but for the moment we treat only these two.) Communities that are entirely subsumed into a larger community are involved in a vertical relationship. Other communities have horizontal relationships. Nation-state to nation-state is a horizontal relationship, as is the relationship between competing corporations. But corporations have a vertical relationship to their home nation-state, as does a corporate subsidiary to its parent firm.

The horizontal-vertical dichotomy helps to identify sources of potential norms applicable to a given ethical decision. A decision concerning safety standards at the Union Carbide plant in Bhopal invokes norms governing safety in both the U.S. and Indian culture. Both nation-states have an equivalent status, and their relationship is horizontal. A recent example of a norm emerging among horizontal communities is reflected in conduct codes among retailers trying to insure that their suppliers don't employ underage workers. In contrast, consider the case in which Seagram's decides to start advertising hard liquor on television. That decision invokes norms of horizontal communities such as the liquor industry and the television networks, but it also invokes the norms of the United States as a whole. The United States is the broader community encompassing both the liquor industry and the television networks. In this case, the relationship is vertical. Because of vertical relationships, individuals are often in two or more communities simultaneously. One is concurrently a member of a corporate subsidiary, the parent company, the home nation-state, and so on. Individuals may also belong to two or more horizontal communities, as in the case of an individual who maintains two residences, or a travel agency employee who is stationed on site at a client. The relationship between communities is relevant to deciding which norms should be given priority.

Identifying Authentic Norms

An authentic ethical norm exists within a group or community whenever a substantial majority of the membership holds the attitude that a particular behavior is right (wrong) and a substantial majority act consistently with that attitude.[11] The most straightforward test for the existence of an authentic norm would entail directly ascertaining the attitudes and behaviors of the requisite population.

The great diversity in the manner in which norms are created complicates the process of identifying norms. Norms may evolve without any expression in words ever occurring. There is no set formula by which norms become established. The process by which norms come to be is, of necessity, sui generis to each group or community. Direct information about relevant attitudes and behaviors is always the best evidence for authentic norms and should dominate when available. But in many, probably most, cases, direct evidence will not be readily available to a manager or ethicist trying to assess whether a given action is ethical. In such circumstances, the options left for identifying authentic ethical norms would be either to evaluate the process by which the norm was created, or to rely upon proxies identifying presumptive authentic norms. We will propose an approach based upon consideration of both process and proxies as a realistic way of generating a workable list of authentic norms. Before suggesting the details of our approach, we first offer a few comments concerning procedural tests, the vital importance of getting authentic norms right, and the difficulties associated with the task.

Because of the great variety of ways in which norms may evolve within communities, the test of an authentic norm cannot be solely procedural in the sense that particular procedures are specified ex ante as guaranteed producers of authentic norms. Although authentic norms are founded upon majoritarian ideals, it does not follow that particular procedures authenticate norms. A majority of community members subscribe to a particular attitude as a result of a wide variety of phenomena. Corporate employees may, for example, adopt an attitude because a highly respected CEO states that it is a proper view to hold. Or, within a Muslim firm, an authentic norm may be the result of a common reading of religious authorities. The majoritarian foundation of authentic norms does not imply that representative procedures will, ipso facto, produce genuine norms. Thus, the test cannot be reduced to ascertaining whether a proper vote was held, or whether every member of the group or community had an opportunity to provide input into the "adoption" of the norm. On the other hand, the process by which a norm is generated may corrupt the norm. As we have cautioned, coercion or deception are highly problematic in reference to ascertaining whether norms are authentic.

Proxies also have their dangers. It is a legitimate concern that norms identified by proxies , such as provisions in a corporate code of ethics, might be found spurious if relevant direct evidence of attitudes and behaviors were available. The H. J. Heinz case (Post & Goodpaster, 1981), commonly taught for many years in business ethics classes, provides a prime illustration. Heinz had an explicit corporate ethical policy stating that "no division should have any form of unrecorded assets or false entries on its books or records." This policy could be seen as a proxy for an ethical norm adopted by a substantial majority of the members of the organization. But in fact, as the perverse effect of a management incentive plan, a substantial percentage of the managers of the firm acted inconsistently with the stated policy. The reality was that an authentic ethical norm forbidding double bookkeeping did not exist at Heinz.

There may be many instances in which putative norms do not deserve the status of authentic norms. Corporate policies pertaining to dress codes, smoking, frequent flier awards, or political activity may not be ratified by the members of the organization. A firm may express a policy of affirmative action, but a majority of the employees of the firm may disagree with the policy and, to the extent that they can, act inconsistently with it. A firm may strongly encourage all of its employees to give blood or to support the United Way annual campaign. Representatives of the firm may claim that "we all support the Red Cross drive," but it may turn out that a majority actually do not, and they only seemingly consent because of the coercive power of the firm.

It is vitally important that the techniques used to identify authentic norms limit the possibility that ersatz norms are identified. Even the scientific methodologies used to identify aggregate attitudes must be carefully monitored. For example, individual attitudes may be based upon mistaken beliefs about what other members of a community think. There is a well-documented tendency for people to believe that others are less ethical than they are and that a great deal of unethical behavior occurs. Systematic cognitive errors such as the self fairness bias, in which one tends to judge one's own contribution on effort while judging others on results (Messick & Bazerman, 1996), may cause individuals to misidentify authentic norms.

The manager who needs to make an immediate judgment and a scholar who is assessing a current course of action generally do not have the luxury of making use of formal research methodologies to identify authentic norms. This option would be more available to a scholar who is trying to judge ex post a particular decision or common business practice. Nor do we think empirical research is necessary in most cases. Instead, the ex ante decision maker can rely on traditional sources of information. A simple framework should work in most cases.

Certain proxies are commonly used and have been shown to be accurate in reflecting the existence of authentic norms. They may serve as the basis for a presumption concerning the existence of a norm.

An authentic norm may be presumed to exist on the basis of the following:

- Many people in the community believe it exists and are able to express it in words
- Inclusion in a formal professional code
- Inclusion in a corporate code
- Commonly listed in the media as an ethical standard for the relevant community
- Commonly referred to as an ethical standard by business leaders
- Identified as a standard in competent opinion surveys

The more sources that support a particular candidate for an authentic norm, the stronger the presumption in its favor.

The presumption in favor of authentic norm status may be overcome on the basis of:

- Evidence of substantial deviance from the putative norm
- Evidence of an inconsistent or contrary norm in the same community
- Evidence of coercion relating to the norm within the relevant community
- Evidence of deception influencing the emergence or evolution of the norm

The more proxies supporting the existence of an authentic norm, the stronger the contrary evidence required to conclude that the norm is, in fact, ersatz.

The type of evidence required for these judgments will generally be commonly known and readily available. It will not require an elaborate amount of research. The presumption will not result in perfect judgments, and there is always some chance of either failing to identify a genuine authentic norm, or of pronouncing ersatz norms to be authentic. On the other hand, we would expect that prima facie norms recognized on the basis of the presumption will generally hold up if subjected to an ex post test. Nor do such tests have to be complicated, expensive, or elaborate. Common techniques such as the use of focus groups chosen as a valid sample of the target community

may be used to test the authenticity of putative norms. In the following paragraphs we discuss some of the general proxies available to
identify authentic norms.

The considerable research conducted over the past two decades in
an effort to identify the ethical attitudes of managers, salespeople,
and other professionals may help to identify important general ethical
norms in business. The researchers typically focus on high-profile
issues and often comment concerning the level of ethical behavior in
business. Some have sought to provide time-series data, replicating
earlier studies (Brenner & Molander, 1977; Akaah & Riordan,
1989). Often, the focus is on variables, such as those pertaining to the
organization, that may serve as predictors of unethical behavior
(Akaah & Riordan, 1990). Underlying all of these studies is an
implicit, if not explicit, assumption, that attitudes reflected in authentic norms guide ethical behavior. Specific ethical norms relevant to
ISCT decision making are ascertainable through reference to this
body of research. Examples of very specific survey questions include:
What would you do if you learned that an executive was padding
his/her expense account by an amount equal to 5 percent of his
annual salary (Brenner & Molander, 1977)? Do you approve of an
employee posing as a graduate student working on a thesis as a technique for getting information from a competitor (Cohen & Czepiec,
1988)? Much of the research on specific issues has also been targeted
to a very specific business community, sometimes to employees of a
particular firm (much of this research is proprietary), and often to
those who are involved with a specific business function, e.g., purchasing agents, marketing researchers, salespeople.

Direct research on attitudes competently done is surely the best evidence for the purposes of identifying ethical norms. The questions
used in the research should ascertain the respondents' views concerning the rightness/wrongness of the behavior. The more specific the
practice identified, the more helpful the research. The usefulness of
the research for making ethical judgments will depend in large part on
the communities represented by the respondents.

Too much of the attitudinal research in business ethics has been
based on convenience samples of students. The attitudes of students
concerning very specific practices within a particular industry or business function are unlikely to be relevant in ascertaining existing
norms. Undergraduates, in particular, may not be knowledgeable
about, or identify with, the community they are supposedly representing. They are unlikely to be familiar with the customs and traditions

of the particular business community, nor will they necessarily appreciate the full context of the decisions that have to be made.

Perhaps students may be thought to represent the broader social community, so that their attitudes could be projected to represent the attitudes of citizens in the broader social or political community. But that seems unlikely also. Ultimately, they are what they undeniably are. Students who have qualified to get into college themselves constitute a group with identifiable demographic characteristics. Thus, they may genuinely represent a category of consumers of a certain age and income. Most especially, they represent a certain segment of the community of college students, which may be highly relevant for surveys pertaining to norms related to academic integrity (McCabe, Dukerich, & Dutton, 1991).

Research is needed to determine the existence of norms relevant to the controversial ethical judgments that have a major impact upon society. This research must be carefully focused to identify context-specific attitudes and behaviors within the relevant communities. Often, there will be multiple communities whose norms are relevant to a particular ethical judgment, as will be discussed in chapter 7. Great care should be taken to insure that those surveyed are representative of the membership of relevant communities and groups.

Even research focused on very general attitudes and very broad communities, for example, expectations concerning the role of business within a given country, may serve to help identify authentic ethical norms. Consider, for example, the extensive research seeking opinions on the debate about company goals engendered by Milton Friedman. Is the role of business limited to maximizing profits for shareholders, or may business firms instead properly incorporate other objectives? One of the largest surveys of this type posed the question to over 15,000 managers as follows:

> Which of these opinions do you think most other people in your own country would think better represents the goals of a company, (a) or (b)?
> (A) the only real goal of a company is making profit.
> (B) a company, besides making profit, has a goal of attaining the well-being of various stakeholders, such as employees, customers, etc. (Hampden-Turner & Trompenaars, 1993: 32).

They learned as a result of this massive survey that in no country of the many surveyed do a majority of managers believe that the only real goal of a company is making a profit. General surveys of this sort help to provide a general background in which to interpret evidence pertaining to specific authentic norms.

Behavior may be even more tricky to measure because of the understandable tendency of individuals to conceal unethical behavior. Direct measurement of the incidence of unethical behavior may be attempted, for example, using aggregate financial data to measure the level of noncompliance with the federal tax laws, or "surveillance shoppers" may be used to determine whether banks are redlining or corporate clients are ignoring the airlines' rules for reduced airfares. One can check responses against aggregate data so that tax evasion can be roughly measured by other indicators of personal income and economic performance. Alternatively, behavior can be measured directly in laboratory experiments, such as in-basket exercises or negotiation games. Many experiments of actual behavior have been conducted, e.g., money is left on the floor in an envelope with a return address, and the rate of return is measured factored by some demographic dimension, as for example, the relative tendencies of economics students and students taking other types of classes (Yezer, Goldfarb, & Poppen, 1996) to return "lost" money.

Lab experiments have been employed to determine how individuals react to certain environments and how they make decisions. The most common of these have been the many experiments involving prisoners' dilemma games, which measure the impact of manipulations of the rules or context on the rate of defection. Other experiments have individuals conduct negotiations to determine tendencies to misrepresent information and to identify factors that influence negotiating behavior. In-basket exercises have also been used, with individuals being asked to play roles on the basis of certain memos and documents. Factors such as the nature of an ethical code or the existence of strong statements about ethical practices by the CEO are manipulated to determine their impact on the individuals' behavior in the laboratory (Newman, 1996).

More commonly, researchers have attempted to estimate incidents of unethical behavior by indirect measures. Respondents can be asked to either identify actual incidents of unethical behavior they have directly observed (Goldberg & Greenberg, 1993), or to estimate the level of unethical behavior based upon their own experience in the industry. An example of the latter is a study asking marketing professionals to estimate the incidence of certain behaviors (deliberate understating by marketing researchers of the amount of time required to respond to a research survey) on the basis of their experience using a standardized scale (e.g., not at all common/slightly uncommon/neither common nor uncommon/slightly common/highly common). The aggregate responses can be taken as representative of the actual incidence of practices within the community represented by the respondents (Akaah & Riordan, 1990).

Research seeking to identify attitudes and behaviors is subject to certain well-known pitfalls, and these must be guarded against in the search for ethical norms. A primary problem for this type of research is social desirability. This involves the respondent to the survey or the subject in the behavioral lab seeking to please the investigator by giving what are believed to be the "correct" responses. Social desirability is a particularly acute problem when the questions are in the domain of ethics. One doesn't want to be thought of as unethical. The standard controlling device is to provide an airtight guarantee of anonymity. One technique is to have each respondent flip a coin in private and provide all yes answers if the coin toss is heads, but to answer truthfully if the coin toss is tails. The data is then analyzed on the basis that 50 percent of the respondents answered all yeses.

Framing problems may also distort results, particularly in studying ethical attitudes, where the phrasing of the question may bias the response by implying that there is an existing ethical norm condemning the practice in question. For example, using the term "bribe" rather than "payment" may be taken as pejorative, resulting in more negative responses. In addition to these concerns, which apply specifically to the field of business ethics, the standard problems of empirical research, such as sample validity, may also come into play.

Although direct measures of attitudes and behaviors are the strongest evidence for the existence of norms, it will often be necessary to rely upon proxies. Professional codes, corporate codes of ethics, corporate credos, statements by influential business organizations such as the Business Roundtable or the Caux Round Table, and speeches by business leaders, among many factors, may serve as proxies for direct evidence of ethical norms in a given circumstance. Judgment has to be used in selecting a proxy to insure that the proxy is relevant to the tradition and character of the target community. Similarly, the proxy must fit the context of the specific decision required. A proxy for one circumstance may not be appropriate for a different situation. Table 4-2 lists types and examples of proxies and norms.

The various proxies sketched in Table 4-2 are familiar to most managers, and one or more should prove helpful in many cases. The table is not intended to be all-inclusive, but instead is only suggestive

Table 4-2 Proxies for Ethical Norms

Proxies	Examples	Specific Norms
Professional codes	American Bar Association: Model Rules for Professional Conduct	Rule 1.6 pertaining to confidentiality
	Direct Marketing Association: Guidelines for Ethical Business Practices	Article 10: every shipment should identify the name and address of the direct marketer
	Institute of Certified Financial Planners: Code of Ethics and Standards of Practice	I.B.d.: Planner must disclose compensation by commissions and fees. Cannot claim "fee only" if receiving commissions from affiliated companies
Credos	Johnson & Johnson	"Our first responsibility is to the doctors, nurses and patients . . . who use our products and services"
	Merck Statement of Corporate Purpose	"We are committed to the highest standards of ethics and integrity. . . . Marketing approaches that present our products with complete honesty and fair balance"
Standards expressed by senior management organizations	The Business Roundtable: Statement on Corporate Responsibility	"Most suppliers . . . expect and need fair purchasing practices and prompt payment"
	Caux Round Table: Principles for Business	Sec. 3: "protect employees from avoidable injury and illness in the workplace"
Corporate codes of ethics	Monsanto Company: Ethical Practices and Conflicts of Interest	V. D.: "The use of funds . . . for any unlawful purpose, including any political or commercial bribery is prohibited. . . . It is Monsanto's policy to permit the making of 'facilitating' payments . . ."

Table 4-2, continued

Proxies	Examples	Specific Norms
	Bethlehem Steel Corporation: Conflicts of Interest	II. F. 4.: "In no event should an employee permit the host . . . to pay for travel tickets or for lodging"
Speeches by senior executives[a]	William C. Ferguson, NYNEX	Pay own way when invited to a golf tournament by a vendor
	D. Van Skilling, Newco, Inc. (credit reporting)	Important to be willing to change inaccurate data immediately
Standards proposed by advocacy groups and economic organizations	Transparency International	Distributes model codes of business conduct as an example of best practices
	OECD	Member nations should stop tax deductibility of bribes
Best practices standards proposed by ethics consultants	Coopers & Lybrand	Direct prohibition of "masking entries" for bribes
	Arthur Andersen	Emphasize "process by which codes, standards, business practices, policies, etc., are developed."[b]

[a] A 1995 Conference Board Survey reported that 31 percent of U.S. CEOs and 40 percent of European CEOs had spoken out about business ethics during the previous year (HR *Magazine*, 1995).

[b] Provided by Barbara Ley Toffler of Arthur Andersen. "The Process by which codes, standards, business practices, policies, etc., are developed is the best practice for proxies for ethical norms. Since a norm is a way of doing things that grows out of a group's culture, the way to stimulate a norm is through the process that involves group/organizational members" (letter to Thomas Dunfee, 4/16/97).

of the types of proxies that might exist. Another important proxy, particularly relevant as a guide to norms in broader sociopolitical communities, is the general reaction when actions are disclosed in the media. If there is indeed a general reaction of "outrage" to a disclosure, then it may be taken as a proxy for a broad social norm. Public disclosure of the payments by Lockheed to Prime Minister Tanaka produced an intense reaction in Japan, which ultimately led to both the resignation of the prime minister and legal changes. This reaction is a clear signal that the authentic norm was the opposite of the putative norm assumed by those who claimed that political bribery was broadly accepted as a way of doing business in Japan.

By definition, most authentic ethical norms will be generally known to experienced practitioners. This reality may help to explain a somewhat disturbing phenomenon. Several studies comparing the attitudes and opinions of students and businesspeople have found that students appear to be more accepting of unethical behavior (e.g., Robertson & Ross, 1995). Some have interpreted this along generational lines, worrying that the seeming lack of ethical values associated with the younger generation bodes ill for the future of business. A more sanguine interpretation of these studies is that students are not knowledgeable about extant ethical norms pertaining to the practices they are evaluating.[12] The managers against whom their answers are compared are aware of these norms and reflect them in their answers. Presumably, when the students become experienced members of the business community, they will learn the norms and adjust their opinions accordingly.

Ethical Implications of Authentic Norms and Moral Free Space

We will elaborate on the way in which a manager may make use of the full scope of ISCT in chapter 7. For now, we assume that decision makers could readily identify authentic norms in the following cases:

■

Tobacco Marketing

Decision: Tobacco company marketing executives must decide what to do with ongoing advertising campaigns.

Authentic norms: In the social community of the United States, the proxies indicate the existence of a new authentic norm condemning any commercial activity encouraging young children to smoke or allowing them easy access to cigarettes. Today, in countries such as Japan or Taiwan, evidence exists of the early stages of an emerging norm that it is wrong to encourage young children, particularly girls, to smoke.

Implications: Ethical obligations of tobacco companies changed. They are now held to a different standard, one with clear and high expectations. A major pitfall is denial concerning changing authentic norms. A systematic consideration of proxies and other evidence of norms may help to identify important changes. When an increasing number of proxies indicate that a firm's perception of current authentic norms is wrong, then it is important to investigate further and, perhaps most critical, to fully understand the ethical obligations that ensue. Once firms understand the nature of relevant ethical norms, they have several options: one is to bring their actions into conformity with the norm. Another, which might be pursued concurrently, is to try to prevent change in preferred authentic norms. Failure to respond to broad social norms of this type in broader sociopolitical communities may result in public policy changes and deteriorating public relations for the tobacco companies. Evolving authentic norms typically requires aggressive changes in the way in which the companies act and present themselves. Sometimes, as in the case of the tobacco advertising issue, the power of the new norms is such that it is best to adopt a proactive strategy and seek to keep ahead of the change. Sadly, that doesn't appear to have been the strategy chosen.

■

Accepting Gifts and Entertainment

Decision: General Motors purchasing manager must decide whether to follow the firm's new policy prohibiting employees from attending golf outings and other entertainment sponsored by a potential supplier. The manager is pressured by the supplier and one GM colleague (who has dealt with this particular supplier for many years) to accept the invitation.

Authentic norms: General Motors has institutionally promulgated a new rule prohibiting the acceptance of certain forms of entertainment from potential suppliers. The official statement of the norm serves as a valid proxy because most employees of General Motors accept such rules as proper behavior for all General Motors employees. Unless there is evidence of widespread rejection of the new rule (as opposed to some isolated dissent), or unless some other proxy indicates a contrary norm, the new rule stands as an authentic norm within General Motors. A contrary authentic norm, e.g., one that allows the acceptance of such benefits, exists for many purchasing agents in the automobile business.

Implications: Even though a particular manager may disagree with the norm and may strongly prefer the norms of other firms and those considered fair by purchasing agents generally, there is an ethical obligation to comply with the General Motors norm. Organizations, operating within their own moral free space, have a great deal of leeway in developing their own idiosyncratic norms. In order for norms to rise to the level of ISCT authentic norms, firms must take steps to insure that their employees/members accept the norms as representing correct behavior.

■

Protecting the Environment

Decision: Shell must decide how to answer the objections of environmentalists and dispose of the Brent Spar Oil Rig.

Authentic Norms: The proxies indicate an authentic norm requiring substantial transparency on the part of global corporations in relation to actions that may have a significant impact on the environment. The norm appears to be process-oriented: firms must communicate to and involve stakeholders in the process. The norm that exists among the public at large does not recognize government agencies as agents for all stakeholders. Just because a government agency signs off does not forestall a significant negative reaction among the general public.

Implications: Authentic norms may relate to what might be thought of as fair or appropriate procedures. Thinking of a procedural norm as substantive results in a focus on outcomes rather than process. Expectations in the relevant community may be more focused on how a firm goes about the decision than on the best science. Misunderstanding this norm, as Shell apparently did, may lead to mistakes and misjudgments. Authentic norms may not necessarily be "rational" when rationality is defined in some scientific sense. Instead, norms such as those involved with the Brent Spar episode may reflect an understanding that there are tradeoffs to be made and that transparency is the best way to insure that tradeoffs are done properly. They may also reflect a general mistrust of a profit-motivated firm in making the best judgment for society as a whole. Although Shell had acted proactively with the British government and was ultimately proven correct on certain aspects of the scientific merits, their actions did not comply with an important authentic process norm at the time.

These examples demonstrate the role of authentic ethical norms within moral free space. They also show that, in addition to the primary ethical obligation to act consistently with such norms, it is generally (but not always) a sound business decision. Authentic norms vary significantly from community to community, even concerning the same business practice. Further, they change and may, in certain circumstances, change rapidly. Many questions remain concerning the nature and implications of authentic norms, particularly within organizations. What happens when authentic norms of firms engaged in a transaction prove to be in conflict? What should be done if no authentic norms can be found pertaining to a given decision? What about dissenters? Can there be repressive norms that should not be considered obligatory even though they are unquestionably authentic? These and other questions will be discussed in chapter 6, Moral Free Space Revealed, and chapter 7, ISCT and Ethical Decision Making: Priorities, Proxies, and Patterns. First, however, we need to say more about the nature of hypernorms.

Appendix

The following formulation helps to clarify the specifications for an authentic norm. Where **ANx** = authentic norm specifying behavior x, **S1** = situation S1, and **S1'** = situations sufficiently similar to S1 to invoke the same ethical issue, where **CAa–z** = common attitude of a majority of the members of a group or community concerning the rightness (wrongness) of any given action alternatives ranging across a nearly infinite number of options from a to z pertaining to S1, and **BTa–z** = behavior consistent with the matching attitude on the part of a majority of the members of a group or community, and **G(1–i)** = any of an infinite number of groups capable of developing a consensus on attitudes and complying behavior supportive of an obligatory norm, and **CEa–z** = a common expectation held by and known to the members of a group that a particular BT1–i represents right (wrong) behavior in corresponding S1–i, then the derivation and effect of an authentic norm can be presented as follows:

GENERATION OF AN AUTHENTIC NORM

1. Within G1, recurring S1 (through whatever means influences members of group G1) produces;

2. CAx, BTx when future instances of S1 are encountered;

3. leading to CEx that BTx is right (wrong) behavior for S1,

4. then ANx supporting BTx for S1 has been established.

Eliminating the behavioral requirement results in the following modification:

GENERATION OF AN AUTHENTIC NORM
(WITHOUT A BEHAVIORAL REQUIREMENT)

1. Within G1, recurring S1 (through whatever means influences members of group G1) produces;

2. CAx, when future instances of S1 are encountered;

3. leading to CEx that CAx establishes right (wrong) behavior for S1,

4. then ANx supporting CAx for S1 has been established.

5

Hypernorms Revealed: The Hypernorm
of Necessary Social Efficiency

The desire for economic prosperity is itself not culturally determined
but almost universally shared. . . . It is not sufficient to say that everyone
eventually arrives at the same goal but by different paths. How a society
arrives and the speed with which it does so affect the happiness
of its people, and some never arrive at all.

—Francis Fukuyama (1995: 354)

Chapters 2 and 3 introduced the critically important concept of
hypernorms. We noted the existence of three basic categories of
hypernorms: substantive, procedural, and structural. Chapter 3 discussed the procedural hypernorms protecting rights of voice and exit
within communities, and provided examples of substantive hypernorms while describing how others might be identified. This chapter
elaborates on the basic concept by detailing at considerable length an
important structural hypernorm. As we noted in chapter 3, the class
of structural hypernorms is broad. It arguably includes noneconomic
norms such as the right to political participation and to fair treatment
by the law. In this chapter, however, we develop only one example of
a structural hypernorm, namely, the hypernorm of "necessary social
efficiency," or the "efficiency" hypernorm. We do so because the efficiency hypernorm has special application to economic activity, the
focus of this book.

The efficiency hypernorm speaks to the need for institutions and
coexistent duties designed to enable people to achieve basic or "necessary" social goods. These are goods desired by all rational people,
such as health, education, housing, food, clothing, and social justice.
The hypernorm we will describe in this chapter provides the basic
underpinnings for liberty and opportunities for exchange essential
to enable individuals to achieve these necessary goods. Two broad
classes of necessary goods are, as we will explain, justice and
aggregate economic welfare. Necessary social goods, unlike many

individual goods, require a range of collective institutions. They are, in turn, achieved through a range of institutional strategies, including the specification of property rights, the structure of systems of economic exchange, and the design of trust-supporting background institutions. The hypernorm we examine here operates to protect a minimal set of property interests while also requiring the imposition of duties and public remedies supporting key business behaviors such as promise keeping. At its broadest, this hypernorm requires observance of duties generated by the multitude of institutions and organizations that taken together provide the basic fabric of a given political economy. It can entail legal as well as business obligations. It may require respect for accounting principles and intellectual property even as it justifies a commitment to obey legitimate law. Beyond that, the hypernorm implies the need to engage in collective solutions to social problems such as unacceptable poverty or (in wealthy countries) poor health.

Necessary Social Goods

We begin by inquiring about the role of systemic efficiency in satisfying fundamental needs whose basic fulfillment is desired by all human beings regardless of culture or time. Consider the following economic actors from markedly different cultures and historical time periods: a magistrate of the early Nara period in eighth-century Japan, a thirteenth-century monk from a monastery in France, and a twentieth-century Wall Street banker. Remarkably, each resembles the others in one respect: each has duties emanating directly from the economic systems in which they participate. A magistrate of the early Nara period in the eighth century participates in a Confucian-inspired economic and social system, which places a premium on mutual obedience and in which failures ripple to other parts of the system (Morton, 1984: 35–48). Likewise, a thirteenth-century monk cultivating vegetables in a Catholic monastery in France possesses duties to the communistic economic system of the monastery. He knows, for example, that his enlightened abstinence, i.e., his refraining from stealing food in the fields before delivering it to the monastic community storehouse, is one of the keys to the system's efficiency. And a twentieth-century Wall Street trader understands that if she and others successfully pass false information about certain firms, the securities markets will misallocate capital resources, with unwanted consequences for society.

It is worth noting that each of these persons, living in dramatically different times and places, have presumptive obligations flowing from the requirement of "necessary social efficiency." Described differently, each owes allegiance to a structural "efficiency" hypernorm that bids them play their part in maintaining the underlying efficiency of whatever system society has chosen to promote aggregate welfare. This is true whether or not their system enshrines or rejects modern concepts of a "market" or of "market freedom."

We note and will elaborate later that not all economic systems qualify as legitimate—they may, for example, be disqualified by a totalitarian or coercive environment, which systemically violates basic procedural and substantive hypernorms. In this circumstance, the proper response is not to support the economic system, nor even to fulfill the duties it imposes, but to reform or overthrow it. Certainly many American revolutionaries in the 1770s took this position about England's oppressive system of mercantilism, as did Russian citizens in response to years of totalitarian communism. African Americans certainly had no hypernorm-derived obligations to support an economic system based upon slavery. Thus, not all systems require allegiance, and no system requires unconditional allegiance.

Yet barring systemic corruption or violations of the above kind, the mere presence and structure of a given economic system entails some duties, and many of these duties are linked to the notion of "efficiency." For present purposes, we shall define an action, policy, or other means as "efficient" *when it contributes toward the provision of necessary social goods sufficient to sustain the least well-off members of society at a level of reasonable possibility concerning liberty, health, food, housing, education, and just treatment.* By "necessary goods," we mean those things that any society anywhere is bound to want more of, such as justice or overall economic welfare.

It may seem odd even to talk of a hypernorm related directly to efficiency, since at first blush efficiency appears to have merely instrumental or hypothetical significance. Why not, one might ask, simply regard it as morally neutral? If we are presented with a goal that is worth pursuing, we readily grant the importance of being efficient in pursuing it. Given the goal of bringing education to the illiterate, or of restoring peace to a troubled country, we are all willing to ascribe value to eliminating illiteracy or restoring peace *more efficiently.* Alternatively, the efficiency of a Nazi death camp is evil. Efficiency, it appears, is neither good nor bad, but depends utterly on the end to which it is directed.

As Piderit (1993) and others note, however, efficiency takes on more than a neutral status when it is related to the attainment of fundamental values. Even in an ideal world, one structured in accordance with the best imaginable principles, people face budget constraints as they choose that bundle of commodities that allows for "participation at the highest level in the fundamental values" (1993: 130). From the vantage point of the individual, "scarcity of resources combined with a commitment to the fundamental values is sufficient to derive efficiency as a principal of justice" (1993: 121). Hence, efficiency as a moral principle (or as a principle of justice pace Piderit) is understandable when we apprehend that some goods may possess intrinsic worth for society, or in other words, are ones that societies must pursue. And, if it happens that such "necessary" public goods do exist, then efficiency in pursuing them is also desirable. In other words, if public goods exist that qualify as *necessarily* good, then efficiency in pursuing them is, likewise, necessarily good—so long, at least, as we make the reasonable assumption that the mere process of their pursuit does not offend some other fundamental social value.

We must ask, therefore, whether any goods might count as necessary social goods. In other words, do goods exist that any society must pursue? First, we follow Rawls in asserting that any "well-ordered" society stands in need of a "public, political conception of justice" (Rawls, 1993: 35). As with Rawls, we shall use the terms "justice" and "fairness" as roughly interchangeable. Although they sometimes fail to recognize it, societies have a fundamental interest in securing justice for their members, something that is true however they wish to define "justice." They have a fundamental interest, that is, in providing to any citizen what Aristotle succinctly calls—as he defines "justice"—the citizen's "due" (1976: 1130–1131). Legal systems throughout the ages have been preoccupied with such issues. Monarchs, presidents, and other potentates have always devoted energy—or at least attempted to create the impression of doing so—to working on behalf of justice for their citizens. Citizens recognize this, and, in turn, the inherently moral aspects of political leadership. For example, the celebrated political wisdom of Solomon, Gandhi, or Lincoln owes as much to these persons' deep-seated compassion as to their managerial skills. Still further, even in corporate organizations, fairness is acknowledged as a worthy goal.

Because efficiency's goodness is relative to the end it achieves, we often fail to realize how important efficiency can be when pursuing an essential good such as justice or fairness. All other things being equal, a judicial system costing twice as much as an alternative system but delivering only the same amount of justice is ripe for reform. All other things being equal, a corporate grievance system costing twice the employee time as an alternative system is equally deficient.

Nonetheless, as we will explain, the bulk of efficiency considerations in economic life lies not with justice or fairness, but with a second kind of necessary social good, "aggregative" economic goods. With Amartya Sen, we affirm that no matter how broadly defined, the demands of fairness or justice (which Sen references under concerns of "equality") can "hardly be the only concern in any basal space, and [that] *aggregative* considerations . . . tend to have an irreducible status" (Sen, 1992: 137, emphasis added). The social arrangements that lead to a maximizing of aggregative welfare are not necessarily those that will lead to a maximizing of fairness. Sen and others have used the term "aggregative" to refer to the *sum total* of what is available for society. More bread, more wealth, more health-care resources, more educational resources—all of these we presume to be good even before considering how the "more" is to be distributed.

We assume then, with Rawls and Sen, that fairness and aggregative welfare constitute necessary goods for any society, no matter how that society is constituted.[1] Other necessary goods may exist, but we assume at least these two. Hence, we may conclude that efficiency in the pursuit of fairness and/or aggregative welfare is desirable.

Figure 5-1 displays the relationships between efficiency and the pursuit of necessary social goods.

Strategic Implications

It is a short step to the conclusion that societies must develop *systems* to pursue the necessary goods depicted in Figure 5-1. What is minimally necessary for this step is that fairness or aggregative welfare is at least sometimes (although not necessarily all the time) achievable better through structured, cooperative action than without it. This point is independent of political persuasion. The mere existence of cooperative problems in forms such as the prisoners' dilemma insures the need for cooperative, structured problem solving (Sen, 1977). For example, even the extreme anarchist, having rejected the legitimacy of all forms of government, must grant that society is often better off having "productive organizations" (Donaldson, 1982, chap. 3) in which people cooperate to pursue economic ends (in modern societies these organizations are frequently for-profit "corporations"). Among other things, productive organizations serve to increase the level of efficiency in transactions by reducing the need to formalize employment relationships (Coase, 1991). Furthermore, they are capable of enforcing cooperative strategies among members through institutionalized systems of rewards, benefits, and punishments. "The normative structures of ordinary working people probably exhibit a large measure of similarity the world over," notes William Jones. "[C]onsider, for example, whether there is any society in which ordinary citizens seek a lower standard of material well-being for themselves and their children" (1994: 547). Jones adds:

> Without cooperation, production of any meaningful magnitude is not feasible. Throughout history, humans have cooperated in foraging and hunting, and in agricultural and industrial production. The mode of cooperation has varied both over time and at the same time, sometimes dependent on hierarchical relations, as in feudal and socialized societies; sometimes dependent on market exchange and the business

Figure 5-1   How Resources Are Used to Achieve Social Good

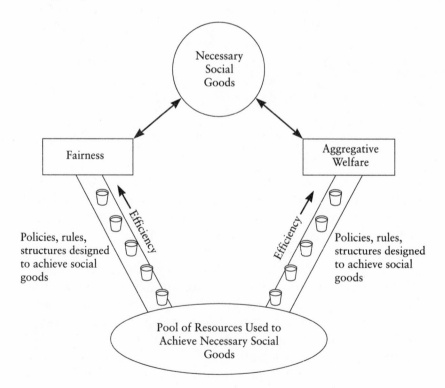

firm, as in modern capitalist economies; and sometimes dependent on less formal understandings, as in relations among family members and extended kinship groups. In each case, the goal is to achieve a form of social organization that maximizes, or at least increases, the returns from economic endeavor (1994: 549).

Supporting Cooperative Behavior

A lack of adequate systems and frameworks supporting necessary cooperative behavior within a given society may have far-reaching consequences. The level of trust within a society has a direct impact on consumer markets and firm operations. Fraud and opportunism impose well-known deadweight losses. Many such losses occur when there is asymmetrical information in circumstances where the disadvantaged party is unable to obtain essential information at a reasonable cost.

One must grant that the costs traditionally associated with asymmetrical information, including search costs, negotiating costs, monitoring costs, and enforcement costs (Jones, 1995) cannot be entirely eliminated by individual actions of trusting. Nor can the costs of other well-known forms of opportunism. An example is the "hold-up" problem, in which an opportunist takes advantage of the reliance of a party making a specialized investment whose full value is dependent upon a continuation of the relationship. But although these and other costs cannot be fully controlled, they may be reduced by the level of trust within a society and the willingness of individuals to forgo profitable short-term opportunism. As Tom Jones argues, "[R]educed opportunism, through the voluntary adoption of such shared values as honesty and integrity, aids the development of smoothly functioning, efficient markets" (1995: 413). Further, it may even be the case that when the aggregate level of trust falls below a certain threshold, an economic system as a whole will lose its ability to function, particularly in circumstances in which background legal institutions are inadequate to sustain the minimum level of ethical behavior. It may also be true, that as Jones suggests, there is loss in perceived quality of life resulting from opportunism at the societal level reflected in "a sense of injustice that results from instances in which opportunists 'get away with it'" (1995: 413).

Much business depends on cooperative behavior among individuals. This dependency holds true at all levels: economic systems and broad markets; specific transactions between firms, among individuals, and between individuals and firms; and interactions among members within organizations. Thus, nations, organizations, and

individuals all benefit from a normative framework providing clear
parameters for ethical behavior in business. The challenge is for communities to develop a normative ethical framework that, in addition
to giving solid ethical guidance, supports predictable and efficient
economic interactions.

Consider business negotiation. Negotiation by definition occurs
prior to reaching an agreement or contract; it is a process of attempting to prepare for, or exploring the possibility of, reaching agreement.
It occurs among strangers as well as friends, and is notorious for
reflecting parties' naked self-interest (Shell, 1991a). Yet in order to be
efficient, even this suspect and uncertain process must occur against a
backdrop of moral norms (Shell, 1991b). To the extent negotiating
information is systematically unreliable, the process becomes clumsy
and time-consuming. Of course, efficiency does not require that all
relevant information be disclosed, or even disclosed accurately.
Shrewd negotiators refuse to show all their cards, and may sometimes
bluff about their intentions (Strudler, 1995). Hence, misinformation
in the form of incomplete disclosure can figure in efficient negotiations, but when it does, it is crucial for purposes of efficiency that all
parties understand certain rules about possible misinformation. In
one context, bluffing about intent may be expected, so that the
expression "I couldn't take less than . . ." is not taken at face value. In
another context, less than complete disclosure about the subject of
exchange may be expected. Again, it does not follow that there is only
one set of efficient ethical rules for all systems of negotiation. When
it is clearly understood within the international rice market that bulk
rice sellers do not expect to provide an exhaustive list of the rice's
defects to purchasing agents, then purchasing agents know that they
must either prod sellers to provide more information or check the rice
themselves. On the other hand, when international rubber buyers
know that sellers will voluntarily disclose information about product
defects, then they need not check the rubber themselves (Kollack,
1992: 1–29). In the instance of the rubber market, failure of full disclosure would be unethical; but in the rice market it would not be. It
is important primarily that there be some ethical framework as a
background condition for efficient negotiation. Some rules must
mitigate uncertainty. In many situations, the choice of one set of rules
over another will not matter, because the existence of any reasonable
set of rules is capable of reducing uncertainty and enhancing
efficiency.

Systems for Achieving Economic Welfare

An increasing number of modern societies use market systems to achieve aggregative economic welfare, and in doing so often combine market mechanisms with political institutions and systems designed to achieve necessary social goods. Other societies use broad systems designed to achieve both fairness and aggregative welfare. For example, the Confucian political/economic system with its historical roots in China, or the traditional Islamic social system inspired by the Koran, are intended to achieve both fairness and aggregative welfare through the same broad political system. But whatever a nation's religious or cultural heritage, it must adopt some cooperation-supporting strategy to pursue its necessary goals.

Rawls's work since 1980, and especially his *Political Liberalism* (1993), offers a compatible perspective. Political justification, according to Rawls, requires four "model conceptional" or "fundamental ideas." These are the ideas of:

1. The citizen,

2. Social cooperation for reciprocal benefit,

3. The well-ordered society and its basic institutional structure, and

4. The norms for discussion and decision making to which fellow citizens can be expected to adhere in arriving at principles of political justice.

Idea 2 refers to the need for society to engage in cooperative schemes designed to achieve mutual benefit, including economic benefit; idea 3 refers to the inevitable institutions that arise to implement such schemes; and 4 refers to the social goal of justice. Taken together, these points exhibit what we have called the "necessary goods" of fairness ("justice") and aggregate welfare or "benefit," as well as the necessity of designing strategies and institutions to fulfill them.

Even the traditions of neoclassical economic analysis, as Hargreaves Heap (1989) has shown, inevitably refer to the "procedural" parts of economic systems. These are the shared procedures, rules, and conventions that form the institutions and do the daily work of a particular economic community. For example, the explanation of wage and price stickiness in the analysis of unemployment in Keynes's General Theory refers to the procedural element of the property

rights system existing in economies that suffer unemployment. Procedures, rules, conventions, and the institutions they comprise constitute the institutional reality that "locates" individuals socially and
historically in an economy.

Efficiency Strategies

The cooperative strategies undertaken by societies or segments of
societies in order to achieve fairness and aggregative welfare may be
called "necessary goal strategies" or "Efficiency Strategies." Because
they reflect a set of shared norms and establish specific expectations
for participants, they often find expression in the form of microsocial
contracts. Their implementation occurs in an amazing variety of
forms, including markets, social institutions, rules, policies, and other
social structures. Figure 5-2 displays the way in which Efficiency
Strategies mediate between publicly available resources and necessary
social goods.

Some Efficiency Strategies are instantiated in formal systems, while
others are expressed through informal norms and habits. For example, the judiciary systems of ancient Egypt, Napoleonic France, and
contemporary England, or the contemporary regulations prohibiting
private monopolies in market economies, qualify as *formal* systems
for the purpose of achieving certain concepts of justice or fairness. In
contrast to this kind of formal system, the norms prevailing in Byzan-
tium from the ninth to the twelfth centuries in accordance with which

---

Figure 5-2   The Role of Efficiency Strategies

Necessary Social Goods
(Aggregate Welfare and Fairness)

↑

Efficiency Strategies
for Achieving Necessary Goods
(Productive Organizations, Markets,
Confucian Social System, etc.)

↑

Public Resources
(Definition: Resources Needed
to Achieve Necessary Goods)

Byzantine emperors gave elaborate brocade robes to powerful local chieftains in exchange for peace and recognition were *informal*. No rulebook prescribed that such robes be offered; and yet, the practice was a critical piece in the political puzzle that successfully maintained peace, and in turn, enhanced aggregate welfare.

Formal institutions exist in many economic systems as strategies for the pursuit of aggregate welfare. Examples include the Federal Trade Commission, the New York Stock Exchange, and the Securities and Exchange Commission in the United States. Other efficiency-related components of the economic system are informal yet no less important. William Jones discusses, for example, how informal social norms often serve to facilitate economic production by encouraging cooperation and accountability while banning predation. They include the ethic of hard work, of saving and investment, and of learning (Jones, 1994). Moreover, the familiar but informal norm of promise keeping, operative in nearly all societies, helps indirectly to promote both fairness and economic prosperity. Unfairness and inefficiency would metastasize if promises were not generally reliable. Even norms establishing the value of equal opportunity and the balancing of unequal results are vital to a productive and cohesive society (Jones, 1994).

The "public resources" depicted in Figure 5-2 are by definition the sort needed to further a given society's conception of fairness and aggregate welfare. Considered as such, they are intrinsically valuable. For instance, some public resources, such as water, air, and minerals, are crucial inputs to the Efficiency Strategies of economic production, while others, such as labor and land, are important not only for strategies of production but also for maintaining systems of fairness and justice. In turn, such resources require husbanding, and most Efficiency Strategies include parameters intentionally designed to economize use of public resources. This aspect of the design of Efficiency Strategies, i.e., the economizing element of Efficiency Strategies, may be called "Efficiency Strategy economizing parameters." Like mathematical parameters, they help determine the specific form of the Efficiency Strategy function but not its general nature.

The most commonplace of informal norms often serve as Efficiency Strategies. For example, the implicit agreement to "do business on a handshake," a norm operative even today in many industries around the world, constitutes a cooperative strategy for efficiently achieving economic fairness and success. Agreeing to do business on a handshake eliminates much of the inefficiency associated with reducing all transactions to formal, enforceable contracts. Here the power is *infor-mal*. On the other hand, the laws prohibiting monopolies in free-market economies are highly *formal* attempts to block market concentrations that could erode the efficient pursuit of aggregate welfare.

Both Robert Frank and Thomas Jones have illustrated how certain largely informal ethical practices in modern corporations can bring about considerable efficiency. As Frank notes, "commitment" problems occur in business when the form of a business relationship resembles a prisoners' dilemma. When companies need employees to develop skills that are company specific, for example, but when these skills are nonmarketable outside the company, ethics can constitute a remedy (Frank, 1996). A reputation for being "ethical" in employment practices, and of seeking to avoid layoffs at nearly all costs, can boost worker confidence, allowing them to develop company-specific skills, with the result that the firm gains a competitive advantage over its rivals. Similarly, when customers are relatively ignorant about the inherent quality of a technologically or scientifically complex product, a company's informal ethical reputation, especially its reputation for "ethical" concern about the well-being of the customer (as the instance of Johnson & Johnson, Inc., and the Tylenol poisoning incident shows) can induce customers to remain loyal to the firm's products (Frank, 1996). Still further, Thomas Jones has discussed the ways in which a subset of other ethical principles, including trust, trustworthiness, and cooperation, can result in significant competitive advantages over time for corporations (Jones, 1995). Trust (Hosmer, 1995) is an especially potent engine of efficiency inside corporations insofar as it obviates the need for expensive compliance structures (Jones, 1995). When managers lack trust in their employees' commitment to the firm, they inevitably develop punitive mechanisms to monitor and influence behavior. And when employees lack trust in management's commitment to their well-being, they respond with self-interested shirking and absenteeism (Greenberg, 1990).

A well-known institution reflecting economizing parameters within Efficiency Strategies is the institution of private property, which may be seen as a device encouraging the most parsimonious yet efficient use of property. One argues with great difficulty for the superiority of the institution of market-based, unconstrained private property as manifested in modern democratic capitalistic society on *moral* grounds alone. At a minimum, formidable challenges arise, and it is difficult to presume the moral superiority of any notion that allows one person to own a million times what another owns. From a moral point of view alone, it is far from clear that the collective ownership systems, i.e., Efficiency Strategies, of primitive tribes in Micronesia or of monasteries in medieval Europe are morally inferior to the "winner-take-all" brand of private property ensconced in modern, capitalistic democracies. Indeed, history has often provided tempting alternative perspectives. In Plato's *Republic* (1968) and More's *Utopia* (1516/1753) we find moral defenses of a less aggressive, less individualistic notion of private property. It is difficult to escape the conclusion that what makes the modern notion superior is not simply its *moral* superiority but its enormous *efficiency* in generating aggregate welfare.

Aristotle (1975, Book II of *Politics*) criticizes Plato's communal property concept articulated in the *Republic*. He notes there and elsewhere that the concept fails to provide the necessary incentive for fueling innovation, hard work, and productivity—all factors society desperately needs in the pursuit of aggregate welfare. People never care for public property, for public facilities and services, Aristotle notes, in the same attentive way they care for their own property. With this master stroke he establishes the superiority of private property over communal property, and does so not on the basis of private property's *moral* superiority, but on the basis of its remarkable role as an economizing parameter—in a market economy.

Even cultural habits surrounding the family and the state function as Efficiency Strategies. Francis Fukuyama has identified a relationship between the level of trust in a society and the ability to amass capital and develop technology efficiently. The higher the level of trust, he believes, the more "spontaneous sociability" exists, and in turn, the greater the willingness to participate in organizations outside the family such as charities, sports clubs, religious groups, and political organizations (Fukuyama, 1995). This psychological willingness to engage in organizations outside the realm of immediate family and friendships helps make cooperative efforts in corporate organizations more successful, and as a result, fuels technological advancement and capital accumulation. In contrast, he argues that "societies that are riven with barriers of distrust, based on class, ethnicity, kinship, or other factors, will face extra roadblocks in their adoption of new organizational forms."

Because the goals of Efficiency Strategies are universal goods, both they and the economizing parameters that they include are capable of imposing duties on members of society. Members of society thus come to have duties not only through their participation in the broader society, but by virtue of their participation in particular systems and institutions designed to secure necessary social goods. These duties, construed in their most general form, may be subsumed under a principle having transcultural significance as follows:

Generic Principle: Utilize efficiently resources in which society has a stake.

This principle has second-order implications (in other words, it is a perspective from which first-order, or micro, perspectives can be evaluated). For this reason it qualifies as a hypernorm.[2] Its normative implication for the specific economic duties that social participants must accept in particular societies (for first-order economic norms) is as follows:

First-Order Duties: Discharge role duties stemming from the economizing parameters of Efficiency Strategies in which you participate.

Figure 5-3   Derivatives of Duties from the Efficiency Hypernorm

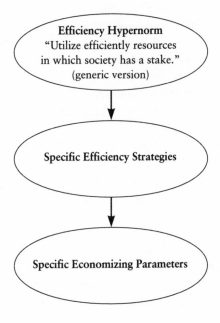

Figure 5-3 exhibits how specific duties flow from the generic hyper-norm, and then are mediated by the Efficiency Strategies and econo-mizing parameters of particular societies.

Cultural Independence of the Efficiency Hypernorm

The generic form of the hypernorm is independent of culture or eco-nomic system. Throughout history, different systems have been imple-mented, or have merely arisen, for the purpose of enhancing aggre-gate welfare. Today we take the presence of markets for granted, but systems other than markets have been used by past societies, and their participants encountered obligations in their activities that were related to maintaining the efficiency of those systems. Consider, for example, the elaborate system of social organization inherited by the Japanese from China in the Asuka period (552–710 A.D.). The revered Prince Shotoku is said to have inspired the so-called Taika Reform that produced a Confucian-style constitution. It was not a constitution in the Western sense at all, but rather a "collection of maxims to guide and exhort those engaged in government along ethi-cal lines derived mainly from Confucian sources" (Morton, 1984: 20). The subsequent organization of the government under Taiho Code in the Nara period reflects economic as well as political goals. The list of duties of the Treasury, for example, included overseeing public accounts, weights and measures, commodity prices, and the mint, as well as lacquer, weaving, and other industries (Morton, 1984: 25). The informal duties of participants to the efficiency of the system went from the lowest farmer to the emperor himself. The emperor stood atop a huge bureaucratic pyramid; in sharp contrast to the previous feudal system, he was the sole ruler at the summit (Mor-ton, 1984: 20). His authority rested less upon force of arms (in the Western fashion) than it did on a shared respect for his position. Indeed, it was upon the balanced judgment of the emperor that much of the efficiency of the system rested. When the emperor was good, the system flourished. When he was not, it declined.

The social structure of ancient Greece similarly reflected an Effi-ciency Strategy with relatively little reliance on market mechanisms. While this structure possessed some minor market components, it rested largely upon the now unfamiliar concept of the freeholding family. A family estate in ancient Greece was more than just a nice place to live. Such "households," which consisted often of many hundreds of people, were the organizational center for the farming, manufacturing, and distribution activities of a remarkably complex economy. It and its successor in the Roman system played key roles in achieving what was for the time exceptional prosperity. The historian Rondo Cameron (1989) has suggested that the general level of prosperity around the Mediterranean near the time of the birth of Christ was not equaled in modern Italy until after the turn of the twentieth century.

The Efficiency Strategies and their economizing parameters in feudal Japan or ancient Greece implied different duties for their participants. Obedience to the emperor had a special significance for the success of Japan's elaborate system in the Nara period. In ancient Greece, the young, well-born student of Aristotle was taught moral and political duties reflecting the "household" economy prevalent at the time. The Efficiency Strategy of ancient Greece relied heavily on hard work and careful property management. These skills and dispositions were keys to success in an economy in which market mechanisms were of only marginal importance. It is little wonder that we see Aristotle writing in the *Politics* of the relative ethical superiority of "productive" labor in contrast to "trading" labor. The former aims to produce something tangible, asserts Aristotle, while the latter (trading) aims only at increasing a merchant's store of money. Such ethical comparisons are, of course, less common today because modern Efficiency Strategies position markets as key economizing parameters (although such comparisons are not absent entirely in the rhetoric of Wall Street critics).

Limits on Strategies

Efficiency Strategies may possess a darker side. Like other forms of microsocial contracts, they can deceive participants into accepting a given norm that violates substantive or procedural hypernorms. Aristotle defended not only the "household" economy of ancient Greece in his economic discussions, but the ethical acceptability of slavery, an institution upon which Greece's household economy relied. It strikes many people as unimaginable that the towering mind of Aristotle, which coined and developed the concepts of "biology," "politics," "physics," "ethics," and "logic" that lie at the heart of modern learning, could have erred so grievously in its defense of slavery. His defense of slavery, ironically, is put unashamedly in his writings, using the same measured, logical tones that characterize his other analysis. Aristotle's error on slavery is more understandable, although not more defensible, when we realize the power of Efficiency Strategies, and of microsocial contracts in general, to bedazzle the ethical imagination. When one grows up, as Aristotle or Jefferson did, surrounded by an Efficiency Strategy whose economizing parameters call for the designation of other humans as agricultural property, the temptation to confuse authenticity with legitimacy, and the requirements of an Efficiency Strategy with fundamental truth, can be almost irresistible. Economic institutions founded on slavery, such as those in ancient Greece and the early United States, do not generate duties justifiable by the efficiency hypernorm.

Duties Derived from the Efficiency Hypernorm

The duties that flow from Efficiency Strategies and their corresponding economizing parameters may be supported by microsocial norms. On the other hand, they may operate independently of ethical norms. Formal, i.e., publicly articulated, norm-related duties abound in institutions where participants frequently have specific role responsibilities defined through such formal principles. For example, the norms expressed in GAAP (Generally Accepted Accounting Principles) bind professional accountants to follow certain formal norms that, when observed, enhance information accuracy and, in turn, business efficiency. Compliance with formal norms is often accomplished by the application of sanctions, including legal liability, in the event of noncompliance. Other duties flowing from Efficiency Strategies and their corresponding economizing parameters may not be enforced by sanctions or even reflected in specific norms. Modern theories dealing with economic production, including game theoretic approaches, converge in believing that no matter how well conceived the design of an organization may be, that is, no matter how nuanced or sophisticated it may be in assessing production and tailoring rewards, it will inevitably fail to align self-interest with broader interests perfectly. Even with perfectly accurate indicators of individual productivity—which we do not happen to possess—*team* or *public* productivity cannot be understood with sufficient precision to determine accurately individual contributions in each instance, and hence to avoid free-riding by some participants. As Amatai Etzioni (1988) notes, if ten of us are pushing a truck out of the mud at midnight, I cannot know how hard you are pushing. And if I cannot know how hard you are pushing, I cannot reward you proportionately for the pushing. In business, situations requiring an informal duty of restraint occur daily. Clients of brokerage firms, or institutional clients of investment banks who purchase complex financial instruments known as "derivatives," may be vulnerable to unscrupulous sales tactics. It is inevitable that some such customers will lack the sophistication to purchase correctly. The broker or investment banker who refrains from exploiting these inevitable customer weaknesses enhances customer trust and contributes to overall economic welfare by preferring an efficient to an inefficient transaction.

Rawls comes close to capturing this notion when he suggests that we may derive a "duty of civility" from the unavoidable defects in any social structure. He argues that this duty obliges us not to manipulate our surrounding system so that its "inevitable loopholes . . . advance our interests." "The duty of civility," he writes, "imposes a due acceptance of the defects of institutions and a certain restraint in taking advantage of them" (Rawls, 1971: 355). The later Rawls echoes this in the notion of "reasonable persons" who "insist that reciprocity should hold within that [social] world so that each benefits along with others" (1993: 50). "Unreasonable people in contrast," he writes, are "unwilling to honor, or even to propose, except as a necessary public pretense, any general principles or standards for specifying fair terms of cooperation" (1993: 50). The duty, then, is to go beyond self-interest and in doing so to refuse to exploit the regrettable but inevitable ways in which institutions fail automatically to align self-interest with broader interests. As Balfour Brickner is said to have remarked, "It is what we do when we are alone, no one is looking, and we know we won't be caught, that makes all the difference between a civilization and a jungle."

When citizens make exclusively self-interested calculations about whether to take the time to vote, democracy deteriorates.[3] And if corporate chieftains make exclusively self-interested calculations about whom to hire, fire, or promote, justice in the organization eventually deteriorates.

This general point has special application to modern business. Even the magic of the market, which since Adam Smith has been championed for turning private vices into public virtues, does not always succeed in transforming the self-interest of the butcher, the brewer, or the baker.[4] Market participants must shoulder systemic responsibilities or else the market suffers. For example, as Julienne Nelson has argued (Nelson, 1994), *because* the assumptions of a perfectly competitive market are not met, certain duties follow. A perfectly competitive market assumes, for example, that:

1. We all have the same information.

2. We all behave competitively in both spot and futures markets (i.e., neither producers nor consumers expect to influence the prices of goods and services offered for sale).

3. We do not use technologies that cause externalities or that exhibit increasing returns to scale at relevant levels of production.

Failure to meet these conditions is an everyday occurrence in business. It follows that we possess duties to "maintain the system" and that the denial of these conditions undermines the morality of the free-market system. (Nelson, 1994: 666). These duties would require, for example, "an informed seller to notify a buyer of hidden product defects" and sellers to "promote accurate and informative advertising."[5]

The efficiency hypernorm has significant implications for critical issues in business ethics, including those of the environment, intellectual property, and bribery. One of the most obvious applications is to environmental issues. The historical business insensitivity to environmental concerns, called "pre-ecological economism" by Paul Steidlmeier, is characterized by faith in technology and the presumption that an irresolvable conflict exists between ecology and economic growth (Steidlmeier, 1990). This attitude, in which ecology is a secondary concern, is clearly inconsistent with the implications of the efficiency hypernorm. Pre-ecological economism presumes what the hypernorm formally rejects—namely, that efficiency is to be measured only by the height of the gross domestic product. The efficiency hypernorm implies, rather, that until we factor into the broad economic equation the value of scarce natural resources, we have an inadequate measure of social efficiency. Thus, the hypernorm is more in line with what Steidlmeier calls "public policy ecology" (Steidlmeier, 1990).

Furthermore, the actions of private business as well as government are obvious factors in the overall level of efficiency conceived by the hypernorm. For this reason, the growing corporate initiatives in the areas of recycling, emergency response, and environmental accounting are perfectly in step with the efficiency hypernorm (Benchmark Corporate Environmental Survey, 1991).

The issue of intellectual property also submits to analysis through the efficiency hypernorm. Consider, for example, a key instance of intellectual property, namely, software. It happens that the ratio of pirated software to legitimately purchased software varies dramatically from country to country. For example, a comparison of key European states shows that in Italy the ratio of pirated to purchased software is roughly eight times that of Great Britain and four times that of Germany. Now what is remarkable is that the laws are virtually identical in all the countries surveyed. They all have laws against pirating software, but in some the rate is sky-high, while in others it is low. Why the difference? Most of it must be attributed to a difference in perspective taken by the users of software about the ethics of piracy. Because the ethical attitudes vary by culture, it is tempting to regard such piracy merely as a cultural phenomenon, to be evaluated only by the scruples of individual cultures and nation-states. Yet consideration under the rubric of the efficiency hypernorm shows that the issues are transcultural, and relate to economizing parameters in the Efficiency Strategies of modern market democracies. What does software piracy have to do with efficiency? Ask yourself: In which country will the bright entrepreneur, given a choice, decide to invent and market her new, path-breaking software? The answer is painfully obvious. Attitudes that respect the economizing parameters of market systems enhance efficiency; those that disregard them, retard it.

Bribery, too, falls within the sphere of relevant issues for the efficiency hypernorm. The issue of bribery, for example, reflects a practice rampant in many sectors of the global economy, which is difficult to examine without reference to the need for efficiency parameters in civil economy. Bribery is business as usual in many societies. It is necessary sometimes for conducting successful business, and is difficult to distinguish from tipping behavior. Because of this, it has long remained an elusive target for business ethicists, finding a surprising number of defenders among both corporate leaders and business theorists. Nevertheless, as we shall see in chapter 8, the deep moral problem of bribery is unraveled utilizing, among other things, the efficiency hypernorm. Bribery's deepest difficulty turns out to be its pernicious impact on efficiency, through fueling unpredictability and the misallocation of resources.

It may not be obvious why it is necessary even to isolate the efficiency hypernorm. Is it not redundant for ISCT? Because most efficiency strategies are instantiated through microsocial contracts, why need we ever appeal to the efficiency hypernorm? Why not simply appeal to the microsocial contract that is relevant?

One of the many practical reasons for invoking the efficiency hypernorm lies in the blurry institutional reality found in many Third World countries. Where forms of modern production are unsophisticated, so too often are their surrounding social institutions. In this context the efficiency hypernorm is potentially a guide or compass. Where efficiency strategies are latent but unrealized, or where they are evolving but not yet mature, managers must penetrate beneath social customs.

For example, a small, less-developed country may be committed to liberalizing its economic institutions and thereby gaining higher levels of economic welfare. Whether from the prodding of the IMF or the World Bank, or from its own bootstrapping initiative, it may have devalued its currency, relaxed its trade restrictions, lowered its public spending, and taken national industries public. The country, then, has clearly committed itself to an efficiency strategy of market-based development. Yet this very efficiency strategy may exist side by side with centuries-old patterns of favoritism, bribery, and environmental disregard. A foreign businessperson may well be excused for her confusion over exactly *which* microsocial norms are relevant. Are they the centuries-old implicit understandings surrounding gift giving, family loyalty, and intellectual property? Or are the relevant norms those of the emerging financial systems, of the professional accounting practices and contractual business relationships? The pursuit of aggregate economic welfare through these emerging market institutions requires the ethical cooperation of a nation's citizens in a way that may clash with older microsocial norms. In such instances, as the efficiency hypernorm suggests, a businessperson is well advised to choose what is best for the country, not what is best for the private interests of a small group of citizens.

Too often, economic systems have been viewed and described simply as composites of laws and business institutions. Instead, as Adam Smith and others have noted, economic systems require the ethical cooperation of their participants. The efficiency hypernorm serves as a moral pathfinder, guiding business transactions where microsocial norms are obscure or inconsistent.

Conclusion

Our discussion of the efficiency hypernorm in this chapter implies no favored status for that hypernorm in contrast to others. Surely economizing parameters in Efficiency Strategies are often less important in global business than, say, hypernorms of discrimination, subsistence, or physical security. Still less is our discussion intended as a disguised argument for freer markets. Freer markets may or may not augment efficiency in certain contexts. In many developing countries, it has been argued that more and better government is a better tonic for enhanced economic efficiency than market liberalization. We take no stand on this issue. Rather, our attempt has been to identify the way in which all economic participants share moral obligations stemming from their very participation in an economic system. In chapter 7 we will explore how this and other structural hypernorms can be identified in the context of specific business decisions, and in chapter 8 we will discuss at length the efficiency hypernorm's implications for the phenomenon of bribery.

6

Moral Free Space Revealed

No written law has ever been more binding
than unwritten custom supported by popular opinion.

—C. C. Catt at Senate hearings on women's suffrage in 1900
(Rousseau, 1995: 13)

Within moral free space, much of the substance of business ethics exists in implicit understandings about right behavior that derive in large part from businesspeople making decisions in response to ever-changing goals and environments. The authentic ethical norms that emerge from this process are typically specific to firms, markets, and forms of transactions. Some, such as those supporting promise keeping and honesty, appear immutable. Others change and evolve over time, as with norms pertaining to the content and use of advertising.[1] What counted as "puffery" in an ad for a mouthwash fifty years ago ("It cleans your breath and fights colds") is regarded as misleading and unacceptable today. Norms in general establish the ground rules for efficient and appropriate behavior within firms, industries, and professions. They reflect and help protect basic human interests in such areas as privacy, physical well-being, and the environment.

ISCT emphasizes the attitudes and behaviors of managers in recognizing obligatory, authentic ethical norms generated within the moral free space of communities. We now explore in some detail influences on behavior and the development of attitudes. We will review existing theoretical approaches and the growing, though still inadequate, empirical research. In the process, we will seek rough answers to very basic questions:

1. To what extent is there a psychological dimension to ethical decision making?

2. Are most humans innately ethical, perhaps as an attribute of their very humanness?

3. Is there a natural process of moral growth by which most people gradually become more mature in their decision making? Can

139

employees develop psychological commitments to their firms? If so, what are the implications for social-contract-based business ethics?

4. What is the relationship between law and ethics? For example, can we ever conclude that someone who has meticulously complied with a law has nonetheless acted unethically?

5. What is the impact of norms on ethical behavior? Are they an important influence, or instead merely guideposts to aspirations?

6. Is there any evidence of implicit contracts between individuals and organizations?

Similarly, we must consider questions pertaining to the basic concept of moral free space and the role of authentic ethical norms. What type of consent is required to justify a community member's obligation to comply with an ethical norm? What about dissenters, those who disagree with a particular community norm that nonetheless satisfies the test of authenticity? Suppose that a community has failed to develop norms that pertain to a given decision—what then? Does moral free space require a certain political environment or a particular set of background institutions? What responses support moral free space against objections raised by relativists or, at the other end of the continuum, universalists?

The answers to these intriguing and important questions are vital to any understanding of business ethics, and they are absolutely critical to a social-contracts-based approach. In the following sections we look briefly at many of the major influences on ethical behavior in business. We evaluate each factor in terms of its implications for the role of norms in business ethics and its consistency with ISCT.

The Role of Norms in Ethical Behavior

The heavy emphasis in ISCT on authentic ethical norms in moral free space finds support in the growing recognition that norms are a powerful influence on human behavior and a significant source for determining what constitutes right behavior in given situations (Symposium on Law, Economics, and Norms, 1996). The phenomenon of giving a gratuity, or tipping, is a well-known example in which relatively elaborate and precise rules evolve out of the general experience of members of a society. Community members know the "rules" of tipping in considerable detail, including the percentage ranges for an acceptable tip, special exceptions in which the practice may be forgone, and the categories of permissible tippees (in much of the United States, employees, but not owners; cabdrivers and barbers, but not toll or gas-station attendants). These norms persist across divergent cultures, although the specific rules may vary quite substantially, particularly as to the expected amounts and the appropriate circumstances. There are, of course, societies in which U.S.-style tipping is not the norm, e.g., China, Australia, and Japan, but even there, strong norms pertaining to similar practices exist, such as gifts necessary to the conduct of certain business practices.

Tipping norms may be enforced and reinforced through the comments and actions of those who believe they have not received the appropriate amount. In some service establishments the billing process incorporates the norm, particularly with regard to large dinner parties in upscale restaurants. But in spite of these limited efforts at coercion, much of the compliance with the norms for tipping appears to result from a desire on the part of the tippers to conform to general societal expectations. It is difficult to build a case for rational egoistic behavior as an explanation for tipping. The persistence of tipping in circumstances in which there is no expected payoff or likely public embarrassment is a source of consternation among some, but not all, economic theorists (Frank, 1988).

A number of models of ethical decision making in business recognize the role of norms as a critical reference point for managers. Trevino explicitly incorporates norms into her model of ethical decision making in organizations by connecting them to organizational culture: "Culture also can provide the collective norms that guide behavior. . . . Collective norms about what is and what is not appropriate behavior are shared and are used to guide behavior. . . . These help individuals judge both what is right and who is responsible in a particular situation" (1986: 612).

Similarly, Ferrell and Gresham (1985), relying upon differential association theory, explicitly incorporate "significant others" as a contingency variable in individual decision making in marketing. Differential association theory "assumes that ethical/unethical behavior is learned in the process of interacting with persons who are part of intimate personal groups or role sets" (1985: 90). Differential association theory further posits that the ratio of contacts with particular types of groups or patterns is a predictable factor governing the ultimate outcome of (un)ethical behavior. Certainly, the core foundation of differential association theory is highly consistent with the idea that social-contract-based ethical norms are a critical dimension of ethical standards and behavior in business.

Reliance on authentic norms in developing a normative framework of ethical behavior is justifiable only to the extent that beliefs and attitudes actually influence behavior. Fishbein and Ajzen (1975) developed a theory of reasoned action that emphasizes the role of behavioral intentions in explaining and predicting behavior. In turn, they claim that attitudes (toward behavior, not objects or persons) and beliefs influence behavioral intentions. There is a substantial body of literature extending and testing this theory. For, example, the effectiveness of the model in predicting behavior has been empirically tested with positive results (Sheppard, Hartwick, & Warshaw, 1988). There has been little direct application of the theory to business ethics, with most efforts limited to marketing ethics (Dubinsky & Loken, 1989), although Kurland (1996) found that a modified version incorporating a variable of the moral actor's perceived behavioral control helped explain ethical intentions of salespeople on straight commission. Randall (1989) summarizes the business ethics literature incorporating the theory of reasoned action (specifically, Fishbein and Ajzen's model) and provides the diagram shown in Figure 6-1.

As Figure 6-1 demonstrates, norms fit into Fishbein and Ajzen's theory of reasoned action. The two key predictor variables for behavior are the attitude of the individual and the subjective norm. The subjective norm is "a function of the person's beliefs about whether significant others think he or she should perform the behavior, weighted by the person's motivation to comply" (Randall, 1989: 875). Awareness of and commitment to authentic moral norms would therefore be expected to have a major influence on behavior.

The models developed by Trevino, Ferrell and Gresham, and Randall are descriptive of the process by which ethical decision making occurs. Other writers have attempted to develop normative frameworks that suggest a process designed to insure business decision makers act ethically. One of the first of this type, developed by Cavanaugh, Moberg, and Velasquez in 1981, tested prospective decisions on the basis of utilitarian, rights, and justice theories. An action was considered appropriate only if it passed the test under all three criteria, subject to certain overriding factors. Others have made similar attempts to develop workable models. A recent variation by Fritzsche (1997) borrows some of the ideas from Cavanaugh, such as

Figure 6-1 Randall's Model of Fishbein and Ajzen's Theory of Reasoned Action

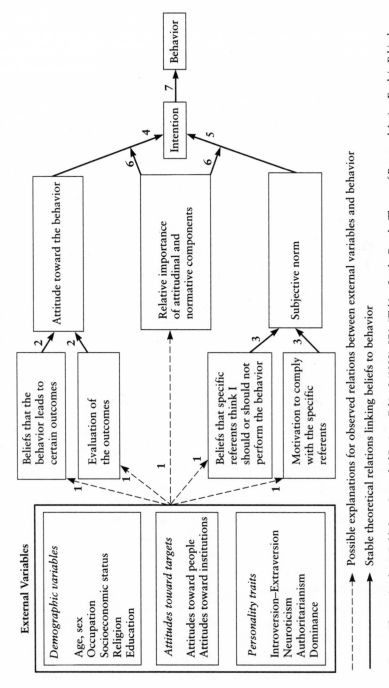

Source: Kluwer Academic Publishers, Journal of Business Ethics 8 (1989), 874, "Taking Stock: Can the Theory of Reasoned Action Explain Ethical Conduct?" Donna M. Randall, figure 1. © 1989 Kluwer Academic Publishers. With kind permission from Kluwer Academic Publishers.

the concept of overriding factors, but extends the model by incorporating more recent concepts pertaining to stakeholder obligations and the role of norms (see Figure 6-2).

Fritzsche offers the model as a way of translating theory into action. His focus is on making sure that actions undertaken meet a minimum acceptance level. His model tests action options on the basis of both community norms, which we assume track closely with authentic norms, and hypernorms. From these examples, it is clear that business ethicists have long recognized the potential of norms as a major influence on ethical behavior in business.

Some models have emphasized other factors, such as the role of senior managers, particularly those at the very top, in determining the moral tone of an organization. Some studies have found the influence of senior executives to be the best predictor of perceptions of ethical problems within firms (Hunt, Chonko, & Wilcox, 1984). Other studies have emphasized the role of ethical climate, corporate codes of behavior and ethics programs, and broader ethnic or social cultures.[2] Although not univocal in the conclusions reached, the extensive empirical literature on environmental and individual moderators is quite compatible with ISCT's emphasis on the role of social contracts as an important source of business ethics.

Linking Reasoning about Ethics to Behavior

Behavior cannot be accurately predicted on the basis of knowledge concerning how an individual reasons about ethical issues. If moral or ethical reasoning were ipso facto to correlate with behavior, the implications for corporate ethics programs and business school education would be clear: teaching current and prospective managers how to use a proper form of ethical reasoning would cause ethical behavior to improve. Unfortunately, perhaps, the sources of ethical behavior appear to be far more complicated. As Trevino (1986) emphasizes, individual characteristics and environmental moderators, such as the context of the decision, the nature of the organizations involved, professional and organizational norms, and the roles of the parties will all have great influence on the ultimate response to an ethical decision.

There is limited empirical evidence concerning how managers reason about ethical issues. In an early study, Fritzsche and Becker (1984) concluded that managers tend to be predominately utilitarian in their decision making. Yet, subsequently, Reidenbach and Robin (1990) were unable to identify significant use of utilitarian thinking in establishing their multidimensional scale for evaluating decision making about business ethics.

Figure 6-2   Fritzsche's Decision Support Model

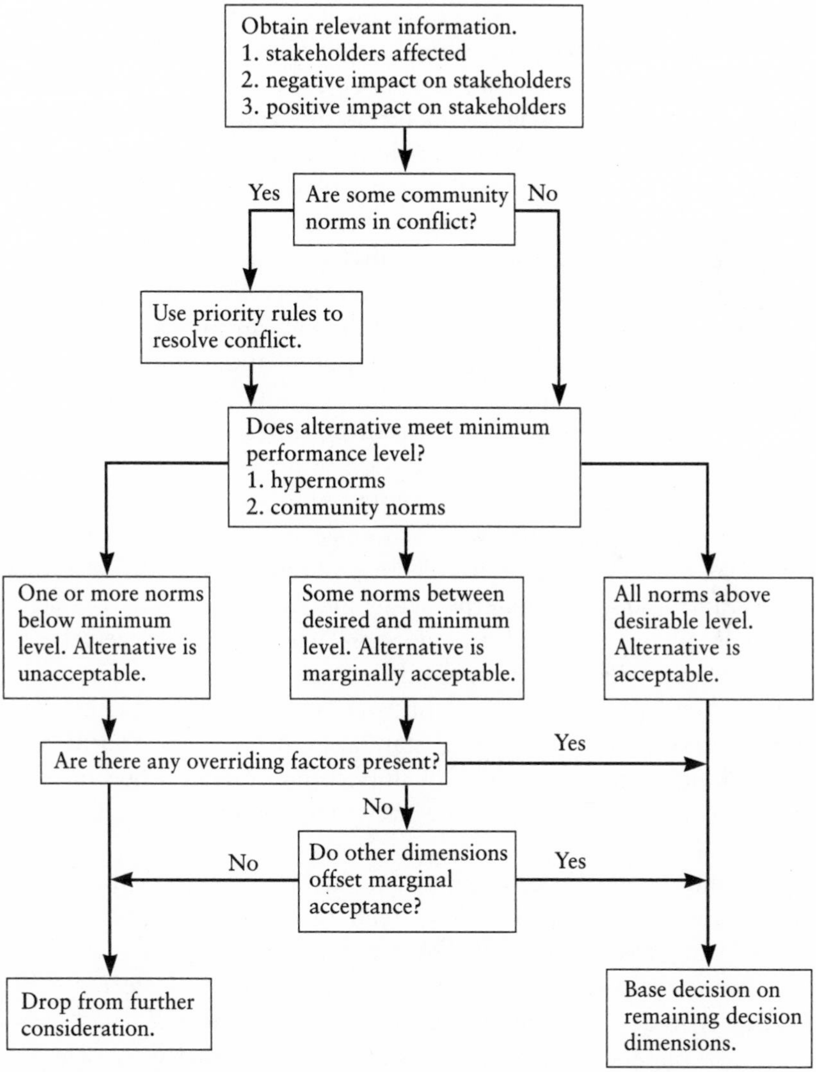

Source: D. J. Fritzche, *Business Ethics: A Global and Managerial Perspective* (New York: McGraw-Hill, 1997), 116. Reproduced with permission of The McGraw-Hill Companies.

The experience of Reidenbach and Robin (1990) in developing a multidimensional scale of individual ethical judgment in business is instructive. They initially emphasized inclusiveness, developing a pool of thirty-three ways of judging (thinking) divided into categories of justice, relativist, egoism, utilitarian, and deontology. After testing the entire list to determine the relative significance of the thirty-three items, Reidenbach and Robin revised their scale to focus on the three core dimensions that appeared to be the most influential. The first of these is a moral equity dimension, incorporating general beliefs about right and wrong, reflected in concepts of justice and fairness. The second is a relativistic dimension incorporating traditional and cultural views of acceptable behavior. The third is explicitly contractual, asking whether or not a proposed action violates unspoken promises or unwritten agreements. They purged references to utilitarianism in the refining stages as "it was obvious that respondents had a difficult time understanding and applying the concepts inherent in utilitarian thinking" (1990: 647). All three core dimensions appear to incorporate factors consistent with the assumptions about the influence of authentic norms on behavior in ISCT. Dimension three is purely contractual, and its reliance on unspoken promises or unwritten agreements tracks closely with the definition of authentic norms in ISCT. Dimension one includes a factor expressed as "acceptable/ unacceptable to my family" coupled with a more general factor of what is perceived as being morally right. These principles appear to be rather open-ended and may be interpreted by individuals as being consistent with compliance with authentic norms. That is, they may perceive as morally right what they believe others expect as right behavior. The second dimension is even more consistent in its reliance on considerations of traditional and cultural standards. A given respondent may be thinking of national norms or implicit agreements when offering the explanation that something is wrong because it is culturally unacceptable.

As things now stand, there are no definitive empirical findings concerning which ethical theories tend to influence managers, consciously or even subliminally. Nor is there any definitive evidence concerning the percentage of the time that managers use formal ethical theory in deciding how to resolve ethical decisions. Related questions also remain unanswered. It is unknown whether those who do rely on a particular ethical theory do so consistently, that is, how many people are distinctly and consistently Kantian or utilitarian.

Nor is it known, in contrast, how many managers are pluralists who vacillate among theories depending on the context of the decision, or their emotional state, or whatever else is influencing their selection of criteria. Nor is there a definitive finding concerning how commonly individuals use any of the theories. As we note above, some evidence supports the importance of norms and implicit agreements in business. For example, Robertson and Ross concluded that "judgment of an act as a breach of a social contract is significantly linked to reduction in likelihood of engaging in the act" (1995: 231).

Hegarty and Sims (1978) suggested long ago that most individuals start with a preconditioned set of values that operate as strong influences on their ethical behavior. These attitudes or values, derived from life's experience, serve as an initial screening device for making ethical decisions. Personal rules of behavior (e.g., never sign your name to something that isn't true) may evolve from experiences with family, school, peers, workplace colleagues, and others. For some individuals, rules may be inspired by familiarity with general ethical theories. For others, personal heuristics may be based upon impressions about the existence of norms, or beliefs relating to general expectations among their peers concerning the boundaries of correct behavior. Across a population of individuals, even within the same organization or culture, one could reasonably expect a substantial variance in the approaches taken to resolving ethical dilemmas.

The variances reported by empirical researchers and implicit in Fritzsche and Becker (1983, 1984), where respondents appear to be utilitarian in making one decision, and then rely on a conception of rights for the next decision, might reflect the limitations of their personal decision systems for dealing with novel ethical challenges. Complex ethical dilemmas at all levels of the organization may simply overwhelm the capacity of individuals' cognitive ethical toolboxes. A recently minted MBA may not be sure how to respond when pressured by colleagues to act inconsistently with the firm's frequent flier policy or rules concerning travel and entertainment. Having to choose between loyalty to close peers and following the rules of the organization may leave the MBA in a state of dithering dissonance. A senior manager who has always strongly supported equality for women in the workplace may not be able to decide whether that value/preference extends to placing women in workplace environments that could be harmful to a fetus. Thus, particularly when one's own values appear insufficient to provide a definitive resolution to a problem, a natural move may be to think about whether general understandings exist concerning the proper way to deal with such a problem.[3]

Fritzsche (1997) has surveyed the existing empirical literature on managers' ethical beliefs and behavior and has concluded that one can be "pretty confident" that "[b]eliefs concerning the ethical nature of specific acts vary among managers" (76–77). This is probably even more true across cultures.

These variances in ways of thinking and beliefs may be problematic for ethical theories that put forward a particular way of thinking as a normative standard presumably superior to other alternatives. In contrast, the domain of moral free space within ISCT is open to a wide range of authentic norms that may result from very different ways of thinking about ethical problems. In this manner, ISCT incorporates substantial diversity, while flexibly allowing for evolution and change in attitudes about what constitutes ethical behavior.[4]

The field of psychology provides further insights into the factors that influence human reasoning and behavior. We now consider how studies in social, moral, and evolutionary psychology can help in understanding moral free space.

Psychological Contracts and Moral Free Space

Psychologists have studied in depth the nature and influence of norms within organizations. One subset of this literature has identified influential "psychological contracts" that help define the relationship between an organization and its members. The aptly named[5] Denise Rousseau summarizes the research concerning psychological contracts in organizations: The *psychological contract* is individual beliefs, shaped by the organization, regarding terms of an exchange agreement between individuals and their organization" (1995: 9). The core of the concept is that implicit agreements arise out of a combination of organizational and personal factors. Formal and informal communications from and within the organization (policy manuals, CEO statements, social cues from coworkers) determine the information that the individual receives. Personal characteristics (cognitive biases, motives) influence the manner in which individual employees and managers filter and interpret the communications. Out of this process, expectations evolve that come to define the workplace relationship, e.g., "I'll be promoted this year if I get above-average ratings" (1995: 34).

Multiple similar individual psychological contracts within an organization will result in a "normative contract" when the individuals share common expectations. Shared normative psychological contracts can be an important source of standards for right/wrong behavior. Pervasive reinforcement involving multiple individuals within an organization strengthens the legitimacy of the expectations. Strongly ingrained expectations may pass on from one set or generation of employees to another. It seems plausible to assume that the influence of normative contracts as behavioral guideposts is directly related to the percentage of people within the organization who hold the common expectations. The more who do, the stronger is the influence as a guide to right/wrong behavior.

Reliance on authentic norms as an important source of standards of business ethics is entirely consistent with the assumptions underpinning psychological contracts. However, the two approaches differ in focus. ISCT is concerned with all types of communities and relationships pertaining to ethical issues in business. The social contract norms found in broader social, political, and economic communities are important in ISCT and may, on occasion, override the "terms" of normative psychological contracts found within a given organization. For example, an organization could conceivably develop normative psychological contracts that approve discrimination on the basis of race, religion, or ethnicity in hiring, or that require that all employees give money to support Democratic Party candidates, or that take race into consideration as a dominant factor in determining whether to extend credit. The terms of such normative psychological contracts are likely to be directly inconsistent with the terms of broader community-level social contracts, and also with hypernorms. Such contracts meet the standards for psychological contracts, but would not constitute legitimate norms under ISCT. Rousseau is not clear on how such problems are to be dealt with in the context of psychological contracts. She notes that "reasonable" third parties are involved in the process of recognizing broader implied contracts at the level of the relationship; and that ethicists would, as outsiders, take a broader view referencing law and concepts of procedural justice (1995: 53).

Beyond the focus on the relationship between individuals and organizations, another important difference between our approach and those of the scholars writing about psychological contracts is the use of the term "normative." Rousseau uses the term to mean an expected practice or standard. Our use focuses ultimately on what constitutes right/wrong behavior with reference to universal standards and authentic ethical norms.

Even so, there is significant commonality between the two approaches, and they do appear to provide conceptual support for each other. The examples and insights concerning how individual psychological contracts, and particularly normative psychological contracts, emerge and can be identified is directly relevant to our approach. Sufficiently widespread normative psychological contracts that focus on right/wrong behavior would represent authentic ethical norms under our approach. In that sense, the literature on psychological contracts supports and informs our approach. At the same time, the broader normative focus on ethics in our approach can be used as a way to judge psychological contracts from outside the organization, and in so doing provides a compatible means for dealing with problematic terms in particular agreements.

Moral Psychology and Moral Free Space

Moral psychology involves the empirical study of human development with reference to moral dimensions. The field evolved from child psychology, where time-series studies of subjects traced the development of reasoning, attitudes, and beliefs in response to moral choices. Scholars in moral psychology, particularly those who have relied upon the work of Lawrence Kohlberg (1981, 1984), emphasize the way in which moral agents think about ethical dilemmas with little consideration of the potential individual or environmental influences on behavior. Based upon studies of the development of moral thinking in young people, these scholars have concluded that humans tend to go through similar stages of development in their moral reasoning. All humans start, as infants, as preconventional egoists who are seeking to avoid pain and to satisfy their basic desires. End points differ, but most humans progress to, and remain at, a conventional level in which they respond to the needs and preferences of those around them, and in many cases to the rules and laws of a broader society. Some advance beyond the conventional stage (my friends, colleagues, or company, right or wrong! my country, right or wrong!) to the postconventional stage in which they engage in reasoning based upon or consistent with formal ethical theory. The basic stages and levels of the Kohlberg hierarchy are listed in Table 6-1 (Dunfee et al., 1996: 153).

There are many controversial aspects of Kohlberg's approach to moral psychology. Gilligan (1982) criticized Kohlberg for relying upon studies of males and drawing conclusions for everyone based upon his gender-specific studies. Her own research on young girls demonstrated that women tend to think in terms of relationships (the ethics of caring), which represents an alternative viewpoint. Others have challenged the hierarchal implications of Kohlberg's work, arguing that the framework lacks philosophical justification, particularly when it implies that a duty-based approach is superior to social contract, or that a law-and-order orientation is superior to recognizing duties to family and close friends. For example, relying on workplace norms may be classified as stage 3 in Kohlberg's hierarchy, implying that such reasoning is significantly inferior to postconventional Kantian or utilitarian reasoning.

Kohlberg's psychology of moral development de-emphasizes the actual decision. Critics note that someone acting in a manner most people intuitively believe wrong may be considered postconventional, whereas someone acting appropriately may be considered to be early-stage conventional. For example, the manager who relies on a utilitarian reason for paying a bribe to a government official to allow importation of a prohibited toxic drug into a developing country (on the

Table 6-1   Kohlberg's Model of Levels and Stages of Moral Development

Level	Stage
Preconventional level (Self-interest)	Stage 1: Avoid pain, get reward Stage 2: Naïve instrumental hedonism; back scratching
Conventional level (Group orientation)	Stage 3: Good boy–good girl; approval of peers, family Stage 4: Law and order; recognize duty to society, obey legitimate authority
Postconventional level (Moral autonomy)	Stage 5: Obey good laws; recognize a social contract; recognize individual rights Stage 6: Act in accord with logical, consistent, universal moral principles

Source: T. W. Dunfee, F. F. Gibson, J. D. Blackburn, D. Whitman, F. W. McCarty, B. A. Brennan, & D. B. Cohen, *Modern Business Law*, 3e (New York: McGraw-Hill, 1996), 153. Reproduced with permission of The McGraw-Hill Companies.

basis that it generates jobs for his firm, and that the cost won't be so high because of low life expectancy in the developing country) reflects a higher level of moral development than a manager who relies upon her company's ethics policy and decides not to pay the bribe.

This brief description leads us to the core question: What relationship, if any, exists between moral psychology and ISCT? How does each fit into the other framework? At first glance, ISCT's emphasis on authentic ethical norms might appear to be stage 3 reasoning. Authentic ethical norms involve individuals relating to peer group or organizational expectations. However, ISCT has developed as an integrated theory, and it is essential to consider the full theory in order to properly fit it into the Kohlberg framework. When all of the ISCT components are recognized, including the macrosocial contract and hypernorms, ISCT properly fits into the category of postconventional reasoning. It is, therefore, either stage 5 because of its similarity to the classical social contract approaches, or stage 6 because of the core values and rights recognized through hypernorms.

Just as interesting are the implications of the Kohlberg framework for ISCT. The empirical studies supporting the framework of moral psychology confirm that people generally are more likely to refer to laws and the norms of colleagues and fellow professionals than they are to employ formal analysis based upon the traditional ethical theories. Presumably, the same holds true for managers and business professionals. Thus, moral psychology appears to support the assumptions undergirding ISCT.

Even so, serious questions exist concerning the applicability of moral psychology to business decision making. Studies of managers have found that they tend to vary the stage of moral reasoning used depending upon the context of the decision (Weber, 1991). This finding is inconsistent with some of the assumptions of moral psychology and may reflect a tendency to compartmentalize ethical decisions in business. Trevino suggests that these situational moderators, as she describes them, may even have an impact on the stage of moral development. The commonly held belief that an unsavory organizational environment may actually lower a susceptible employee's stage of moral development is consistent with this view and inconsistent with Kohlberg's assumptions concerning the normal progression of moral development. Weber and others have confirmed that most managers appear to be at stage 3 or stage 4 of moral development and are therefore similar to the population as a whole.

Moral psychology provides insights about how people tend to reason and thus how they may go about developing attitudes that may support authentic ethical norms. The framework and tests designed to place individuals within the framework, such as the Defining Issues Test developed by Rest (1979), do not appear to be directly applicable to ISCT. Authentic norms evolve out of populations composed of people reasoning at various stages of moral development. The resulting norms represent some sort of convergence or aggregate viewpoint. The Defining Issues Test does not appear useful as a means of identifying specific authentic ethical norms in moral free space.

Evolutionary Psychology and Moral Free Space: Are Humans (Managers) Hardwired to Be Ethical?

Ultimately, every ethical theory and approach should be tested against what we know about human evolution, particularly from the fields of biology and psychology, to determine whether its assumptions and requirements appear to be compatible with our understandings of human nature. The relatively recent field of human evolutionary psychology is concerned with the impact of biological evolution on patterns of human behavior (Wilson, 1978). As popularized by writers such as Robert Wright (1994), evolutionary concepts have been applied to moral behavior. Wax (1996: 309) summarizes Wright's argument as follows: "[T]he process of evolution has equipped man to create morality and to abide by moral precepts." The essential issue is the extent to which particular moralities (or moral tendencies) have proved essential to the success of human cultures. Wright's answer is direct:

> Beneath the global crazy quilt of rituals and customs, [Darwinian anthropologists] see recurring patterns in the structure of family, friendship, politics, courtship, morality. They believe the evolutionary design of human beings explains these patterns: why people in all cultures worry about social status (often more than they realize); why people in all cultures not only gossip, but gossip about the same kinds of things; why in all cultures men and women seem different in a few basic ways; why people everywhere feel guilt, and feel it in broadly predictable circumstances; why people everywhere have a deep sense of justice, so that the axioms "One good turn deserves another" and "An eye for an eye, a tooth for a tooth" shape human life everywhere on this planet (1994: 7–8).

A different way of framing the question is to ask whether people who deceive and act unethically would be expected to prevail in the long term over those who generally act honestly and ethically. The question is not so much whether coarsely unethical people would come to dominate, because it is easy to make the case that they would be found out and constrained. Instead, the question needs to be asked of the "smart cheaters"—the people who act with guile and who do their very best to develop winning strategies, even going to the lengths of trying to appear ethical whenever that would advance their goals.

Robert Frank, among others, has argued that the smart cheaters will not dominate over time, because individuals who are intrinsically trustworthy "will be much sought after as a partner in situations that require trust" (1988: 18). Humans signal their ethical orientations through emotional leakage. Even though smart cheaters may do everything possible to fake credibility, in many instances they will fail. Their emotions will give them away. Others will be able to see through their disguise and identify them as untrustworthy (DePaulo, Zuckerman, & Rosenthal, 1980). True, the process of emotional screening is not perfect. There are people who are able to beat lie detectors. Further, the means of assessing emotional leakage may be culturally dependent, making identification of potential defectors more problematic in cross-cultural transactions. But, at the margin, in economic transactions generally, many potential defectors will be found out and thus lose out on attractive opportunities. In addition, it has been argued that smart cheaters often make mistakes in estimating the likelihood that they will be found out, or that the victim of the chicanery will be unable to retaliate. The business media is full of stories in which individual misdealings have been discovered and have produced unexpected consequences for the perpetrators. It seems reasonable to believe that results such as these may reflect natural values that lie at the heart of the persistence of ethical values in business.

Bill Frederick has recently engaged in an extended quest to apply a synthesis of the natural sciences, social science, and philosophy as a means of identifying and understanding core business values. Among the sets of ideas Frederick considers is the role of natural evolutionary processes in creating modern business values.[6] He argues as follows:

The original values of business arise as manifestations of natural evolutionary processes. The forms they take reflect the operation of basic physical processes of the universe. This evolutionary embed-dedness gives them their distinctive function in organized life and causes them to be an essential component in sustaining life itself. Although ... these values have an acquired cultural meaning, they are rooted firmly in biophysical and biochemical processes that gave them their first significance (1995: 27).

Are the powerful ideas pertaining to the hardwiring of humanity supportive of business ethics? Wright (1994), Wilson (1993), and others argue that morality is natural to the human condition. Business ethicists, encountering skeptical managers who assert that business ethics is an oxymoron, take comfort from such science-based claims. They turn the analogy around. Those who doubt the existence and importance of business ethics are the ones making the unnatural assumptions. In ignoring the reality of a naturalistic basis for morality, the skeptics act at their own peril by denying the forces of nature.

Others may be tempted, as Frederick apparently is, to use these new scientific perspectives as a basis for parsing out fundamental business values. Certainly, to the extent that fundamental human traits exist relevant to moral behavior in business, then any ethical theory based on assumptions incompatible with those traits will at best be irrelevant and at worst will constitute a self-condemnation of humanity as an immoral species. Wright (1994) emphasizes a utilitarian framework as a background for much of his discussion. If he is correct that utilitarian concepts are consistent with human evolution, does it therefore follow that other approaches based on, for example, Kantian ethics or social contracts are inconsistent?

This is an important question to consider in any discussion of a social-contracts-based approach to business ethics. Under ISCT, authentic ethical norms are the product of human interaction. They reflect the attitudes and behaviors of the people within the community in which the norm is generated. Communities are constantly generating new norms, and existing norms change whenever circumstances are appropriate. The norm generation process, which is singular to each community, is open to the changing needs, values, and preferences of the people within the community. There are no preset conditions based upon certain assumptions about human nature that have to be met in order to have an authentic social contract norm. ISCT authentic norms incorporate the views of Kantians, utilitarians, and others whose particular ways of thinking are part of the input into the processes by which norms are recognized or created. They, too, become part of the evolutionary process through the device of the social-contract-based norms. Thus, evolution is intrinsic to the process by which norms generate and change. It is not an external factor that must somehow be identified and then used as a Procrustean device to measure norms.

The "integrative" dimension of ISCT connects a focus on actual ethical norms with a theoretical analysis that, among other things, justifies reliance on empirical evidence about attitudes and behaviors. Thus, the social-contracts-based approach of ISCT incorporates the natural, behavioral dimensions of business ethics. Social psychology, organizational behavior, and many other academic disciplines provide insights concerning how authentic norms come into being, how they change, how community members come to know they exist, and so on. In this chapter we have connected the treatment of authentic norms to several other approaches to demonstrate, by example, some of the interrelationships that exist. We believe that the framework of ISCT raises a number of important research issues concerning the connection between behavioral business ethics and authentic ethical norms, and we encourage such research.

The Role of Law in Moral Free Space

Law critics may believe reliance on authentic ethical norms is unnecessary because law provides a fully sufficient basis for ethical judgments. Reflected in the familiar comment, "if it's legal, it's ethical," this approach accepts the idea that the law represents a satisfactory boundary of mandatory ethical behavior. Acting beyond what the law requires is seen as purely discretionary, something that may be praiseworthy in certain circumstances, but that may also involve a breach of obligations to maximize wealth for shareholders in others. This attitude underlies decisions to pay facilitating payments where the law allows it even though the payments harm others or violate authentic norms. Or a firm may limit adoption of environmental controls to what the law requires, refusing to consider any other justifications for protecting the natural environment. Before exploring the implications for our understanding of moral free space, we need first to identify and consider the possible attitudes managers might hold concerning compliance with law.

Contrast the reasoning of two managers facing a decision about whether to comply with an environmental regulation forbidding the release of certain pollutants into the atmosphere. One, Ty, follows a strategy of efficient breach. Ty makes a calculation concerning the benefit to the firm if they release the pollutants and avoid incurring the costs of legal disposal. He then makes a judgment concerning the likelihood of getting caught and the probable fine if caught. Ty multiplies the probability of getting caught and the expected fine and then determines whether the benefits or the costs are greater in deciding whether to comply with the law. Included within the analysis is the cost of any strategies to reduce the chances of detection and the full cost of any enforcement proceedings that might be brought against the firm. Ty then makes the decision that he believes most advances his personal career. Ty's attitude toward the law is clearly adversarial. Ty views law as nothing more than a cost imposer.

Cy takes a different approach. He consults with a lawyer to determine what the law clearly specifies. Once that is done, Cy complies with the law's command. He does this out of respect for the law, and perhaps out of a desire that others will act as he does. Cy believes that a world in which all act in compliance with legitimate law is the most desirable state of affairs. By personally complying with the law in his role both as a manager and as an individual, Cy sees himself helping bring about the type of environment in which he would prefer to live. Cy sees the law as a reflection of the community's political will, and although he personally may disagree with some policies and choices, he is willing to accept all law as prima facie legitimate.

The Kohlberg framework, independent of its scientific validity, provides a useful perspective on the approaches taken by Ty and Cy. Ty is clearly at a preconventional level, perhaps even stage 1, where the objective is to avoid or minimize pain and to achieve egoistic goals. If the law is not an efficient deterrent, then some Tys in the world will place the lives and health of other people at risk in order to achieve their economic objectives. Cy, in contrast, is at stage 4, where his inclination is to comply with the law for its own sake. It is difficult to measure how managers divide between these two strategies in actual practice. The successful Tys do not willingly reveal their legal breaches.

To the extent that there are a substantial number of Tys in any given society, they lessen the power of the law to control behavior, particularly in areas in which enforcement is costly or detection is difficult. We know that there is substantial, even massive, noncompliance with the law in many societies, particularly the United States.

But law is not the only means by which behavior may be constrained. As Eric Posner (1996) suggests, social (and ethical) norms of behavior may often be more powerful influences on behavior than formal law.

> Most people do not take their disputes to lawyers and judges. Norms, rather than laws, provide the rules of conduct; friends, relatives, and coworkers, rather than juries, make findings of fact; shame and ostracism, rather than imprisonment or legal damages, punish the wrongdoer. Court is not in a courthouse, but in homes, work places, and neighborhoods, among networks of kin, friends, and associates. In a sufficiently close-knit group, where norms are well defined and nonlegal sanctions are effective, the law has little impact on behavior (1996: 133).

On the other hand, surely some managers think that the law defines what is ethical (Paine, 1994). Under this "convergence" view, the law defines the full scope of the ethical obligations for a manager. Under a stronger extension of this argument, the law synthesizes ethical conflict within a society. Legal process is the means by which deep divisions on issues such as abortion or genetic research are resolved. Thus, under this view, the law becomes the definitive reference point concerning the scope of mandatory ethical obligations for managers.

Where moral views have not yet converged to create a sufficiently broad consensus, the law may help to bring about a change of attitudes. Examples include the role of law in the 1950s and 1960s to change attitudes concerning racial discrimination and segregation, and the view that one of the purposes of the Federal Corporate Sentencing Guidelines is to bring about a change in compliance-related ethical attitudes and behavior on the part of the subject corporations (Nagel & Swenson, 1993; Laufer, 1996).

As Paine (1994) forcefully argues, the convergence view is not an adequate unequivocal standard for business ethics. The legal system is not intended as a definitive guide for moral standards, nor is there clear evidence that it is an efficient substitute for extralegal morality.

This analysis provides a powerful justification for the role of authentic norms within ISCT. The contrast with law, which many people assume intuitively to be a powerful moderator of behavior, helps to dramatize the potential influence of ethical norms on individuals. Ethics is not something at the periphery affecting only relatively insignificant matters. Instead, it goes to the heart of human behavior and relationships. The significance of norms in moral free space leads to a related question. We have seen how law relates to and influences ethics within the framework of ISCT. What about the opposite? How do ethical norms affect the evolution and implementation of the law?

As law clearly influences both ethical behavior and the evolution of moral standards, attitudes about morality may often influence the evolution of legal standards indirectly, and sometimes even directly. Velasquez writes: "Our moral standards are sometimes incorporated into the law when enough of us feel that a moral standard should be enforced by the pressures of a legal system; and laws, on the other hand, are sometimes criticized and eliminated when it becomes clear that they blatantly violate our moral standards" (1998: 38).

Ethical practice, community moral values, and, particularly, strong authentic ethical norms may affect the law in at least three basic ways: (1) by influencing the enactment of legislation, as for example, in the cases of the Foreign Corrupt Practices Act or antiscalping laws, both of which appear to be grounded, at least in part, on moral sentiments; (2) in the judicial interpretation of legislation; and (3) in the judicial creation and development of common law doctrines.[7] Examples abound. Shell identifies doctrinal areas in which the "courts have increasingly relied on generalized, ethical standards to decide disputes between business" (1988: 1198). He highlights his analysis by focusing on the interpretation of the states' so-called little FTC acts, which tend to use language such as "unfair," "good faith," "bad faith," "deceptive," and "unconscionable." Reference to ethical standards can help the fact finder determine whether a particular legal standard has been met. For example, the literature on corporate social responsibility and risk management may help a jury determine whether a defendant has acted with "reckless indifference" sufficient to sustain a conviction of manslaughter in the context of an amusement park fire.[8] Similarly, ethical analysis concerning the relevancy of corporate personhood may assist a court in legislative interpretation essential for determining whether a corporation should be held criminally liable.[9] In civil suits, evidence concerning ethical attitudes should help inform fact finders required to determine whether a requisite standard of outrageous conduct has been met in order to justify imposition of punitive damages. As Paine (1994) demonstrates by using the E. F. Hutton check-kiting case and the Salomon Brothers treasury-bidding scandal, actions producing intense moral condemnation may be ultimately determined to be illegal, although the actions may not have been technically illegal at the time they occurred.

Law without reference to ethics and community moral values is in danger of becoming disconnected from the public will.[10] In a democracy, strongly held moral attitudes and widely recognized habits and practices must be considered in the interpretation and application of the law. Among other things, this is the way in which a sense of community is developed and community virtue nurtured. This is not to say that such attitudes and practices should always dominate other considerations, but only that they should be given due consideration. Authoritarian dismissal of all ethical sentiments in the creation and interpretation of law is not only inconsistent with fundamental liberty and quintessentially undemocratic, but it is also inefficient. Legal interpretations at odds with strongly held community attitudes and values make enforcement problematic and may even weaken the institution of the law itself.

Law, therefore, is not the preemptive source of all human behavior, as some might claim. Nor is it properly viewed as the ultimate moral arbiter. Moral norms and attitudes and values pertaining to ethical standards are also a critical source of influence on behavior and, under ISCT, a core element in determinating what constitutes ethical behavior in business. Similarly, morality is an appropriate and effective lens through which to judge laws. The traditional example of the laws permitting slavery, which existed for nearly a century in the United States, demonstrates that immoral laws are possible. Ethics, though intimately intertwined with law, exists well beyond legal rules and institutions. Law is not a firm constraint on ISCT, but instead is an element that operates in a defined way within the parameters of ISCT. Law helps us to understand ethical norms and how they come to be. Law does not definitively answer the question of what constitutes ethical behavior.

Consent and Dissent within Organizational Moral Free Space

Recognition of authentic ethical norms within ISCT does not require unanimity for either attitudes or behaviors. Requiring unanimity would be unrealistic, impractical, and unnecessary. Unanimity is not commonly found among business communities. There may be norms, such as those stigmatizing certain forms of sexual harassment, which may be supported by the attitudes of a substantial majority of the employees of an organization. At the same time, a few employees may believe that the firm has gone too far in condemning what is considered to be sexual harassment, and that some of the condemned activities are perfectly acceptable. Yet, within the organization, virtually all members, including those who disagree, understand the anti-sexual-harassment norm to be authentic to that community. Everyone is expected to comply, and this is known throughout the organization. Those who act inconsistently with the standard will be ostracized within or formally punished by the organization. Observers of these reactions may experience positive feelings when they believe that justice has been served, or conversely, experience anger when they believe that someone has gotten away with unjust actions (Trevino, 1992). Those who breach strong justice-based norms may themselves expect to be punished (Butterfield, Trevino, & Ball, 1996). Such reactions may be part of the process by which norms are established. Ethical norms are in fact established without unanimous agreement on the part of the members of the group. Further, we believe that a requirement of unanimity (see discussions of the issue in Simmons, 1979, 1988) is unrealistic, even idealistically naive. Viable standards of business ethics cannot coexist with a requirement of unanimous consent.

Moreover, requiring unanimous behavior among community members in support of a norm would not be realistic. It should be sufficient that a substantial majority of the membership of a community act consistently with a putative norm. Norms vary in the strength of their influence on human behavior. Some (those prohibiting pedophilia, cannibalism, or incest) are powerful and constrain all but a few. Others (one should not jaywalk) are far weaker (at least in certain U.S. cities) and are treated as suggestions to be followed if there aren't good reasons for an exception. As our purpose is to identify norms that should be obligatory based upon implicit understandings among the members of a group or community, it is necessary to focus on stronger norms. The test of substantial majority compliance eliminates weak or more suggestive norms, and coupled with the attitudinal requirement, serves to pinpoint norms that can fairly constitute part of the core material of business ethics. However, there is an important qualification. If there is evidence that behavior in support of a putative norm is coerced, then a contrary norm based on persuasive attitudinal evidence may be recognized.

The nature of the consent that exists for the macrosocial contract was discussed at length in chapter 2. We now discuss how the concept applies in the context of moral free space. Here, the consent focuses on membership in a community, rather than consent to every individual authentic norm. The circumstances of consent to community membership are specified by the macrosocial contractors who are willing to accept recognized participation in a community as evidence sufficient to bind individuals to authentic ethical norms. Phillips (1997) has expressed concern about the sufficiency of this approach to consent, arguing that (1) ISCT microsocial contracts appear to rely upon acts that imply consent that in fact fail to establish consent, and (2) a fairness-based principle works better in establishing moral obligations. In reference to the latter claim, Phillips essentially argues that the macrosocial contractors would prefer a more substantive definition of consent, one that has very specific requirements and applicability (e.g., "that there be a mutually beneficial scheme of cooperation requiring sacrifice or contribution on the parts of the participants . . . [with the possibility of] . . . free-riding" [1997: 57]). We believe that it is difficult to justify such a conclusion on the part of the macrosocial contractors who will represent many cultures and orientations. Instead, we recognize that it is perfectly possible certain communities may adopt authentic ethical norms consistent with Phillips's fairness principle, and furthermore, if they do, such norms would not violate hypernorms.

As to Phillips's first argument, we should note, as he clearly recognizes, that his arguments do not pertain to the manner in which authentic norms are recognized. There, by definition, consent must be given by the supermajority whose attitudes and behaviors are necessary to support an authentic ethical norm. In that context, when there is a question concerning whether an action implies consent, it is appropriate to use further means, such as scientific surveys of attitudes, to determine whether consent is genuine. Phillips's arguments, instead, focus on the consent to membership within a community. Under ISCT, the ultimate test is whether or not one has sufficient association with a community to allow for an attribution of moral obligation. This may be based on a formal, contractual connection, but it may also be based on entering into a transaction environment in which one acts within the boundaries of a self-recognized group and participates to fulfill some particular desire.

The right to exit the community undergirds this broad conception of consent. It denies individuals the ability to "cross their fingers" and disclaim any obligations associated with participation in a group. Ultimately, the definition is instrumental and pragmatic. There will always be a few extreme cases where the sufficiency of consent may be dubious. It is quite appropriate for communities to develop authentic norms restricting the impact of consent. It may be the case, for example, that a community might excuse the elderly or infirm from certain obligations of membership, effectively on grounds that there is insufficient reason to assume consent to authentic norm obligations. In most of the basic cases of business ethics, we do not believe that this issue of consent to membership is a serious problem. Employees are bound by legitimate corporate morality, doctors are bound by the authentic ethical norms of the medical profession, participants in an auction are bound by the authentic ethical norms of the auction, those who trade securities are bound by the authentic ethical norms of the securities industry, and so on.

There will, of course, be individual dissenters from authentic ethical norms. Norms become ethically obligatory on the basis of the consent of the majority of community members, as reflected in supportive attitudes and behaviors. In order to be fully legitimate, norms must also be compatible with hypernorms. Individuals have an ethical obligation to comply with legitimate norms, even those they personally find inappropriate, wrong, or distasteful. There cannot be a requirement that each person must consent to a legitimate norm in order for it to constitute an obligation. Such a requirement would invite ethical anarchy.

In organizations in which there is an authentic ethical norm supporting affirmative action, dissenting employees have an obligation to act consistently with the norm. Similarly, an individual who disagrees with an authentic norm against sexual harassment in the workplace has an obligation to comply. The same would be true for a pro-animal rights employee of a drug company who objects to the firm's authentic norm-based policy to use rats in research, or equally, to an anti-animal rights employee who objects to her firm's decision not to use animals in research.

What, then, are the options available to the dissenting employee?[11] The first is to exercise "voice" to try to bring about a change in the authentic norm within the community. The term "voice" is broadly defined to include any means of communication that may influence the attitudes and behaviors of other community members. Some actions have the effect of influencing changes in extant norms; others defend the status quo. Voice plays a critical role in the emergence and evolution of authentic ethical norms. Voice helps to clarify understandings concerning the specifics of authentic norms. An important implication is that artificial restrictions on the exercise of voice within a community can stifle the generation of norms.

Within organizations, ethical voice is not limited to formal mechanisms such as hot lines, suggestion boxes, ombudspersons, and open-door policies. Coalition building, networking with colleagues, and other less formal means of interaction may be far more powerful change agents. In an important sense, ethical voice is whatever works within a given community. The best method will vary significantly depending on the context, the community, or the individuals involved. The water cooler may be far more influential than the hot line.

In what circumstances might restrictions on voice be so severe as to stifle the ability of a community to generate authentic norms? In the business environments of the industrialized world, oppressive restrictions on voice should be quite rare. Background political institutions protect the exercise of voice in most forums, with some protections extending to the environment within organizations. Some, though not all, of the rights and protections extended by governments reach inside corporate walls, even the thicker enclosures surrounding global firms. Informal discussions among employees can bring about changes in ethical norms. The test of voice cannot be limited to whether or not an organization has in place certain specific types of voice mechanisms (e.g., a particular type of grievance procedure).

Organizations have incentives to allow for sufficient voice to develop ethical norms. Ethical norms often constitute a critical influence on organizational success. A drug company must insure the quality of its products. An airline must take the rules pertaining to aircraft maintenance seriously. Active expression of opinions and values help to foster the employee attitudes supportive of such goals as safety and integrity. Further, stifled voice may result in a greater tendency for employees to seek release by whistle-blowing outside the firm, resulting in considerable harm to the organization. In contrast are firms with open environments encouraging development of efficient ethical norms that help guide employees through rough spots. Problems find resolutions quickly in-house.

When dissenters are unable to bring about change in objectionable ethical norms, they have the ultimate option of deciding to exit the organization. In many instances, this will be an appropriate response. Someone who works for AT&T and objects to the company making philanthropic contributions to Planned Parenthood can quit and move to another firm. So too can the claims processor who objects to handling reimbursement forms for abortions. To be clear, we are limiting our discussion to instances in which an organization has an authentic ethical norm; a majority of the members of the organization support the norm and act consistently with it. We are not suggesting that exit is an appropriate solution in the face of clear wrongdoing by some individuals within an organization in violation of authentic ethical norms. Exit is not a satisfactory option when one knows that strawberries sold to elementary schools and misrepresented as U.S.-grown are increasing the chance that children get hepatitis.

Certainly, exit may not be a sufficient response to a violation of a hypernorm. As recognized by the classical social contract scholars, a failure to exit cannot always be taken as consent to community membership and the accompanying obligation to comply with legitimate authentic norms. A community may impose restrictions on exit that exceed reasonable bounds, thereby corrupting the essential voluntariness of a community or group. Extreme examples can be given of restrictions that represent the modern equivalent of indentured laborers or the old coal-mining company towns. Stories of modern workplace slavery are unfortunately commonplace today. Sweatshops have been found in Los Angeles and New York. Physical restraints added to more subtle barriers of language, lack of knowledge about legal rights, and fear of government agencies operate to immobilize immigrant workers. Similar stories have been told about Brazilian Indians who have moved from their home areas in hopes of a better life, only to end up in draconian work camps without the money or means to escape. Where mobility is legally or physically restricted in an unreasonable manner,[12] the norms generated by the community, even authentic norms satisfying the tests of attitudes and behavior, cannot be considered binding. But if the only factor constraining exit is financial and personal to the community member, then it should not be considered sufficient to affect the obligation to comply with legitimate norms. The fact that an employee would have to take a pay cut to escape the authentic norm supporting donations to Planned Parenthood does not represent a restriction on exit sufficient to undo the community's capacity for generating obligatory authentic norms.

The Political Dimensions of Moral Free Space

ISCT is intended to provide guidance about business ethics irrespective of the political environment in which firms operate. ISCT is equally applicable to firms based in the United States, Japan, Nigeria, China, France, Korea, the U.K., Germany, and all other nations. At the same time, ISCT has certain political implications that should be briefly considered.

Although the idea that implicit understandings among people should provide insight into the boundaries of right/wrong behavior may seem intuitive, even obvious to many, as we emphasized beginning in chapter 1, there is a long-standing philosophical tradition skeptical of deriving an "ought" from an "is." Fear of this "naturalistic fallacy" (Moore, 1903/1951) has led some to the extreme position of rejecting all consideration of human practice or attitudes as having any relevance to an ultimate normative judgment. Rejecting any role for practice or beliefs leads to a sterile approach in which ethics is disconnected from the realities and complexities of business practice. In contrast, recognizing the role of ethical norms respects human autonomy, supports the equality of human beings, sustains democratic majoritarianism, and allows for an appropriate emphasis on individual consent and choice. Further, this approach should be familiar to managers and professionals.

Human autonomy is respected when the opinions of those whose behavior is at issue are incorporated into the process of rendering normative judgments in business. Authentic ethical norms by definition represent a consensus across a group of individuals. Each individual starts with an opportunity to provide input into the process by which norms come into being. Their own attitude counts, and they may also actively attempt to influence the attitudes held by others.

Under the approach of ISCT, each person who is a member of a community capable of generating a norm has equal value in determining whether a norm exists. In order for an authentic norm to exist, a substantial majority of the members of the community must hold an attitude supporting the norm. If enough people disagree about the propriety of a putative norm, it is not authentic. Consider a common example. A consulting firm specializing in competitive intelligence is thought to have an authentic norm condemning the use of lies (e.g., by employees misrepresenting themselves as reporters or students) to obtain information about a client's competitor. There will be such a norm if a substantial majority of the people working at the consulting firm hold the attitude that lying in such a circumstance is wrong. On the other hand, if the senior managers of the firm hold that ethical attitude, but a majority of the entire staff of the firm does not, then the firm does not have an authentic ethical norm condemning lying. Note that the equality principle in this social-contracts-based approach does not extend to an equality of power, position, or ability to influence others' attitudes. The senior managers of the firm may be in a much stronger position to influence the development of norms through their oversight of the development of ethical codes and programs, employee training, compensation systems, and so on. Unless they are successful in actually bringing about particular attitudes in a majority of their staff, they will not have established an authentic ethical norm.[13]

As emphasized in chapter 4, in order to be authentic, a norm must be consistent with the attitudes and behaviors of a substantial majority of the members of the organization. Authentic norms do not exist in a company merely because of an attitude held by the company's CEO or a few senior managers of an organization, nor can they be established merely by drafting a new section in the organization's ethics code or employee handbook. In order to become authentic, norms must be internalized by the membership of the organization. Thus, the concept of an authentic norm is substantively democratic. There must be consent of the majority, as reflected in attitudes and behavior.

More broadly, business-political relationships in many different countries have been described in the media by references to social contracts (Dunfee, 1991). A common usage is to refer to the employment relationship as governed by a social contract. Framing the relationship in contractual terms often leads to the decrying of a "breach" of that relationship. As a typical example, in the management newsletter *Executive Excellence*, Barbara Strandell (1991) wrote, "There is an implicit *social* contract that management of our large publicly held corporations have with *shareholders, customers* and employees. . . . The social contract with employees is being broken." She then went on to list various examples of breaches, which included the following:

- asking employees to take "time off without pay" over the holidays

- implementing "fixed" employee contests

- using company resources to remodel the homes, cabins, or vacation condominiums of executives

- providing retired . . . executives with lucrative consulting contracts in the midst of hiring freezes[14]

Rousseau (1995: 13) states that "*[s]ocial contracts* are cultural, based on shared, collective beliefs regarding appropriate behavior in a society" and then goes on to note that "[s]ocial contracts in business are evident in pervasive notions regarding what is fair treatment." A social-contract-based analysis incorporating assumed ethical norms has been commonly used in support of public policies. Examples include prohibiting insider trading (Scheppele, 1993), formulating regulatory policies for public utilities, justifying user primacy in corporate financial reports, and dealing with time-consistency problems in capital taxation (see Dunfee, 1991). Professional codes in business have been described as "essentially a social contract that outlines group values, norms, and responsibilities" (Buchholz, 1989: 62). It is very common to see references to the social contract of particular nation-states (Dunfee, 1991). These recurring references to the concept constitute significant evidence that recognition of real social contracts, setting real standards for business behavior, is as familiar and intuitive to business managers and professionals as it is to academics and politicians.

Ethics beyond ISCT: What If No Authentic Norms Exist?

The definition of an authentic ethical norm under ISCT requires that a substantial majority of the members of the community hold supporting attitudes and engage in consistent behavior. Phillips (1997) argues for an even more stringent definition of consent under ISCT, while questioning whether there will be enough instances of authentic norms to support ISCT as an adequately general theory for business ethics. Phillips's question deserves serious consideration. In order to fully discuss its implications, we need to first identify the circumstances in which authentic norms may be lacking.

There are several identifiable circumstances where one might expect to encounter a paucity of authentic norms. One is where a community is closely divided over a difficult issue, such as abortion within the United States. There are many analogues in business. Telemarketing, employee dating, religious practices in the workplace, and drug-testing processes may all invoke controversies in which there are strong advocates for contrasting positions and no apparent consensus supporting any particular approach.

Secondly, new processes or techniques may unveil novel ethical issues where, because information is lacking or the context is unclear, there has yet to be a coalescence of attitudes or behavior around a particular solution. Issues raised by new scientific technologies fall into this category. If we have the capacity to clone human beings, should we actually use it? Or, as genetic testing enables identification of tendencies toward certain diseases, how should we use such information? If, for example, we now have the ability to produce artificial human growth hormones, should the market be the primary allocator of access, or should health-care professionals be able to override the desire of parents to use the hormone to increase a son's chances of playing basketball? The ability to have caller identification raises questions as to the limits of its use. Similarly, new techniques for taping telephone calls or for intercepting conversations raise questions concerning how to respect personal privacy interests. Intellectual property is particularly affected by new technologies, which make it far easier to copy and transfer information. This is transforming the publishing industry, and it has opened issues concerning what constitutes proper behavior on the part of ordinary people.

Third, there may be an interim period in which there is a gap or void while new norms replace long-standing authentic norms. Old norms, even ones that have existed for many years, may lose their support. Attitudes change, and members of the community no longer believe in the old norm. People stop acting consistently with the old norm. Yet, for a while there is no new consensus of attitudes and behaviors. This may be true in the late 1990s with the marketing of tobacco products and the advertising of hard liquor.

As the above examples indicate, there may be very good reasons why a community consensus is lacking concerning a particular ethical decision. The fact that the members of a community do not see a bright-line resolution to the problem is significant information in and of itself, information that should be respected in judging the actions of others. ISCT deals with this situation in a straightforward manner. There may be hypernorms that serve to guide the decision, and if such are found to exist, they answer the question. Even though a chemical manufacturing company has not developed authentic norms about assisting dictatorships in developing chemical weapons, there are hypernorms that should resolve this issue. If, however, for a given decision, there are no hypernorms, then the question becomes whether there are other communities that may have dominant authentic norms relevant to the decision. If the chemical firm is a U.S. firm, there may be norms in the U.S. community as a whole that would resolve the issue. Finally, if there are no hypernorms or dominant authentic norms of other communities, then we would recommend that managers act consistently with the traditions and values of their firms, even where those values and traditions have not risen to the status of authentic ethical norms.

The rigor applied to the definition of authentic ethical norms is a strength of ISCT, not a weakness. Ethical theories may be overbroad in the sense that they may condemn a wide scope of activities that many people believe constitute proper behavior. Such theories may be ineffective because they are seen to be disconnected from business realities and human experience. They may also seem arbitrary and to involve the pushing of the values of their devotees upon the rest of humanity. ISCT, in contrast, is grounded in the fundamental attitudes and behaviors of all of those who participate in or are affected by business activities.

Relativist and Universalist Objections to Moral Free Space

In chapter 1, and in subsequent sections, we have developed at length the arguments explaining why ISCT's reliance on authentic norms in moral free space is not relativism. Hypernorms, dominant norms of other communities, and the rights of exit and voice taken together provide strong mitigation against any form of relativism, even the rather mild form of social group relativism of concern to Freeman and Gilbert (1988). They define social group relativism as justifying actions by reference to the enduring norms of social groups: "morality is simply a matter of following the norms that are accepted practice" (33). In addition to the standard arguments against relativism, they also challenge social group relativism on grounds of pluralism and followership. In the former case, they argue that social group relativism is impractical because there are no good ways to deal, in a principled manner, with conflicting norms among communities. This objection does not apply to ISCT, which places great emphasis on criteria to establish priority among conflicting norms. Their second objection, followership, is based on the argument that "[a]ccepted practice is an inherently conservative idea," which does not allow for improvement and which makes impossible "[l]eadership in the moral realm" (34). As we have demonstrated in chapter 4 and in the examples used in this chapter, not only do authentic ethical norms change, sometimes rapidly, but they are also a force influencing behavior in the business community, often in very positive ways. Leadership is a key component in the evolution and creation of authentic ethical norms in business.

Perhaps more serious are objections from the other end of the continuum. Strong universalists would be expected to object to the extent that ISCT recognizes legitimate authentic ethical norms at odds with what the universalist believes to be dominating ethical principles. On first impression, Marxists and religious fundamentalists are likely to reject the idea of moral free space. Consider the well-reasoned argument put forward by Pava:

> While the Jewish perspective is sympathetic to the notion than an authentic business ethics hinges on the degree of consent of the members of relevant communities, consent alone is not a sufficient criterion to establish authenticity. For example, from a Jewish perspective authentic norms need to fit with the historical understanding of what it means to be a good Jew. Regardless of whether or not a majority of contemporary Jews accept or reject a particular norm, it is difficult to suggest that such a norm—with no grounding in traditional Jewish sources—is an authentic Jewish norm (1988: 78–79).

Presumably, Pava's argument could be restated to say "regardless of whether all contemporary Jews accept or reject a particular norm," which leads to the fundamental question of what constitutes a valid interpretation of "the historical understanding of what it means to be a good Jew." Surely, the fact that most or virtually all Jews might have a contrary understanding is highly relevant to identifying the behaviors associated with being a good Jew.

Under ISCT, any principle of sufficient strength and recognition to constitute a hypernorm would override an authentic norm found among a community of Jews. Pava recognizes this in referring to ISCT's "forceful and unapologetic recognition of hypernorms" (1988: 80). On the other hand, if an interpretation of "the historical understanding" does not satisfy the hypernorm test, the case for relying upon authentic norms is strengthened. We note that a community may have authentic norms based upon reference to historical or even spiritual sources, something particularly likely to hold true for religious communities.

Discussing the issue of universalist objections to moral free space in reference to the benign example of orthodox Judaism downplays the malignant potential of other universalist challenges. Any narrow conception of the "good," be it Marxism, neoclassical economics, or National Socialism, may serve as the foundation for those who wish to impose their views and judgments upon others. Such partisans may conclude that when persuasion fails, a community with authentic norms inconsistent with the "good" is problematic. A predictable response may be the employment of physical or intellectual force to override the "bad" ethical attitudes of community members. Total repudiation of moral free space—a form of totalitarianism—denies the right of a community to choose core components of its own morality. ISCT seeks a middle ground on this issue, setting a high standard for hypernorms as a means of limiting the imperialistic tendencies of those eager to impose their morality on others.

The Instrumental Value of Moral Free Space

We assume that rational macrosocial contractors would rely upon moral free space as a means of generating the contextual, flexible, and reasonable morality essential to sustain productive economic relationships. As evidenced in many of the examples used previously, and in the discussion of the efficiency hypernorm in chapter 5, authentic ethical norms are often essential foundations for business relationships. ISCT provides a strong justification for an ethical obligation to act consistently with legitimate ethical norms. Following the legitimate norms of one's industry usually serves the social good even as it is good business. Such legitimate norms are not hard to find. Here are some examples of what we believe are authentic, legitimate norms that it makes good sense to follow:

- Brokers and dealers in the securities industry should honor oral promises.
- System administrators at universities should respect the privacy of personal e-mail.
- Lawyers should respect the confidentiality of client documents and revelations.
- Doctors should respond to emergency situations regardless of liability.
- Salespeople ought not overpromise delivery dates.
- Employees should be granted the opportunity to respond to charges of improper conduct.
- When possible, a whistle-blower should go through internal channels before disclosing his information to outsiders.
- MBA students interviewing for jobs ought not to double-bill two different firms for the same trip.
- With rare exceptions (e.g., apartheid), managers should willingly comply with the criminal law.

- Distributors should not markup marketing expenses passed on to suppliers without disclosure.
- Profitable corporations should engage in philanthropy.

There are millions of examples of norms like these. Taken together, they provide the foundation for much of the substance of business ethics. In practice, the proliferation of norms raises practical problems for decision makers. For one thing, conflicting norms may seem to apply to a given decision. In that case, which norm should prevail? For another, with so many potential norms out there, how far should the search for norms extend? Is it necessary to consider every possible authentic norm before making a decision? These and similar questions are considered in the next chapter, which is devoted to the use of ISCT by decision makers and ethicists.

7

ISCT and Ethical Decision Making: Priorities, Proxies, and Patterns

A strange justice that is bounded by a river! Truth on this side
of the Pyrenees, error on the other.

—Pascal (Note, 1990)

In this chapter, we explore how to make ISCT useful in day-to-day decisions. We consider how firms, their managers, and others, including those making ethical judgments ex post, can learn to apply the concepts at the core of ISCT to the ethical dilemmas they face. Special emphasis will be given to the daunting problems encountered in moral free space, where one confronts competing sets of legitimate ethical norms all having some connection to a decision. We begin by describing two recurring challenges in business decision making: gifts and safety standards.

Cases of Conflicting Standards

DuPont has a simple rule for the safety standards to be followed in its overseas plants. "If our safety standards are higher, we use ours. If the other country's are higher, we use theirs" (Hofmann, 1988). Implicit in this standard is a recognition that DuPont, as a global firm operating plants in many countries, unavoidably encounters differing community standards concerning plant safety. By establishing a priority policy, DuPont is setting forth a rule to govern foreseeable cases of conflicting standards. On the face of it, the policy of following the highest standard seems highly praiseworthy and uncontroversial. Yet, as DuPont's experience demonstrates, even such a laudable policy may result in unexpected difficulties.

Consider DuPont's experience in Korea. Korea has appallingly low plant-safety standards as a nation. In 1990 alone, 2,336 workers were killed, and 132,983 hospitalized for at least four days by workplace injuries. When DuPont responded to this environment by putting their corporate safety standards into effect in two plants at Ichon, workers walked off the job several times in protest against the stringent safety requirements. Presumably the Korean workers were reflecting local norms and expectations by protesting against the more expensive and time-consuming policies implemented by DuPont. Apparently the Korean workers' expectations for risk in the workplace were such that they would personally prefer a more dangerous environment if they thought that the tradeoff was lower salaries or less job security. If injured, they would expect to be paid, but presumably at a level far below that of injured workers in the United States. Recognizing the implications of this environment, *The Far Eastern Economic Review* (Clifford, 1991) concluded, "As long as it is cheaper to recompense workers and their families for industrial accidents, safety-conscious companies such as DuPont will be the exception in South Korea."

How should DuPont's decision be viewed? By failing to adopt the less expensive, more risky plant-safety standards in Korea, did DuPont management violate an obligation to its shareholders? Is it ethical imperialism for DuPont to impose its home standards on Korea, particularly in the face of protests by the workers? Or, contrariwise, was DuPont ethically obligated to follow its higher standards in Korea?

Contrast the DuPont case with a different case, this time involving gift-giving standards. Each year in anticipation of the holiday season of gift-giving and entertainment, a number of U.S. firms send what are known as "no-presents letters" asking suppliers to respect their policies concerning the size and nature of gifts, if any, that they allow employees to receive. The following is typical of the genre:[1]

UNITED TECHNOLOGIES–SIKORSKY AIRCRAFT

Ladies and Gentlemen:

The Christmas Season is fast approaching and I want to take this opportunity to acknowledge with gratitude the continuing contribution made by your organization to the success of our enterprise. I would also like to record with you our feelings on a topical subject of great importance to us both.

It is quite natural that personal friendships and associations

develop between our representatives and yours. This may lead to
expressions of friendship which, viewed strictly in the light of personal relationships, may be considered proper. But, unfortunately, it is
often virtually impossible to identify the difference between commercial and personal relationships. What may be offered simply as a
token of friendship and goodwill may be construed, as we know, as
not only a breach of ethics but even a criminal action under the Anti-
Kickback Act, which applies to U.S. Government prime contractors
and subcontractors alike.

Our policy at Sikorsky Aircraft has always been that soliciting, giving or receiving gifts by our employees is prohibited. This includes use
of property or facilities, gift certificates or favors extended to employees or their families. We continue to ask for your cooperation in making this policy effective, enabling us to maintain the conditions of
arms-length impartiality and mutual respect essential to both of us.

In the "no-presents" letters, Sikorsky Aircraft makes quite clear
that when its practices and standards differ from those of their suppliers, it expects its own policies to be followed. Is this an example of
ethical imperialism? Is there some ethical obligation on the part of the
suppliers to honor these policies? Can such an obligation exist without the consent of the supplier? Suppose that a supplier sends a letter
to Sikorsky indicating that they purchased desk organizers for all of
their clients, valued at $50, and that they intend to offer them to all
the purchasing agents with whom they deal, as they have always done
since they first entered the business? Would such a "notice-of-presents
letter" override any obligation to honor a "no-presents letter"?

The plant-safety and gift and entertainment examples involve the
same challenging dilemma, namely, how should corporations respond
when policies and expectations differ significantly from their own
policies in the business communities in which they operate? Both
examples pertain to common yet vitally important decisions confronted by managers. The plant-safety issue directly involves the
physical well-being, even the very survival of workers. The gift and
entertainment policies respond to the potential for fundamental corruption of the corporate purchasing process, which if it occurs can
endanger the viability of the firm. But at the same time, it is understandable that there would be varying practices among different
firms, industries, and cultures. Plant safety ultimately comes down to
choices. Enormous sums can be spent to produce paltry increases in

individual safety. A policy of doing everything possible to eliminate all risks from the workplace is neither rational nor realistic. Instead, managers and government officials, acting within their respective domains, must draw lines concerning the limits of acceptable risk in plant safety. Their decisions are necessarily influenced by their differing environments and objectives as well as circumscribed by limited information.

The kaleidoscopic environment surrounding gifts and entertainment also spawns confusion. Contrary to the views of those who see it as a calculating science, business remains an activity in which personal relationships, fueled in part by gifts and social activities, provide important advantages. In this realm cultural factors, delineating the nature and context of personal relationships, become important in assessing the boundaries of permissible conduct. Korea, Japan, and Saudi Arabia are just a few of the nations that are well known for highly ritualized gift giving within business relationships. In the United States massive sums are spent on corporate "Superboxes" for sports events and for other types of entertainment. Each of these nations is sufficiently distinctive in its practices that both a lavish gift considered appropriate in Saudi Arabia and lavish entertainment common in the United States might be seen to violate the boundaries of proper behavior in a third country such as Japan.

One extremely important point needs to be made at the outset. As discussed at length in the chapters 2 and 3, whenever any authentic norm violates any form of hypernorm, it immediately fails the test of legitimacy. In addition, in certain contexts hypernorms will specify minimal standards, for example, a mandatory threshold level of safety for chemical plants around the world. In a case such as safety, the vantage point of transcultural principles will not require that every bell and whistle of current safety practice be implemented, but it will require that firms meet certain minimal standards. If the Korean norms reflected in the DuPont example fall below such minimal standards, then they are no longer candidates for legitimate norms.

But, even in a case where lives are at stake, such as conflicting plant-safety norms between Korea and the United States, there will be some room for variance among legitimate norms, thus requiring a managerial decision as to which competing legitimate norms to follow. Firms through their policies, and individual managers when confronting novel situations, must make hard decisions concerning the boundaries of ethical behavior. Often there is no middle ground, and no easy way of finessing the decision. Dawai Bank in the 1990s had to make a decision about whether to report to U.S. authorities the actions of a rogue trader who had violated government regulations. The formality of such a report differed significantly from the way that the transaction would be handled in Japan, where banks and securities firms have traditionally had a very close, informal relationship with the regulatory authorities. The failure of Daiwa Bank to make the correct decision resulted in substantial costs to the firm and subjected it to intense scrutiny.

Might ISCT have helped the bank make a better decision? Under the framework of ISCT, each community (firms, governmental bodies, and so on) acts within moral free space to establish authentic norms providing guidance concerning business decisions with ethical implications. Again, if an authentic norm is consistent with obligations under hypernorms, then it is a legitimate norm. But when two or more competing legitimate norms come into direct conflict, the otherwise useful notion of moral free space provides insufficient guidance. Two (or more) communities, each having acted legitimately within its own moral free space, may make contradictory claims about the morality of their actions. How should the conflict be resolved? Neither can claim a preference based solely on the fact that their norm is the legitimate product of its own norm-generating process, for the other can make the same claim! Something more is needed, that is, some other criterion that transcends claims made at the community level.

In the following sections of this chapter, we will explore at length criteria that may be helpful in resolving conflicting legitimate claims. The chapter then closes with a look at strategies for applying ISCT to ethical dilemmas in business.

Sources of Conflicting Norms

As a first step we require a better understanding of how conflicting legitimate norms may arise. A variety of relationships may exist among communities. Some communities exist entirely within a larger community, as in the case of corporate subsidiaries, where, for example, Burger King exists as a subsidiary of the British firm, Grand Metropolitan. Identifying and specifying the different relationships that exist among communities can help us understand the basic contexts in which recurring problems of competing, conflicting legitimate norms arise. Consider the three following kinds of community relationships.

Communities within Communities: Vertical Relationships

It is common for relatively autonomous communities to be within the ambit or control of a broader community. Often this community, in turn, is under the control of a still larger community. A public affairs office attached to the research subsidiary of SmithKline Beecham in King of Prussia, Pennsylvania, reports to the Public Affairs Office of SKB in Philadelphia, which is ultimately under the control of the parent firm in the U.K., which in turn is under the jurisdiction of both the governments of the United Kingdom and the United States.[2] All of these communities may generate norms concerning the propriety of certain types of activities, for example, lobbying. These norms, say those regarding disclosure of the lobbyist's source of funding, may come into conflict in specific contexts. A key issue for ISCT, as we will see, is whether a given community has a subordinate relationship to a larger or broader community.

Transactions Crossing Communities: Horizontal Relationships

Business is commonly conducted across communities by firms that have no previous formal relationship. Such "horizontal" relationships may involve transactions, such as mergers, in instances where the parties are entirely independent from one another. For example, a New York–based company and a Texas-based company in the same industry might consider merging, as happened in the infamous Pennzoil-Texaco case, or, commonly, a sales transaction may take place between companies from different countries, as when Volkswagen contracts to buy parts from General Motors. Many of the examples of conflicting norms given in prior chapters and in the next chapter involve such horizontal relationships. In some instances, the transaction takes place between two communities within a larger neutral community whose only role lies in providing the environment in which a contract is formed or a sale made. Stock exchanges are examples of such "matchmaking." In other cases, the two transacting parties constitute a kind of "host" community in which the physical transaction takes place and in which the parties play host to an "outsider" who comes into the host community environment to transact business. When Ford acquires Mazda and then operates Mazda within the Japanese economic system, Ford is an outsider operating within the host community of Japan. The nature of this relationship will also often have significance for resolving conflicts among competing legitimate norms.

Conflicts within Communities: Tug-of-War Relationships

Even though it may seem counterintuitive, a single community may be found to have mutually inconsistent norms. For example, a community may hold separate values that in a given context may come into conflict. The more general the form in which norms are expressed, the greater their potential for conflict. Thus, the community of the University of Texas may simultaneously hold preferences for equal opportunity, for not basing decisions on racial characteristics, and for remedial affirmative action as a response to historic patterns of racial discrimination. When a particular decision is required, say as to a system of affirmative action for admission into the University's law school, these norms come into direct conflict. The members of the community believe in all three values, and there appear to be no clearly established norms that could resolve the conflict. Thus, within the moral free space of a single community, there may be competing norms in the context of a single decision. These internal tugs-of-war also turn out to be significant characteristics in the resolution of conflicting norms.

Resolving the Conflicts

A choice is often required between two competing standards, where neither standard violates any reasonable characterization of universal principles. Appealing to hypernorms may not help, since both standards may be consistent with hypernorms. Nor will appealing to moral free space help insofar as each of the communities has a right to moral free space.

In the next sections, we discuss various principles that may serve to guide a decision maker in making these difficult choices. As we will emphasize, the principles or "rules of thumb" are not presented as a

formal calculus for norm conflict dilemmas. Instead, taken together
they constitute a process of general guidance aimed at identifying the
circumstances in which a particular norm enjoys priority.

The moral stakes are lower here than when discussing legitimacy.
Whatever the outcome, the norm selected will be consistent with
hypernorms. This might lead one to conclude that the simplest rule
would be for the decision maker to act always on the basis of her own
norms. Such an operating principle would recognize the cogency of
the decision maker's own moral free space and would provide a clear
and clean decision rule. An advocate of this approach might note that
since the decision will be consistent with hypernorms, no harm follows from allowing such a preference for one's own norms.

There is, however, a major problem with such an approach. When
its full implications are considered, it becomes obvious that it would
sometimes endorse open-ended moral imperialism on the part of business decision makers. So long as hypernorms are not relevant to the
situation, this approach offers carte blanche to decision makers to
ignore the norms of other communities and always prefer their own
approach—even when negative implications arise for the other community. This would mean, for example, that a firm should always
prefer its own policies concerning gifts and entertainment regardless
of the customs and preferences of other parties.[3]

The "follow one's own norms" approach is best interpreted as a
rebuttable presumption. If there isn't a clear-cut argument on behalf
of following the norms of another party, it is fair to apply one's own
norms. In the general decision models that are discussed at the end of
this chapter, we illustrate the value of this rebuttable presumption in
favor of one's own norms.

The Basic Nature of Rules of Thumb

So far, we have established the need for a set of rules or principles to
help arbitrate conflicts of norms among communities. What, then,
would a set of priority principles look like? Under ISCT, they must, of
course, be found to be consistent with the assumptions and terms of
the macrosocial contract.

Such principles, or "rules of thumb," would be analogous to legal
principles that concern conflicts among laws, and also to legal doctrines pertaining to the extraterritorial application of substantive
(rights-determining) laws. It will be helpful to explore this analogy in

more detail. Analogous judicial standards arise out of the problems faced by court systems when they must deal with legal actions involving people and/or issues that fall under two or more legal jurisdictions. For example, questions may arise as to whether the United States should be able to apply its antidiscrimination or environmental laws to any of the following: (1) U.S. firms operating a subsidiary in a foreign country, (2) foreign firms operating a subsidiary in the United States, (3) foreign firms employing U.S. citizens in their operations entirely outside of the United States, and so on? Another sample question might be, should a court in Maine apply Washington state law in a lawsuit in which a Maine citizen injured in the crash of a Boeing 727 in Illinois is suing claiming that Boeing improperly designed an airplane component in its research labs in Seattle?

In such "choice-of-law" contexts, the "forum court" actually deciding the case must determine whether to recognize or apply the substantive law of another jurisdiction. It is an accepted principle of choice-of-law conflicts jurisprudence that the forum court will apply its own rules of procedure, although questions often arise about what constitutes procedural as opposed to substantive law in a given case. Significantly, in the context of the rebuttable presumption proviso for "following one's own norms" that we identified earlier, law courts long ago abandoned the assumption that they should invariably utilize the laws existing in the jurisdiction in which the contract was finalized or the tort occurred. Instead a "contacts" principle evolved, in which courts applied the law of the jurisdiction that had the greatest number of contacts with the litigation. These formalistic approaches based on applying the law of the forum or of the state with the most contacts did not work well in practice, where other considerations often seemed paramount. Many courts have adopted a more flexible "governmental interests" approach, which incorporates a consideration of contacts but also seeks to determine the respective interests of each community with some claim on the litigation and to apply the law of any state with a paramount or overriding interest in the transaction.

Of course there are many important differences between legal and ethical dimensions. Certain hoary legal doctrines applicable to conflicts such as sovereign immunity or the act-of-state doctrine rarely have analogues in ethical decision making. Further, the comparable judicial decisions often have to be considered within broader legal and political contexts in a formal manner not fully relevant to ethical decision making. On the other hand, this rich and extensive jurisprudence has dealt with comparable issues and contexts and is full of valuable insights for our purposes. The primary lessons are (1) that a flexible, nonformalistic approach is essential when multiple diverse interests are involved, and (2) that some means is needed to identify as accurately as possible the goals and interests that underlie the competing norms.

Six Sample Rules of Thumb

The following sections discuss a set of six rules of thumb for choosing among competing legitimate norms. The rules, all consistent with the macrosocial contract, derive in large part from principles recognized in choice-of-law and extraterritorial jurisprudence. They are offered as samples of principles, not as an exhaustive set. Although the list is extensive, there may well be other rules worthy of consideration, and we encourage the search for additions to the set. These six rules were stated in slightly different language in each of the two foundational ISCT articles (Donaldson & Dunfee, 1994, 1995).

1. Transactions solely within a single community, which do not have significant adverse effects on other humans or communities, should be governed by the host community's norms.

This principle is directly consistent with the important ISCT principle of community moral free space. Ceteris paribus, the "forum" community (the firm or other community making the decision or judgment at issue) should act in a manner consistent with its own legitimate norms. Two factors are particularly important in applying this rule. First, one must be extremely careful in evaluating the impact of the decision on outsiders. Otherwise one may miss the key externalities that this rule is designed to guard against. Second, particularly in the context of rendering an ex post ethical judgment, one should exercise care in the determination of the relevant community. There may be other communities having a claim or relationship to the transaction that may not be readily apparent. In vertical community relationships there may be some broader community, a corporate parent or a political body, having norms relevant to the decision. Thus, a corporation that has an internal human-resources policy recognizing seniority may be at odds with norms in its surrounding political community that recognize unfettered equal opportunity. The norms of both communities are relevant to the transaction, and to the extent that both are consistent with hypernorms, any conflicts among them should be resolved through the priority rules of thumb.

2. Existing community norms indicating a preference for resolving conflicts of norms should be utilized, so long as they do not have significant adverse effects on other individuals or communities.

Because certain conflicts-of-norms situations, including those detailed at the beginning of this chapter, occur quite often, it is not surprising that many communities develop their own norms concerning how anticipated conflicts among norms should be resolved. These internal rules of thumb specify how future conflicts will be arbitrated, and they may also constitute signals to third parties showing how they should deal with comparable issues. The "no-presents" letters are a prime example. The firms sending the letters realize that their own employee gifts and entertainment policies may be challenged by their suppliers' provisions of favors and social outings. In essence, the letter states that "we recognize that we may have different norms and values concerning what is appropriate for holiday giving and entertainment. We want you to understand what our policies are, and we would like for you to respect them."

A broader, and perhaps more dramatic, example of this type of priority rule of thumb is the Foreign Corrupt Practices Act in the United States. Assuming that the FCPA constitutes an authentic norm for the United States,[4] it thereby represents a community-based standard for resolving conflicts between U.S. norms censuring bribery and more accepting norms of other communities. In essence, the norm is both a statement of an expectation concerning how members of the U.S. community will act when confronted with conflicting norms about bribery, and an announcement to other communities concerning what they should expect from members of the U.S. business community when conflicting bribery norms are at issue.

The weight given to such an internal norm should depend, in part, on whether the community takes a consistent position when the reverse situation occurs. As noted in the next chapter, many countries, Germany for example, used to support the payment of bribes in other economic environments while strongly condemning them when they occurred within German markets. A community statement of a preference rule based on raw self-interest should not be entitled automatically to preemptive status.

This rule is also supported by the concept of moral free space emanating from the macrosocial contract. The contract extends moral free space insofar as it recognizes that communities may anticipate and respond to classes of foreseeable conflicts between their own norms and norms of other communities. As such, it is an important factor, and when done consistently should be given considerable weight in the resolution of conflicts-of-norms situations.

Yet another context shows the importance of this rule. Many firms, particularly those with very strong core values, have set up internal rules for dealing with problematic conflicts-of-norms situations. Levi Strauss (LS), for example, has set up standards determining the circumstances under which it will allow production of its products in other countries. LS recognizes that other firms and cultures may have norms at a direct variance with those of LS concerning the minimum working age, work conditions, support for employee education, and so on. LS not only specifies how they will resolve their own conflicts, but they make it very clear that they will follow rigid rules in dealing with contractors, requiring, in essence, that their contractors implement specified LS norms on these issues. Although hypernorms may resolve some of these issues, others may fall outside their range and therefore require resolution under the rules of thumb.

Rules of thumb such as those followed by Levi Strauss (and also AT&T and Motorola, among others) may result in the firms being classified as "corporate imperialists" (Dunfee, 1996). Even though the term "corporate imperialist" may sound pejorative, in this context it should be treated as a compliment. There are circumstances in which a very strong case can be made for the superiority of a decision maker's values over competing claims. This rule recognizes that fact.

3. The more extensive or more global the community that is the source of the norm, the greater the priority that should be given to the norm.

This rule of thumb implicitly recognizes the potential for vertical relationships among communities. To the extent that one of the communities is at a higher level, e.g., a corporate parent or a regional political community, its norms should have some consideration for priority over the norms of subservient communities. Several justifications may be given for this preference. First, the broader economic community often formally contains constituent communities. Therefore, it stands in a position of authority with respect to constituent communities. Second, the broader and more global the community, the more likely it is that its norms will approach hypernorm status. In chapter 8, we further demonstrate the implications of this argument.

A dramatic example (May 1998) occurred with the effort to establish an authentic norm against bribery in the twenty-nine-nation regional group, the Organization of Economic Cooperation and Development (OECD). The OECD, after a long period of negotiations, formally adopted a plan to reduce bribery in global business transactions. As the OECD policy achieves status as a norm, and as more nations adopt the norms of the OECD, the appropriate weight assigned to the norms increases. Ultimately, as efforts are made toward developing an international treaty condemning bribery, the policy should come to have dominant priority for those dimensions of bribery that fall outside substantive and structural hypernorms. Here, too, the rule is consistent with the concepts of hypernorms and moral free space (and the authentic norms generated therein).

4. Norms essential to the maintenance of the economic environment in which the transaction occurs should have priority over norms potentially damaging to that environment.

Many norms develop out of the need to provide boundaries limiting opportunism in market transactions. While not rising to the level of the efficiency hypernorm (also called the hypernorm of necessary social efficiency) examined in chapter 5, such norms are nonetheless significant components of the transaction environment. They may include, for example, familiar rules for the operation of an auction where norms clarify issues of representation, signaling, and financial backing. Other examples include principles of confidentiality, truth telling, and fairness in securities transactions. Implicit unwritten rules of confidentiality serve as important foundations for transactions involving intellectual property. Similarly, confidentiality may be an implicit understanding in the rendering of professional services, including the practice of law, psychological counseling, and financial planning. What these various norms have in common is that they are tailored to the needs of the particular transaction community. They will therefore vary according to the needs of the specific form of transactions they support. For example, bond auctions would be expected to have norms insuring speed and liquidity, whereas real estate auctions would have norms supporting financial security and recognizing formal legal requirements for the transfer of title.

All other things being equal, when a decision is required in an environment where one of the conflicting norms helps sustain necessary background institutions, that norm should be given priority. Failure to follow supporting norms of the transaction environment may ultimately weaken, and even cause the failure of, the transaction environment. The chaos that would ensue from widespread breach of the norms of a particular form of auction, for example, may render future operations impossible. Assuming that the decision maker wants to make future instrumental use of the auction, failure to support these norms would be irrational. But, if decision makers have no future expectations for using the auction, they may be tempted to prefer their own norms to those of the auction. This priority rule of thumb provides some, but not unlimited, protection to the transaction environment. It is grounded in the macrosocial contract in two ways. First, it is consistent with the assumption of a desire on the part of the macrosocial contractors to establish an economic environment in which they can act to achieve their particular desires and wants. Second, it is consistent with the macrosocial contract term recognizing structural hypernorms such as the efficiency hypernorm.

5. Where multiple conflicting norms are involved, patterns of consistency among alternative norms provide a basis for prioritization.

In some very complex situations, there may be many communities with diverse norms having some connection to the transaction. For example, actions involving the natural environment may have an impact on many, many communities, thus triggering consideration of a wide range of norms. Consider the case discussed at the beginning of chapter 1, namely, Royal Dutch Shell's decision to dismantle the Brent Spar oil platform in the North Sea. The decision as to how to dispose of the platform had potential impact on a vast array of communities, as it had significant implications for fragile ecosystems and human well-being. The oil and fishing industries were directly involved, but so were numerous countries that had shorelines neighboring the vicinity of the platform. The scientific community also held important interests, not the least of which was that the decisions reflect good science and the current state of knowledge. The decision could affect employment in the U.K., the purity of the water in Norwegian fjords, and the availability of fish to complement chips. Presumably there were a large number of norms at issue among the relevant communities. Some supported a decision to sink the platform, others to tow it to ground where it could be safely dismantled, while others supported a more complete on-site dismantlement.

Across this array of communities, a norm opposed to the sinking of the platform gradually emerged. As this occurred, the pressure on Royal Dutch Shell increased, leading them ultimately to abandon their initial plan for dismantling, even though they continued to believe that there was significant scientific support for their initial choice. In fact, some of the estimates of potential environmental impact made by other groups, e.g., Greenpeace, were ultimately discovered to be substantially overstated. Even so, that did not prevent the evolution of a consensus among many of the potentially affected communities challenging Shell's initial plan. Shell's example demonstrates the importance of the rule of thumb concerning patterns of consistency. Where a norm is identified in diverse cultures, and there is some convergence (short of obtaining hypernorm status) in favor of a norm in conflict locally with other norms, the more broadly recognized norm should be given some priority. An emerging convergence may reflect nascent substantive hypernorm status. At the least, when diverse communities are involved, partial convergence demonstrates that numerous people have found comparable norms responsive to common problems. This gives the norm validation that extends beyond the moral free space of a single community and is thereby consistent with the general assumptions and terms of the macrosocial contract.

6. Well-defined norms should ordinarily have priority over more general, less precise norms.

This final rule, recognized in law in the principles used to interpret ambiguous contracts, recognizes that norms vary in their form and scope. Some norms may be translated in highly general terms such as "act with integrity." The meaning of such unfocused norms is often unclear. Does the "act with integrity" principle mean that a young soldier who is torn between enlisting in the army to defend his country and staying at home with his aging mother should do one or the other? Many of the most valuable norms, emphasized within ISCT, are those that are context specific. Thus, a norm indicating that a drug company is expected to fully disclose all information about side effects that might be of concern to a prospective customer, regardless of what the law requires, is more precise than the general "act with integrity" norm. The more precise norm deals with the particular context of the marketing of retail drugs and is a strong candidate for priority.

Applying the Six Rules

As we argued in earlier writings, the rules of thumb here described "have a ceteris paribus condition and must be weighed and applied in combination" (Donaldson & Dunfee, 1994: 270). We assign no ordinal ranking to the rules. We envision that the rules would be applied in a commonsense manner somewhat analogous to the way in which the courts have applied the rules of statutory interpretation. Over the years the courts have developed an extensive set of rules that help them achieve their basic objective of determining legislative intent in the interpretation of controversial statutory language. A few examples of the many rules include (1) the "plain meaning rule," where when the language of a statute is clear on its face, the courts will not add to or subtract from that language, (2) "implied repealer," where a later enactment that is inconsistent with earlier language is considered to take precedence, (3) "in derogation of common law," where statutes that repeal well-established doctrines of judge-made law will be strictly construed, and (4) *ejusdem generis*, in which more specific terms are used to define and limit more general terms. Often in a given case, particular rules of statutory construction will point in different directions. Further, in many individual cases, some of the rules may seem to be more pertinent than others. The courts do not take an excessively formalistic approach to statutory interpretation. They do not, for example, merely count how many rules of interpretation embrace a particular construction over the alternative.

As a first step in addressing conflicts of norms, we believe that clarifying existing norms, using the techniques of specification advocated by Richardson (1990), will serve to resolve many false conflicts. By pressing to determine more precisely the meaning of the norms at issue, it is often possible to make seeming conflicts dissolve. Second, we believe that greater precision is brought to the process by following a weak presumption that if the priority rules of thumb fail to give a clear signal preferring a particular norm, then the decision maker should act consistently with her own norms. Because the choice is always among legitimate norms, giving some preference to the norms generated in the moral free space of the decision maker constitutes an appropriate recognition of the macrosocial contractors' desire to resolve issues outside the boundaries of hypernorms by establishing contextual legitimate norms. We also recognize that there will likely be circumstances in which a decision maker is unable to choose among conflicting norms by using the priority rules of thumb because of a lack of information or a lack of time. This derivation of bounded moral rationality also justifies allowing decision makers to fall back on their own norms in such circumstances. Beyond these approaches, we believe that a strategy of flexible judging is best. No precise formula is available, or desirable, at this time. Instead, parties required to resolve conflicts should use their best judgment and moral imagination.

Taka (1996a) has proposed a "transparency test" that involves a useful way of thinking about conflicting norms. Under Taka's transparency test, the decision maker assumes that members of all affected communities are aware of all of the competing norms at issue. The task then is to identify the norms that would emerge as authentic across this broader community. Those that survive "are judged to be transparent and are assumed to be ethically preferred norms" (1996a: 9).

Applications of ISCT by Others

Several theorists, including us (Donaldson & Dunfee, 1995), have applied the set of rules of thumb to cases of conflicting norms. In some cases in which competing, conflicting norms were confronted, it was impossible to construct a rational argument for the dominance of one of the conflicting norms without more information. This was the case with Puffer and McCarthy's analysis (1997) of conflicting norms in Russia in relation to the laying off of workers justified by economic necessity, and also with Donaldson and Dunfee (1995) on conflicting norms surrounding company policies requiring that employees completely abstain from smoking. Nelson (1996) undertook a sophisticated application extended by social choice analysis concerning the Sunday operation of Richard Branson's Virgin Megastore on the Champs Élysées in Paris. Nelson identified three competing norms: (1) ban all retail sales on Sunday, (2) empower local officials to allow sales of leisure goods and services in tourist zones on Sunday, and (3) empower local officials to allow, at their discretion, Sunday sales of any type. Nelson identified the various communities supporting each of the norms and then attempted to determine, in a manner not dissimilar to the process advocated by Taka, whether any norm was dominant. Nelson was unable to establish a superior norm. Our view is that in circumstances such as these, it then falls within the moral free space of the decision maker to prefer his own norms, and that such actions should be shielded from ethical criticism.

We note that establishing priority among conflicting norms may resolve some of the hard cases discussed in chapter 3, where those applying ISCT have been unable to pinpoint applicable hypernorms. In their analysis of ISCT, Mayer and Cava (1995) were concerned that they could not identify a hypernorm to resolve the issues in a case involving a female employee of a U.S. bank who is given a rotating assignment in Mexico. The woman finds her authority restricted by paternalistic policies that handicap her ability to perform her job. In this case, two authentic norms appear to be at issue. The norm of gender equality followed by the U.S. bank and the norm restricting the access of female professionals to clients followed by the corresponding bank in Mexico. The norm of the Mexican bank does not appear to be supported by any of the rules of thumb save perhaps rule 6, and then only to the extent that the norm restricting opportunities of female managers would be considered well-defined. The Mexican norm clearly has adverse effects on other humans and communities and thus is not supported by rule 1. Nor is it essential to the maintenance of the economic environment as required by rule 4. In fact, the Mexican norm probably erodes efficiency. On the other hand, the gender equality norm of the U.S. bank is supported, at the least, by rule 3 (more global community) and rule 5 (patterns of consistency among alternative norms), so that the U.S. norm would prevail as a matter of priority. Thus, although Mayer and Cava were not able to reach the result they desired through hypernorms, they could have reached it through the application of the priority rules of thumb.

Poindexter (1995) extends the use of priority rules of thumb in two distinct ways in her analysis of the siting issues that surround urban brownfield redevelopment. First, she broadened the scope of the rules of thumb by explicitly considering the magnitude of the impact of applying a norm in a given context. Second, she explicitly included the application of priority rules in the extensive stakeholder analysis that constituted her primary focus.

As the above discussions show, in some cases applying the rules of thumb will produce very clear guidance concerning preferred norms. In other situations, the results will be mixed, making it difficult to conclude that one of the competing norms should be given priority. In a third category of cases there will be a weak signal pointing toward a particular norm. In almost all cases in which there is a strong internal preference for one of the competing norms, we believe that norm should be applied. When the application of the rules of thumb provides no basis for choosing among competing norms, then the decision maker should act consistently with his own norms. In the middle category where there is a weak signal, we believe it best to compare the relative strength of the firm's own norms with the relative strength of the priority rules-of-thumb signal in order to determine which should be followed.

As is true with the process of establishing authentic norms and identifying substantive hypernorms, it may be necessary to use proxies to generate empirical evidence in order to apply the rules of thumb. We note with interest that Strong and Ringer (1997) found tentative support for the concept of priority rules of thumb in their effort to empirically validate ISCT.

User-Friendly ISCT Decision Making

In this section, we offer a few tools for managers to use in interpreting ISCT.

Background Considerations

The process of ethical decision making is influenced by the timing of the activity and the relationship between the party making the judgment and the decision context. As illustrated in Table 7-1, two critical variables are

1. whether the judgment is made before, i.e., ex ante, or after, i.e., ex post, a given decision, and

2. whether the judgment is made by the actual decision maker or someone directly affected by the decision, or instead, by a relatively disinterested observer.

The term "disinterested observer" is used in application to a category including professional ethicists, politicians, regulators, managers, consultants, journalists, and others. Managers may find themselves in the role of disinterested observers whenever they evaluate the actions of others concerning decisions in which they themselves have no direct interest or involvement.

It is well to remember that the timing of a judgment may have a major influence on its quality. Judgments made ex ante may be constrained by a lack of information and by time pressures. Decision makers cannot obtain full information concerning the existence of potentially relevant norms when they have to make a judgment on the spot. A demand from a customs official for a small payment to allow a shipment of ripe bananas to pass through customs quickly requires an immediate response. One does not have the time to check out the claim that such payments are common for fruit passing through the port.

Judgments made ex post allow the luxury of gathering information and reflecting on the results. On the other hand, judgments made after the fact are easily susceptible to bias. The party making the judgment may be unable to avoid being influenced by the reaction to or consequence of the decision. In judging the decision to go ahead and launch the Challenger space shuttle, it would be impossible to ignore the knowledge that the O-ring seal failed and the shuttle was destroyed. This may result in an overbroad identification of questionable norms or practices assumed to exist at the time of the judgment. The potential unfairness of "Monday morning quarterbacking" is as pertinent to ethical judgments as it is to other dimensions of life.

Table 7-1 The Context of Ethical Judgments		
	Ex Ante Decisions and Policies	Ex Post Judgments and Evaluations
Business decision makers	Making a decision with ethical implications, devising a policy for foreseeable ethical choices	Assessing the propriety of policies and prior judgments for purpose of correcting mistakes
Outside observers	Advising about future decisions and policies	Assessing the propriety of policies and prior judgments for purpose of understanding role of ethics in business, policy implications, etc.

The Nature and Structure of the ISCT Decision Process

The central steps in applying ISCT are straightforward and can be simply stated:

1. identifying key communities relevant to the judgment, using presumptions based on proxies if necessary;

2. identifying key norms relevant to the judgment within the specified communities, using presumptions based on proxies if necessary;

3. determining that all putative key norms are authentic;

4. determining that all key authentic norms are legitimate as tested by hypernorms; and

5. resolving any conflicts that remain among legitimate norms.

Applying ISCT, no less than applying any financial model or ethical theory, requires the exercise of judgment. Discretion is essential; it is not merely the structured exercise of a decision-making calculus. The basic model for applying ISCT is provided in Figure 7-1. The figure diagrams the relatively straightforward situation in which (1) only a single norm is responsive to the decision required, or (2) multiple norms are identified, but they turn out to be consistent with each other. After discussing this basic decision procedure, we expand it to deal with the more complicated situation in which two or more legitimate norms compete. For academics and professional ethicists willing to wade through considerable detail, we have provided a much more formal and elaborate model in an appendix to this chapter.[5]

Ethical judgments differ in kind from scientific measurements such as cholesterol levels in a blood sample, or from judgments concerning the best treatment for a particular medical problem. As Aristotle noted long ago, we ought only to expect of the subject matter the level of precision that it allows, and the subject matter of ethics, he notes, allows for less precision than other sciences such as physics or biology. Yet precision in ethics is eroded even further in instances where decisions are ex ante rather than ex post. As we noted above, the quality of any ethical judgment will be influenced by the information available and the time available for the judgment. Obviously less definitive judgments are possible in ex ante judgments.

In turn, time-pressured ex ante decisions imply that precision must frequently bow to practicality. This is true to some extent for all theories that fall into the category of practical reason, including those of management, finance, and marketing. Once again we see that ISCT ought not be interpreted as a formal calculus, subject to scientific validation. Instead, its greatest value is as one of the growing set of diagnostic tools now available to guide and augment ethical judgment.

Yet another inevitable source of vagueness exists. Community norms defining ethical behavior lie at the heart of ISCT, and while in some cases clear evidence will exist identifying accepted norms, in other cases the evidence will be more ambiguous. The fact that in certain cases the evidence about norms is ambiguous should not be seen as a failing of ISCT. Instead, it is likely to be a signal of lack of consensus within a community that should be, in and of itself, an important consideration in the decision. The strength of the evidence available about the identity of authentic norms is a factor in applying ISCT. The most powerful norms, those that should be considered in any ethical judgment, are, by definition, likely to be well known and generally understood. The weaker or more diffuse the evidence surrounding a given norm, the weaker the role it is able to play in an ISCT interpretation. Thus, in many cases evidence indicating the strength of the norm will signal how much weight to give the norm in an ethical judgment.

As dramatized by Figure 7-1, once a decision with ethical dimensions has been identified, the following four core questions are involved in applying ISCT to the case of a single controlling norm:

1. What groups are likely to have a norm relevant to the decision?

2. Within the relevant groups are members able

   a. to leave the community if they so desire?

   b. to influence the development of shared conventions within community traditions?

3. Within the relevant groups are there shared understandings about the boundaries of correct behavior relevant to the decision?

4. Do any of the shared conventions

   a. violate widely recognized understandings about fundamental principles of correct behavior?

   b. seriously compromise principles of good citizenship, for example, principles that enhance the ability of the broader economic community to create efficiently necessary goods and services?

Each of these key questions can be demonstrated by short case examples. In order to emphasize different components of the ISCT

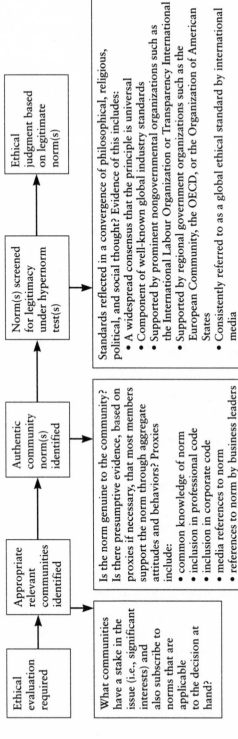

Figure 7-1 The ISCT Decision Process (Single Controlling Norm)

decision-making process, we will use a small set of three cases for purposes of illustration. The short problems (some based on actual incidents) are selected to dramatize different dimensions of ISCT.

■

Lamott Core Drilling and Russian Taxes

Lamott Core Drilling, a U.S. mining firm, begins operations in Russia. After its first year, Lamott determines that they have earned 100 million rubles under the Russian system of accounting for taxable income. The Lamott executives are told by their Russian partner to report earnings of 25 million rubles. They check around with other Western firms and discover that most, including their competitors, report approximately 25 percent of their actual earnings to the Russian tax authority.

Would it be ethical for Lamott to report earnings of 25 million?

■

Watchdog Incorporated and Drug Testing

Watchdog Incorporated (WI) provides on-site guards for corporations and institutions. WI guards are typically entrusted with keys and security codes and have access to valuable assets. In order to insure the integrity of their workforce, WI follows a very elaborate system of checks on its prospective and current employees. All prospective employees must provide urine samples for drug tests. All current employees are spot-checked for drugs on a random basis. Employees who test positive for drugs (initial positive readings reconfirmed) are dismissed.

Is the WI approach to drug testing ethical?

■

Morning Baking Corporation and the Poisoned Cookies

Lynn, a corporate attorney for Morning Baking Corp. (MBC), knows that Jane, a product manager for MBC, has poisoned packages of a competing product, causing three deaths. Jane swears she won't do it again, and Lynn believes her. The CEO of MBC is aware of Jane's actions, but no action is taken. Does Lynn have an ethical obligation to disclose information about the poisonings to outsiders (Dunfee & Maurer, 1992)?

Identifying Relevant Communities

Numerous communities may have a valid interest in a business decision with ethical implications. A critical first step in applying ISCT is
the identification of relevant communities, making sure no community that might have a significant stake in the decision is left out of the
process. If the members of a community believe that their norm is
applicable to the decision, then the norm should be evaluated as part
of the decision process. As will be discussed in chapter 9, it is at this
point that the extensive literature concerning stakeholders is most relevant. However, even though one would expect a substantial overlap
in results, the test for identifying relevant communities under ISCT is
somewhat different from those found in the stakeholder literature.
We do agree with the general presumption of stakeholder theory that
communities having a "stake" in management's decision are owed
special consideration. Under ISCT, however, the basic issue is to identify a community possessing a norm applicable to the decision at
hand; that potential norm may or may not be one that reflects traditional stakeholder obligations.

Hence, the search for potential relevant communities should start
with the primary parties affected by or involved in the decision. If the
parties constitute communities themselves, as would be the case with
the employee community of Watchdog, they should be included. If,
instead, one or more of the primary parties are not communities, then
the question becomes whether they are members of broader communities that might have norms relevant to the decision. An example of
this in the Morning Baking case would be Lynn's membership in the
legal profession. One must consider the possibility that a broader
community may have norms applicable to the transaction. In the
cases of both Morning Baking and Watchdog Security, broader communities are relevant. One such community is the general citizenry.
The general citizenry of a nation-state, in this instance the United
States, has an interest in the level of effective security (relevant for the
Watchdog case) and in the safety of the products they consume (relevant for the Morning Baking case). Similarly, one should anticipate
that there may be subcommunities having norms diverging from
those of a broader community at the focal point of a decision. Thus,
in the case of Watchdog's drug-testing policy there may be a community of employees who do not perform guard work, e.g., the in-house
counsel for the firm, who have a quite different norm concerning the
propriety of random drug testing. That is, the lawyers for the firm

may believe it is inappropriate that they be subjected to random drug tests, although they believe such testing is highly appropriate for the security guards. When a decision is made that has implications across an entire corporation, it is particularly important to stop and consider subgroups within the organization having a norm considered, at least by their members, to be applicable to the decision.

Communities directly affected by a decision should always be carefully evaluated for relevant norms. In the Lamott Core Drilling case, the failure to pay the full amount of the taxes may have an effect on the Russian people as a whole as well as on other global business firms. It may well be that the norms of those communities will ultimately justify the 25 percent payment, but that is not the issue at this point. Instead, in this first step, the task is to make sure that all potential sources of relevant norms have been identified. Communities such as the Russian Orthodox Church, or even the entire Russian society, should be considered at this stage.

One of the most valuable aspects of using ISCT to clarify ethical decisions is this step, in which one carefully considers the existence of communities that might have norms applicable to the process. Often, many different communities hold the same norm. The key is to include all important norms. On the other hand, judgment needs to be exercised in the selection of communities. It is neither helpful nor necessary to identify every possible combination of communities that might conceivably have a norm, particularly when the norms overlap, as would be the case for many different subgroups of employees within an organization. For the short cases, key relevant communities would be as follows:

Case	Key Relevant Communities
Lamott Core Drilling	Russian government, Lamott Core Drilling, Western firms doing business in Russia, U.S. government/society
Watchdog	Watchdog Incorporated, political jurisdictions in which policies are implemented (state, national governments), staff employees or other subgroups who might not agree with the firm's policy
Morning Baking Corporation	legal profession, general public of political jurisdiction in which poisonings took place, Morning Baking Corporation

Determining the Legitimacy Status of Relevant Communities

Norms of communities in which exit is unreasonably restricted, or in which any meaningful participation in the norm generation process is denied, are not given consideration in the ISCT framework. This requirement provides a check and some balance against the majoritarian emphasis of ISCT. In addition, the recognition of the norms of subcommunities also provides some protection for dissenting subgroups within a larger organization. A community in which workers are physically restrained, as in the case of sweatshops in urban centers in the United States, cannot generate legitimate norms. This is true even though the norms produced in such a community meet the attitudinal and behavioral requirements for an authentic norm. Even though individuals willingly agree to the norms, the environment in which this agreement is produced is sufficiently tainted to invalidate the resulting norms.

How then may such communities be identified? In general, a firm or other community constituting a coercive environment in which employee mobility is restricted or where employees accept extreme risks is illegitimate. Warning flags should go up, for example, when a firm in a developed country hires itinerant or foreign workers at very low wages and employs them in a substandard work environment, particularly where the employees' freedom is hampered by language and cultural barriers. Other indicators of coercion would include indebtedness of employees to the firm, unusual contractual arrangements, and repeated allegations of extremely unsafe working conditions. The notorious case of the Film Recovery Company in Chicago, where criminal charges were ultimately filed in response to employee deaths caused by unprotected handling of extremely hazardous materials by workers who could not read warnings posted in English, involved an illegitimate community for purposes of ISCT.

The issue is more difficult when one is dealing with firms in developing countries. Coercive cultural environments, particularly those involving totalitarian governments, are likely to foster illegitimate business communities. Blagov (1996) has noted that Russian business organizations, particularly during the initial stage of privatization, placed significant restrictions on exit that might compromise their ability to generate authentic norms. The communities involved in the short cases are very probably legitimate.

Identifying Authentic Norms

The basic task in this third step is to determine the nature and scope of shared understandings of proper behavior that are held by the members in the identified communities. The process of identifying authentic norms was discussed at length in chapter 4, where a number of proxies were identified that could be used to establish presumptive norms. The proxies include seeking to identify conventions or norms that are common knowledge or part of the conventional wisdom of the designated group. One method for applying this test is by engaging in a hypothetical thought experiment. Candidate norms could be tested by envisioning the likely reaction if those norms were listed as such in community publications, as for example a corporate newsletter circulated to all employees. Proxies such as professional codes of ethics, corporate codes and credos, industry standards, benchmarking studies by consultants and others, and speeches by business leaders may also constitute significant clues about authentic norms.

In the Watchdog and the Lamott Core Drilling cases, establishing the norms of the relevant communities would appear to be fairly simple. The Lamott case shows common knowledge of the norms and evidence of behavior consistent with the putative norms. In Watchdog, norms are indicated by common knowledge, assumed inclusion in the corporate code of ethics, and supporting opinion surveys and media references. The Morning Baking case, however, involves a challenging task of ascertaining the existence of an authentic norm. One norm at issue would be whether or not the lawyer, Lynn, had a professional obligation to protect the confidentiality of her client by withholding the information about the poisonings. In some jurisdictions, an important proxy on this issue, i.e., the published norm of the legal profession, would bind a lawyer to confidentiality so long as the information possessed does not pertain to a possible future crime. But controversial published norms of the legal profession may not represent an authentic norm under ISCT, because a majority of the lawyers in the relevant legal community may not agree with the norm and may believe that revealing the crimes constitutes proper behavior for Lynn. Since such views are seldom made public, it may be quite difficult to ascertain accurately the scope of an authentic norm, if, indeed, any norm exists at all pertaining to this issue.

Presumptive norms likely to be discovered relevant to the decision in the three cases are as follows:

Lamott Core Drilling Case

Relevant Community	*Norm*
Russian government	Pay taxes as described in the formal statement of confiscatory tax rate
	Accept (informally) practices that yield considerably less in taxes than a strict interpretation of the tax law would imply
Lamott Core Drilling	Report numbers accurately (from the company's corporate code)
Western firms doing business in Russia	Don't comply with senseless laws
	Pay taxes on only a proportion of the official rate
U.S. government	Refrain from "cooking the books" for U.S. reporting

Watchdog Case

Relevant Community	*Norm*
Watchdog Incorporated	Random drug testing necessary and appropriate for all employees
Corporate attorneys and staff managers	Drug testing not appropriate for attorneys and managers
Political jurisdictions in which policies are implemented (state, national governments)	Drug testing, subject to certain safeguards, is permissible, particularly where safety and security are involved

Morning Baking Case

Relevant Community	*Norm*
Legal profession	Lawyer may not disclose evidence of prior corporate crime except in narrowly defined circumstances (assuming majority of lawyers agree)
General public of political jurisdiction in which poisonings took place	Lawyer should disclose evidence of past heinous crimes
Morning Baking Corporation	Any information harming the reputation of firm should not be disclosed

Are the Authentic Norms Legitimate?

The fourth step involves testing the identified authentic norms against hypernorms in order to determine whether they are legitimate. They must be compatible with all three kinds of hypernorms identified in chapter 3: procedural, substantive, and structural. One of these three determinations of compatibility has already occurred. Since the process of legitimating a given community involves determining whether community practices are consistent with procedural hypernorms, we may presume that community norms are already consistent with procedural hypernorms. It then remains to test the norms against substantive and structural hypernorms. This entails asking, first, whether any of the authentic norms are inconsistent with widespread understandings concerning correct behavior, i.e., substantive hypernorms. Next, one must ask whether the norms violate any structural hypernorms, for example, norms that systematically promote the ability of the broader political community to efficiently provide necessary goods and services to the community, i.e., the efficiency hypernorm.

As discussed in chapter 3, there are a number of proxies that could be used to determine the scope and nature of substantive hypernorms. Relevant questions may include the following: Do any of the authentic norms conflict with global understandings of right and wrong? With well-known global industry standards? With norms of regional government organizations such as the European Community? With precepts of major religions? With principles supported by global business organizations such as the International Chamber of Commerce? With precepts of major ethical philosophies? With principles supported by relevant international community professionals such as accountants or environmental engineers? Managers may find it helpful to try a thought experiment in which they imagine how the readers of global newspapers would respond to a claim that universal principles support their resolution of an ethical problem. All three cases should be evaluated for the potential implications of hypernorms. For example, in the Morning Baking case, the implications for public safety are dramatic. Most of us would wish to live in a world in which people who murder others with tainted cookies are punished and prevented from killing again. This fundamental intuition qualifies as a hypernorm. The need to prevent Jane from striking again, and perhaps even to punish her, would override any contrary confidentiality-based authentic norm (assuming such exists) of the legal community.

The following norms (which may well be authentic) seem likely to clash with hypernorms:

In the Morning Baking Case

Community	Norms that Fail to Pass the Hypernorm Test
Legal profession	Lawyer may not disclose evidence of prior corporate crime except in narrowly defined circumstances
Morning Baking Corporation	Any information harming the reputation of firm should not be disclosed

Resolution under Figure 7-1 Approach

Lamott Core Drilling

Here to the extent that there are conflicting legitimate norms among the communities involved, it is necessary to go on to the next stage of analysis to resolve the case. We assume that the norm of the Russian government does not violate the hypernorm of necessary social efficiency, since taxes are collected in a systematic way. If the Russian system were to be found to greatly handicap the ability of the government to collect necessary taxes and thereby to function, then the norm would violate a structural hypernorm and would be excluded from further analysis.

Watchdog

Here to the extent that there are conflicting legitimate norms among the communities involved, it is necessary to go on to the next stage of analysis to resolve the case.

Morning Baking

The norms requiring that the lawyer in the Morning Baking case not reveal the information about Jane's crime are illegitimate from the standpoint of hypernorms. The authentic norms of the broader political society, along with hypernorms compelling disclosure, create an ethical obligation to disclose the information.

Cases Involving Conflicting Legitimate Norms

Figure 7-2 extends the ISCT decision process model to encompass situations involving conflicting legitimate norms. The search here is for the existence of dominant norms, e.g., those for which a compelling case can be made that they should prevail over the alternatives. If the application of the rules of thumb discussed in the first part of this chapter fails to identify a dominant norm, then the decision maker is permitted to act consistently with her own community's norms and values. In this circumstance, actions consistent with any of the legitimate norms are ethical.

The extended model would apply to the remaining two cases in the following way. In the Lamott Core Drilling case, the norm of the U.S. government/society prescribing that reports to other jurisdictions ought not "cook the books" may be resolved by greater specification of the scope of the norm. So long as the actions taken in Russia do not affect the reporting required by the U.S. tax and securities authorities, there probably is no direct conflict. Thus, it should be possible

Figure 7-2   The ISCT Decision Process
(Multiple Conflicting Legitimate Norms)

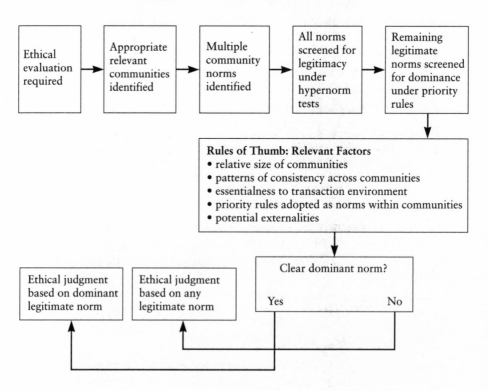

to act consistently with the norms of the Russian government *and* Western firms in Russia without violating the U.S. norm. The remaining conflict is between Lamott's own code provision and both the norms of other Western firms in Russia and the formal specifications of the Russian government. The correct decision would depend in part on the clarity and specific nature of the norm at Lamott, and whether Lamott clearly intended the norm to be an internal rule of thumb. If the norm was meant to be a rule of thumb, then Lamott should follow its own principles. On the other hand, if the Lamott norm turns out to be relatively weak and lacking in clarity, and particularly if exceptions have been recognized in the past, then the local Russian norm should be followed.

In the instance of Watchdog's drug-testing policy, the rules of thumb do not appear to give a clear signal concerning which of the conflicting norms should dominate. That being so, Watchdog should simply act in a manner consistent with its own norms and values. In short, Watchdog management is free to continue its drug-testing policy.

Appendix

Figure 7A-1   Hanna/Dunfee Model for the Application of ISCT General Overview

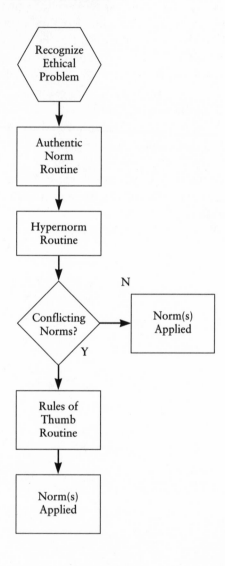

Figure 7A-2 Integrative Social Contracts Theory
Norm Evaluation Process

Authentic Norm Routine

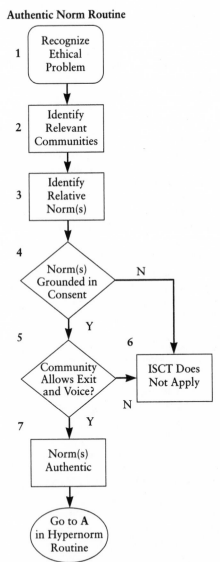

Tests/Comments

1. Use this process chart to determine whether ISCT is applicable and whether relevant **authentic** norms exist.

2. Look for relevant communities that have a stake in the application of the norm, and that themselves possess norms applicable to the decision.

3. Look for convergence of available information concerning shared understandings, unwritten promises, or unspoken agreements. Look at survey data regarding members' attitudes and/or behavior as well as proxy data such as leader statements, laws, codes, professional standards, etc.

4. Consent (expressed or implied) must be informed and noncoerced.

5. Capacity for exit and voice are indicators of noncoercion. Lack of resources to enable exit implicates this test.

6. Failure of test 4 or 5 implies that a true social contract does not exist.

7. Characteristics of **authentic** norms: The norm is genuine to the community, meaning that a substantial majority of the membership hold the attitude that a particular behavior is right (wrong) and a substantial majority act consistently with that attitude.

Figure 7A-3 Hypernorm Routine

Hypernorm Routine

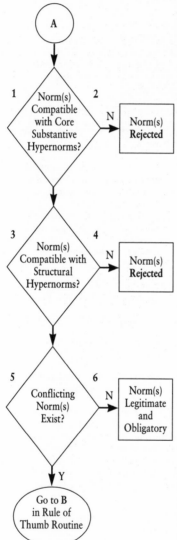

Tests/Comments

1. and **2.** Inquire whether authentic norms violate widespread understandings of right and wrong (hypernorms). Evidence for hypernorms can be found, for example, in:

- A widespread consensus that the principle is universal
- Principles that are well-known global industry standards
- Principles supported by prominent nongovernmental organizations such as the International Labour Organization or Transparency International
- Principles supported by regional government organizations such as the European Community, the OECD, or the Organization of American States
- Principles consistently referred to as a global ethical standard by international media
- Principles known to be consistent with precepts of major religions
- Principles supported by global business organizations such as the International Chamber of Commerce of the Caux Round Table
- Principles known to be consistent with precepts of major philosophies
- Principles generally supported by a relevant international community of professionals, e.g., accountants or environmental engineers
- Principles known to be consistent with findings concerning universal human values
- Principles supported by the laws of many different countries

3. and **4.** Inquire whether authentic norms are incompatible with structural hypernorms, such as the hypernorm of necessary social efficiency, i.e., the efficiency hypernorm.

5. and **6.** An authentic norm consistent with hypernorms is considered to be both legitimate and obligatory. Legitimate norms of relevant sociopolitical communities having priority may also be considered obligatory.

Figure 7A-4   Rules of Thumb Routine

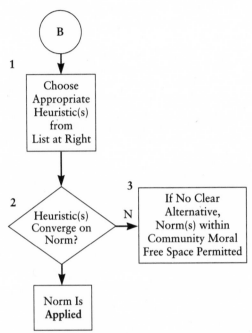

Tests/Comments

1. ISCT rules of thumb (abbreviated):
   A. Local community norms have priority unless adopting them harms members of another community.
   B. Local community norms designed to resolve norm conflicts have priority unless adopting them harms members of another community.
   C. The more global the source of the norm, the greater the norm's priority.
   D. Norms essential to the maintenance of the economic environment in which the transaction occurs have priority over norms potentially damaging to that environment.
   E. Patterns of consistency among alternative norms add weight for priority.
   F. Priority is given to well-defined norms over less well-defined ones.

2. If a number of the rules of thumb converge on a norm, that norm may be considered obligatory.

3. In the case where there are conflicting norms without a clear basis or prioritization, communities are permitted substantial discretion to respond to the claims and interests of its members.

8

When Ethics Travel: The Promise
and Peril of Global Business Ethics

Honesty and frankness make you vulnerable. Be honest and frank anyway.

—Anonymous

Global managers often must navigate the perplexing gray zone that arises when two cultures—and two sets of ethics—meet. Suppose:

You are a manager of Ben & Jerry's in Russia. One day you discover that the most senior officer of your company's Russian joint venture has been "borrowing" equipment from the company and using it in his other business ventures. When you confront him, the Russian partner defends his actions. After all, as a part owner of both companies, isn't he entitled to share in the equipment (Puffer & McCarthy, 1995)?

Or, competing for a bid in a foreign country, you are introduced to a "consultant" who offers to help you in your client contacts. A brief conversation makes it clear that this person is well connected in local government and business circles and knows your customer extremely well. The consultant will help you prepare and submit your bid and negotiate with the customer . . . for a substantial fee. Your peers tell you that such arrangements are normal in this country—and that a large part of the consulting fee will go directly to staff people working for your customer. Those who have rejected such help in the past have seen contracts go to their less-fussy competitors. (Anonymous case study)

What should you do in such cases? Should you straighten out your Russian partner? How should you deal with the problem of bribery? Bribery is just like tipping, some people say. Whether you tip for service at dinner or bribe for the benefit of getting goods through customs, you pay for a service rendered. But while many of us balk at a conclusion that puts bribery on a par with tipping, we have difficulty articulating why.

Most Western companies' codes of ethics never dreamed of cross-cultural challenges like these. How can managers successfully maneuver the disturbing gray zones that lie at the intersections of different cultures? Issues such as these have tended to bedazzle many modern multinational corporations. Companies are finding—and stumbling over—ethics issues abroad as never before. Corporate ethics and values programs are in vogue; and many companies are asking whether they should take their ethics and values programs global. But confusion abounds.

Some companies, recognizing cultural differences, simply accept whatever prevails in the host country. This is a mistake because it exposes the company (and its brand names) to corruption and public affairs disasters, and because it misses the opportunity to find the glue that cements morale and cooperative strategy. It neglects the important role we have identified repeatedly in this book for hypernorms. It substitutes unmitigated relativism for good sense. Years ago, foreign companies operating in South Africa broke the South African apartheid law that required segregated washrooms for employees. Not to break that South African law, and to leave the washrooms segregated, would have been unethical. Consider a more recent example:

The SS *United States*, arguably the most luxurious ocean liner during the 1950s, was loaded with asbestos and would have cost about $100 million to be refurbished for luxury cruising. In 1992 it was towed to Turkey, where the cost of removing the asbestos was only $2 million. Turkish officials refused to allow the removal because of the danger of cancer. In October 1993 it was towed to the Black Sea port of Sebastopol where laws are lax. It will have more than one-half million square feet of carcinogenic asbestos removed for even less than $2 million, and in the context we can predict that the safety standards will be even lower (Satchell, 1994: 64).

Few would argue that exposing workers to hazardous asbestos is the ethically correct policy. A company must sometimes refuse to adopt host-country standards even when there is no law requiring it. Yet it is all too possible to make exactly the opposite mistake. Some companies attempt to export all home-country values to the host country. Wanting to duplicate successful ethics and values programs, these companies "photocopy" home-country ethics initiatives. Photocopying values is a mistake because it is disrespectful of other cultures. It neglects the important role of moral free space that we have consistently outlined in this book.

To create and succeed with a clear, consistent overseas policy, any company must face up to home-/host-country conflicts in ethics. It must develop responses and craft relevant policies. It must anticipate that sometimes the policies it discovers in other countries will appear to fall below its own standards. The Gordian knot of international business ethics is formed around the vexing question, how should a company behave when the standards followed in the host country are lower than those followed in the home country?

This chapter will show ways in which ISCT can provide a practical guide for corporations operating globally. In particular, it will demonstrate how cutting the Gordian knot of international business ethics means utilizing two key aspects of ISCT: hypernorms and microsocial contracts. First, it is important to make use of hypernorms, especially the structural hypernorm of necessary social efficiency discussed in chapter 5. Second, many problems dissolve when relevant microsocial contracts are carefully identified and the proper priority is established among them. In order to illustrate the application of these and other concepts in ISCT, we will look once again at the issue of corruption. As we will see in this chapter, ISCT is capable of unraveling such problems, and it has obvious application to many other problems in international business, including those of intellectual property, host government relations, sourcing, and environmental policy.

Mapping International Business Ethics: Is There Evidence of Microsocial Contracts and Moral Free Space?

No one denies that cultural differences abound in global business activities. That much is indisputable. The real question is whether these differences add up to different microsocial contracts with different authentic, legitimate norms being affirmed by different cultures: in other words, attitudes and behaviors operating in true moral free space. Might it be the case, instead, that in every instance of cultural difference, one side is invariably more "right" than the other is? If so, the task of an international manager turns out to be simply one of discovering what the "right" norms are, and acting accordingly. ISCT's notion of the microsocial contract provides a tool for interpreting the significance of ethical differences, a tool we will use in this chapter.

Kluckhorn (1955), Hofstede (1980), Turner and Trompenaars (1993), and many other management theorists have shown the importance of cultural differences to business—but the further issue of the ethical implications of many of these differences remains unexplored. For example, researchers have documented the importance of understanding the time sensitivity of the Swiss in contrast to the time laxity of South Americans, or the group orientation of the Japanese in contrast to the individualism of the Americans. Not understanding such differences, most business managers now recognize, can trigger missteps and financial losses. But the importance of understanding ethical differences among cultures is much less well understood; this is a puzzling oversight, since ethical differences often take a volatile, sensitive form.

On a positive note, a clearer picture of the significance of cultural differences has slowly been emerging in the last decade, and a few of these have shed light on implicit ethical differences. In one study (Turner & Trompenaars, 1993), for example, thousands of international managers around the world responded to the following question:

> While you are talking and sharing a bottle of beer with a friend who was officially on duty as a safety inspector in the company you both work for, an accident occurs, injuring a shift worker. The national safety commission launches an investigation and you are asked for your evidence. There are other witnesses. What right has your friend to expect you to protect him?

The choices offered as answers to the question were these:

1. A definite right?
2. Some right?
3. No right?

Here the explicit ethical notion of a "right" and the implicit notion of the duties of friendship come into play. The results of the questionnaire were striking, with cultural patterns perspicuous. To cite only one set of comparisons, approximately 94 percent of U.S. managers and 91 percent of Austrian managers answered "3," i.e., "no right," whereas only 53 percent of French and 59 percent of Singaporean managers did.

As noted in chapter 4, surveys of international managers also show striking differences among cultural attitudes towards profit. When asked whether they affirmed the view that "[t]he only real goal of a company is making profit," 40 percent of U.S. managers, 33 percent of British managers, and 35 percent of Austrian managers affirmed the proposition, in contrast to only 11 percent of Singaporean managers, and only 8 percent of Japanese managers selected (Turner & Trompenaars, 1993).

Or, consider studies that show striking differences among ethical attitudes toward everyday business problems. One study revealed that Hong Kong managers rank taking credit for another's work at the top of a list of unethical activities, and, in contrast to their Western counterparts, they consider it more unethical than bribery or the gaining of competitor information. The same study showed that among Hong Kong respondents, 82 percent indicated that additional government regulation would improve ethical conduct in business, whereas only 27 percent of U.S. respondents believed it would (MacDonald, 1988: 835–845).

Not only individual but group ethical attitudes vary. This clearly holds for corporations; different corporations can have strikingly different cultures and sets of beliefs. ISCT implies that companies as well as cultures vary in microsocial contract norms. But what is it that stamps a company's culture as unique from the vantage point of ethics? Theorists have recently begun distinguishing global companies in terms of their distinctive styles of ethical approach. George Enderle, for example, has identified four types of approach, each of which is analogous to a posture taken historically by nation-states (Enderle, 1995). These are:

- Foreign Country Type
- Empire Type
- Interconnection Type
- Global Type

The first, or Foreign Country, type does not apply its own, home-country concepts to host countries abroad. Instead, as the Swiss have historically done in Nigeria, it conforms to local customs, assuming that what prevails as morality in the host climate is an adequate guide. The second, or Empire type, resembles Great Britain in India and elsewhere before 1947. This type of company applies domestic concepts and theories without making any serious modifications. Empire-type companies export their values in a wholesale fashion— and often do so regardless of the consequences. Next, the Interconnection type of company is analogous to states engaging in commercial relations in the European Union, or NAFTA. Such companies regard the international sphere as differing significantly from the domestic sphere, and one in which the interconnectedness of companies transcends national identities. In this model, the entire notion of national interest is blurred. Companies don't see themselves as projecting or defending a national identity.

Finally, the Global type abstracts from all regional differences. Just as the phenomenon of global warming exhibits the dominance of the international sphere over that of the domestic, so the Global type views the domestic sphere as irrelevant. From this vantage point the citizens of all nations, whether they are corporate or individual citizens, must become more cosmopolitan. The nation-state is vanishing, and in turn, only global citizenry makes sense.

It is helpful to analyze these basic types of corporate approaches from the standpoint of ISCT's two key concepts, i.e., moral free space and hypernorms. Each type may be seen to have strengths and weaknesses explainable through these concepts. What is ethically dangerous about the Foreign Country type is that nothing limits the moral free space of the host-country culture. If a given culture accepts government corruption and environmental degradation, then so much the worse for honest people and environmental integrity. From the vantage point of the Foreign Country type, no rules of thumb restrain granting an automatic preference to host-country norms—whatever they are.

Both the Global and the Empire types succeed in avoiding the vicious relativism that characterizes the Foreign Country type, but manage to fall prey to exactly the opposite problem. Since each type acts from a fixed blueprint of right and wrong, each suffocates the host country's moral free space and leaves no room for legitimate local norms. The Empire type displays a version of moral imperialism. It is bedazzled, as it were, by its own larger-than-life goodness. Just as the nations of Western Europe have so often in the past colonized others in a smug, self-righteous manner, so too a company adopting the Empire posture sees itself as the bearer of moral truth. The Global type, too, suffocates the host country's moral free space, but for a different reason. Instead of imposing its home morality on a host culture, it imposes its interpretation of a global morality on a host culture. Because only global citizenry makes sense, the company can be numb to the moral differences that mark a culture's distinctiveness. The opportunity for host cultures to define their moral and economic identity is lost; it is dissolved by the powerful solvent of global Truth, administered by the all-knowing multinational.

The Interactive type alone satisfies ISCT by acknowledging both universal moral limits and the ability of communities to set moral standards of their own. It balances better than the other types a need to retain local identity with the acknowledgment of values that transcend individual communities. Its drawbacks are practical rather than moral. As noted earlier, the entire notion of national interest is blurred in this model, an ambiguity that may make it difficult to integrate the interests of any nation-state in the corporation's deliberations. Even so, it manages to balance moral principles with moral free space in a way that makes it more convincing than its three counterparts.

As intriguing as the differences in global ethical attitudes in business are, they leave nagging questions in their wake. Granted, differences in global ethical attitudes abound, and granted also that it may be possible to map and identify those differences. As Enderle suggests, even global companies may be seen to vary along ethical dimensions, and these differences, too, can be mapped. So far so good. But does it follow that those differences entail the existence of moral free space? It did not turn out to be true, as noted earlier, that in every instance of cultural difference, one side is simply more "right" than the other is. If such an explanation were true, then the task of an international manager would be simply to discover what the "right" norms were, and to act accordingly. Moral free space, and in turn, the need for corporations to attend to subtle differences among cultures, would vanish.

As mentioned in earlier chapters, evidence does exist to confirm the existence of different, legitimate norms in domestic contexts. For example, in the area of employee drug testing, Strong and Ringer (1997) have shown that microsocial contracts differ among employee and nonemployee populations, with nonemployees affirming significantly different norms for privacy in such testing than employees, even when the views of both populations appear authentic and legitimate.

New evidence suggests global ethical differences exist that are not only quite subtle, but that represent beliefs treated as both legitimate and authentic by ISCT. They are beliefs, in other words, residing in what we have called "moral free space." Bigoness and Blakely (1996) used measures drawn from Milton Rokeach's Value Scale to investigate cross-national differences in managerial values. A total of 567 managers from twelve nations participated. Their data indicated that different values not only existed, but also converged neatly in most instances on a national basis. The Rokeach value matrix contains values such as "responsible," "honest," "clean," and "broad-minded," none of which are likely to be overturned by hypernorms. And yet groups differed significantly by national type. For example, analysis by means of Duncan multiple range tests showed that Japanese managers assigned a significantly higher priority than did managers from other nations to the value dimension that included the characteristics "clean, obedient, polite, responsible, and self-controlled" (Bigoness & Blakely, 1996: 747). The three other available value groupings were:

- Forgiving, helpful, loving, and cheerful
- Broad-minded, capable, and courageous
- Imaginative, independent, and intellectual

Swedish and Brazilian managers, for their part, assigned much higher significance than their global peers did to the category of "broad-minded, capable, and courageous."

Differing Advice from Academics

Having seen evidence that business ethics vary from country to country, and that at least some of these constitute authentic, legitimate norms, the obvious question for a multinational manager is, What should I do? How does a manager navigate these moving, complex currents of international values?

Many business writers lack clear solutions and give sharply differing advice. Some seem hopelessly callous, and others idealistically impractical. At one extreme, Boddewyn and Brewer (1994) have defended the view that managers should consider the host-country government on a par with any other competitive factor. The government is seen merely as another factor of production, or set of "agents" that international firms can use in the management of their chain of economic value-adding activities in cross-border activity (Boddewyn & Brewer, 1994: 126). For his own part, Boddewyn (1986) has even argued that when companies seek competitive advantages, bribery, smuggling, and buying absolute market monopolies are not necessarily ruled out.

At the other extreme, DeGeorge (1993) has postulated ten guidelines for multinational corporations. The second of these ten guidelines specifies that every company must "produce more good than harm for the host country." This claim seems innocent enough until one realizes that it entails information and decision-making requirements possessed by few if any large multinational corporations. How is a company to know with confidence that on balance it is doing more good than harm? This is an enormously challenging requirement involving an all-things-considered assessment of, for example, pollution effects, wage labor effects, hypothetical alternatives (what would have happened if the MNC had not done business in the country), host-country government effects, and so on. It would at a minimum require a separate moral "accounting" process. That DeGeorge means for the evaluation to be intentionally undertaken is obvious, for in explaining the guideline he remarks, "If an American chemical company builds a chemical plant in a less developed country, it must ensure that its plant brings more good than harm to the country" (DeGeorge, 1993). While the requirement is reasonable as a general principle, it imposes accounting requirements that may divert corporate resources in an inefficient manner. It exists in stark contrast to Boddewyn's blunt, self-seeking prescriptions, and reflects well-wishing idealism.

The ISCT Global Values Map

In the face of such conflicting and confusing advice, the application of ISCT categories to global problems is helpful. The broadest categories for sorting authentic global norms through ISCT may be displayed in a diagram (see Figure 8-1).

The concentric circles represent core norms held by particular corporations, industries, or economic cultures. Particular values of a corporation, as expressed through its actions and policies, may be plotted as points within the circles.

- *Hypernorms:* As we saw in chapter 3, these include, for example, fundamental human rights or basic prescriptions common to most major religions. The values they represent are by definition acceptable to all cultures and all organizations.

- *Consistent norms:* These values are more culturally specific than those at the center, but are *consistent both with hypernorms and other legitimate norms,* including those of other economic cultures. Most corporations' ethical codes and vision-value statements would fall within this circle. Johnson & Johnson's famous "Credo" and AT&T's "Our Common Bond" are examples.

Figure 8-1   Categories of Authentic Global Norms under ISCT

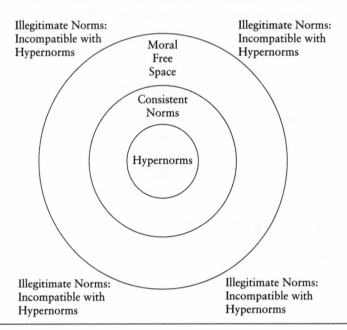

- *Moral Free Space:* As one moves away from the center of the circle to the circle signifying moral free space, one finds norms that are inconsistent with at least some other legitimate norms existing in other economic cultures. Such norms can be in mild tension with hypernorms, even as they are compatible with them. They often express unique, but strongly held, cultural beliefs.

- *Illegitimate Norms:* These are norms that are incompatible with hypernorms. When values or practices reach a point where they transgress permissible limits (as specified, say, by fundamental human rights), they fall outside the circle and into the "incompatible" zone. Exposing workers to unreasonable levels of carcinogens (asbestos), for example, is an expression of a value falling outside the circle.

Navigating Using the ISCT Map:
The Case of Bribery and Sensitive Payments

To gain an understanding of the implications of ISCT for international business, it helps to apply it to a single, concrete instance. Accordingly, we shall probe the issue of corruption—in particular, the question of bribery or "sensitive payments." Although a single example, it is one with ringing significance for contemporary global business. It is widely known that sensitive payments flourish in many parts of the globe. Once this illustrative application is complete, we will draw— later in the chapter—implications of ISCT for a much broader array of international cases.

Consider two typical instances of sensitive payments. First, there is the practice of low-level bribery of public officials in some developing nations. In some developing countries, for example, it is difficult for any company, foreign or national, to move goods through customs without paying low-level officials a few dollars. The payments are relatively small, uniformly assessed, and accepted as standard practice. But the salaries of such officials are sufficiently low that the officials require the additional income. One suspects the salary levels are set with the prevalence of bribery in mind.

Or consider a second kind of instance where a company is competing for a bid in a foreign country, and where in order to win the competition a payment must be made not to a government official, but to the employee of a private company. Nonetheless, it is clear that the employee, instead of passing on the money to the company, will pocket the payment. In a modified version of this scenario, the bribe may even appear one level deeper. For example, a company competing for a bid may be introduced to a "consultant" who offers to help to facilitate client contacts. (See the example that begins this chapter.)

It is not obvious where the norms and issues that arise from such cases should be situated on the ISCT map, if indeed they belong there at all. Are practices involving such payments examples of authentic norms, thus qualifying them to be located on the map? Are payments invariably direct violations of hypernorms and hence located outside the circles in the "illegitimate" arena? Or, instead, do some practices tolerating payments qualify as expressions of moral free space?

As we saw earlier in this chapter, ethical views about business vary around the globe. Bribery is no exception. Not only does the incidence of bribery vary, so does its perception as being unethical. In one study, for example, Greeks perceived the actions in some bribery scenarios as being less unethical than Americans (Tsalikis & LaTour, 1995). In another, Hong Kong managers were shown to be somewhat less critical of bribery than their American counterparts (MacDonald, 1988). Tsalikis (1991) showed that ethical reactions to bribery vary, with Nigerians perceiving some scenarios being less unethical than they seemed to Americans.

From the vantage point of ISCT, then, are there ethical problems with bribery? The answer is "yes," as the following list clarifies:

1. From the standpoint of the bribe recipient, the acceptance usually violates a microsocial contract specifying the duties of the agent, i.e., the bribe recipient, to the principal, i.e., the employing body, such as the government, a private company, etc.

Perhaps the most obvious problem with bribery is that it typically involves the violation of a duty by the person accepting the bribe to the principal for whom he acts as an agent. Note that in both the illustrative cases above, the bribe recipient performs an action at odds with the policies established by his employer. In the case of the customs official, he accepts money for a service that he was supposed to provide anyway. In the case of the company competing for a bid, the employee pockets money in violation of company policy, and the company is shortchanged. In other words, if the money belongs to anyone, it belongs to the customer's company, not the individual employee. Such policies may or may not be written down. Often they are explicit, but even where they are not, they usually reflect well-understood, implicit agreements binding the employee as agent to the interests of his employer (the principal). In short, even when not formally specified, such duties flow from well-understood microsocial contracts existing within the relevant economic community.

But while this rationale shows one ethical problem with bribery, it is inconclusive. To begin with, it shows an ethical objection to accepting a bribe, but says nothing about offering a bribe. Has the person making the payment also committed an ethical error? Second, although violating a duty to an employer is one reason for considering an act unethical, it remains uncertain whether this reason could not be overridden by other, more pressing reasons. Perhaps other microsocial contracts in the culture firmly endorse the ethical correctness of bribe giving and bribe taking. Perhaps these microsocial contracts, along with an employee's legitimate interest in supporting his family, etc., override the prima facie obligation of the employee to follow the policies of his employer. It makes sense to explore the further implications of ISCT.

2. Bribery is typically not an authentic norm.

The mythology is that bribery is accepted wherever it flourishes. This image is badly distorted. Despite the data mentioned earlier that shows variance in the degree to which various people regard bribery as unethical in comparison with other unethical activity, there is a surprising amount of fundamental agreement that bribery is unethical.

All countries have laws against the practice. This is a striking fact often overlooked by individuals who have something to gain by the practice. "There is not a country in the world," writes Fritz Heimann, "where bribery is either legally or morally acceptable." That bribes have to be paid secretly everywhere, and that officials have to resign in disgrace if the bribe is disclosed, makes it clear that bribery violates the moral standards of the South and the East, just as it does in the West" (Heimann, 1994: 7).

Some countries, even ones where the practice has flourished, not only outlaw it, but prescribe draconian penalties. "In Malaysia, which is significantly influenced by the Moslem prescriptions against bribery, execution of executives for the offense of bribery is legal" (Carroll & Gannon, 1997). In China in 1994, the President of the Great Wall Machinery and Electronics High-Technology Industrial Group Corp., Mr. Shen Haifu, was executed by a bullet to the back of his neck for bribery and embezzlement offenses.

Many broad efforts are currently being made against bribery. The OECD is among the leading organizations mounting such efforts, in part due to U.S. pressure resulting from a provision in the amendment of the Foreign Corrupt Practices Act, which requires the President to take steps to bring about a level playing field of global competition. At a symposium held in Paris, France, in March 1994, the OECD launched a campaign aimed at reducing the incidence of bribery in trade transactions, especially in international contracts. (Yannaca-Small, 1995, in an OECD publication discussing the campaign). And in 1996 an OECD committee, with support from an international nongovernmental organization (NGO) dedicated to eradicating bribery, Transparency International, passed a resolution requiring that all member countries pass laws prohibiting the tax-deductibility of bribery in foreign transactions undertaken by their domestic firms. The outcome of this last effort is unclear at the time of this writing; but the OECD is clearly ramping up its battle against bribery. Reflecting this same spirit, some academics have suggested (Laczniak, 1990) the implementation of a worldwide code against bribery and the use of ethical impact statements by corporations. Many leading accounting firms, among them Arthur Andersen, KPMG, and Coopers & Lybrand, now offer services that enhance the ability of internal auditing functions to control the payment of bribes.

When one of the authors of this book (Donaldson) interviewed CEOs in India in 1993, he discovered that they were willing to acknowledge that their companies constantly engaged in bribery and payoffs. (They justify their actions on grounds of extortion—the practice began with the Indian government, and they were forced to bribe.) More surprising, however, was their disgust for the practice. They had no illusions about the propriety of bribery, and were aware that its most pernicious aspect was its effect on efficiency. Under ISCT this implies that even among a community of bribe payers, bribery cannot necessarily be established as an authentic norm.

Philip Nichols (1997) cites specific references from each of the world's major religions condemning bribery. "Corruption is condemned and proscribed," he writes, "by each of the major religious and moral schools of thought. Buddhism, Christianity, Confucianism, Hinduism, Islam, Judaism, Sikhism, and Taoism each proscribe corruption. Adam Smith and David Ricardo condemned corruption, as did Karl Marx and Mao Tse Tung" (Nichols, 1997: 321–322).

In short, in many if not most instances, the necessary condition imposed by ISCT that the norm be authentic—i.e., that it is both acted upon and believed to be ethically correct by a substantial majority of the members of a community—cannot be met. To the extent that this is true, most instances of bribery would fail the ISCT test.

3. Bribery may violate the hypernorm supporting political participation as well as the efficiency hypernorm.

Even this last consideration, however, leaves a nagging doubt behind. In particular, is bribery only wrong because most people dislike it? Is there nothing more fundamentally wrong with bribery? Suppose, hypothetically, that the world came to change its mind about bribery over the next thirty years. Suppose that in some future state, a majority of people finds bribery morally acceptable. If so, would bribery be ethically correct? In such a world, would reformers who spoke out against bribery be speaking illogical nonsense?

The answer to this question turns on the further question of whether a hypernorm disallowing bribery exists. For if such a hypernorm existed, then no legitimate microsocial norm could support bribery, and, in turn, it would deserve moral condemnation even in a world whose majority opinion endorsed it.

At least two hypernorms may be invoked in seeking a more fundamental condemnation of bribery. The first is rather obvious. To the extent that one places a positive, transnational value on the right to political participation, large bribes of publicly elected officials damage that value. For example, when Prime Minister Tanaka of Japan bought planes from the American aircraft manufacturer Lockheed in the 1970s, after accepting tens of millions of dollars in bribes, people questioned whether he was discharging his duties as a public official correctly. In addition to the fact that his actions violated the law, the Japanese citizenry was justified in wondering whether their interests, or Tanaka's personal political interest, drove the decision. Implicit in much of the political philosophy written in the Western world in the last three hundred years—in the writings of Rousseau, Mill, Locke, Jefferson, Kant, and Rawls—is the notion that some transcultural norm supports a public claim for the citizenry of a nation-state to participate in some way in the direction of political affairs. Many (see, e.g., Shue, 1980; Donaldson, 1989; and Universal Declaration of Human Rights, 1948) have discussed and articulated the implications of this right in current contexts. If such a right exists, then it entails obligations on the part of politicians and prospective bribe givers to not violate it. In turn, large-scale bribery of high government officials of the sort that the Lockheed Corporation engaged in during the 1970s would be enjoined through the application of a hypernorm. It would thus be wrong regardless of whether a majority of the members of an economic community, or even the majority of the world's citizens, endorsed it.

This, then, is the first hypernorm that may affect an ISCT interpretation of bribery. But notice that it, too, leaves nagging questions unanswered. Suppose it is true that large-scale payoffs to public officials in democratic or quasi-democratic countries are proscribed by considerations of people's right to political participation. In such countries, bribery may defeat meaningful political rights. But many countries in which bribery is prevalent are not democratic. Bribery in countries such as Zaire, Nigeria, and China may not have a noticeable effect on political participation by ordinary citizens, since that participation is directly repressed by authoritarian governments.

Many other troubling questions may be raised. What about much smaller payoffs to public officials? And what about bribes not to public officials, but to employees of corporations? It seems difficult to argue that small, uniformly structured bribes to customs officials, or that bribes to purchasing agents of companies in host countries, seriously undermine people's right to political participation. These questions prompt the search for yet another hypernorm relevant to the issue of bribery.

The second hypernorm that appears relevant to the present context is the efficiency hypernorm, discussed in chapter 5. That hypernorm, again, requires that economic agents efficiently utilize resources in which their society has a stake. As explained earlier, the hypernorm arises because all societies have an interest in husbanding public resources, developing strategies to promote aggregate economic welfare (Efficiency Strategies), and, in turn, developing economizing parameters to do so. Indeed, nations and NGOs that oppose bribery most commonly couch their opposition in terms of the damage bribery does to the economic efficiency of the nation-state.

Is bribery inefficient? It certainly appears to be. As the economist Kenneth Arrow noted years ago, "a great deal of economic life depends for its viability on a certain limited degree of ethical commitment" (Arrow, 1973: 313). To the extent that market participants bribe, they interfere with the market mechanism's rational allocation of resources, and their actions impose significant social costs. When people buy or sell on the basis of price and quality, with reasonable knowledge about all relevant factors, the market allocates resources efficiently. The best products relative to price, and, in turn, the best production mechanisms, are encouraged to develop. But when people buy or sell not on the basis of price and quality, but on the basis of how much money goes into their own pockets, the entire market mechanism is distorted. By misallocating resources, bribery damages economic efficiency. As economists Bliss and Di Tella (1997) note, "Corrupt agents exact money from firms." Corruption affects, they observe, the number of firms in a free-entry equilibrium, and in turn increases costs relative to profits. In contrast, "the degree of deep competition in the economy increases with lower overhead costs relative to profits; and with a tendency towards similar cost structures" (Bliss & Di Tella, 1997:1). Corruption can even be shown to take a toll on social efforts to improve economic welfare, including industrial policy initiatives (Ades & Di Tella, 1997), and on predictability in economic arrangements.

A striking example of the effect of corruption on predictability occurred recently in Brazil. When a large U.S. company's crates were unloaded on the docks of Rio de Janeiro, handlers regularly pilfered them. The handlers would take about 10 percent of the contents of the crates. Not only did the company lose this portion of the contents, it also never knew which 10 percent would be taken. Finally, in desperation, the company began sending two crates for every one sent in the past. The first crate contained 90 percent of the merchandise normally sent; the second contained 10 percent. The handlers learned to take the second crate and to leave the first untouched. The company viewed this as an improvement. It still suffered a 10 percent loss—but it now knew which 10 percent it would lose (Donaldson, 1996)!

Interviews with Indian CEOs in 1993 revealed that they were well aware that inefficiency metastasizes as decisions are made not on the basis of price and quality, but on the basis of how much money people are getting under the table. This they acknowledged as their principal reason for concern about the widespread phenomenon of Indian bribery. Again, the market is a remarkably efficient tool for allocating resources, but it only works if people buy based on price and quality—not clandestine payoffs. A trip to the streets of Calcutta in 1993 would have brought home the bitter fruits of corruption. The Indian economy in 1993 was one so inefficient that even dramatic redistribution of wealth would leave most of its inhabitants in dire poverty. The poverty is so stark that social activists have given up their attempt to enforce child labor laws, and have turned instead to advocating better working conditions for children—better conditions, for example, for eight-year-old children in match factories. Most of the Indian executives interviewed believed that a great deal of India's economic inefficiency was driven by the presence of massive corruption.

NGOs and government bodies usually cite the negative impact of bribery on efficiency as their principal rationale for attempting to eliminate it. From 1993 to 1997, the OECD targeted bribery as one of its key concerns. Its rationale has focused almost exclusively on the way corrupt practices hamper development of international trade by "distorting competition, raising the cost of transactions and restricting the operation of free markets" (Yannaca-Small, 1994).

As David Vogel notes, the conviction that bribery harms efficiency is especially pronounced in the United States, the only country to pass a comprehensive act against bribery that prohibits bribes to officials of non-U.S. countries, i.e., the Foreign Corrupt Practices Act. He writes, "The U.S. view that not only bribery but other forms of corruption are regarded as inefficient . . . [helps] account for the fact that during the fifteen year period from 1977 to 1992, the United States fined or imprisoned more corporate officers and prominent businessmen than all other capitalist countries combined (Vogel, 1992).

The rejection of bribery through ISCT, using an appeal to hyper-norms, refutes the claim often heard that bribery is inevitably the product of primitive, nonuniversalistic perspectives. For example, the philosopher David Fisher once commented:

> Bribery, as a practice, belongs to a pre-modern world in which inequality of persons is assumed, and in which moral obligation is based on (1) birth into gender and class, (2) birth order, and (3) personal relationships that define duties. The theoretical perspectives of modern ethics, such as those of Kant or Mill, have little to offer those who inhabit such worlds, because they construe moral identity in ways that deny the universalism implied by all forms of modern ethics (Fisher, 1996).

This seems wrong-headed. Developing countries possess at least as many universalistic conceptions as developed ones. To think otherwise is to indulge in the kind of moral imperialism that brought well-educated scientists in the nineteenth century to regard all primitive people as "savages." Recent studies of the moral development of people in Belize, for example, found that they scored higher on Kohlberg-style moral development tests than did people in the United States. A comparative field study evaluated the moral reasoning used by U.S. and Belize business students in resolving business-related moral dilemmas. The Belize business students, inhabitants of a less-developed country, though with a Western heritage, resolved the dilemmas using higher stages of moral judgment than did the U.S. business students (Worrell et al., 1995).

Nonetheless, at the level most individual managers confront it, bribery has no satisfactory solution. Refusing to bribe is very often tantamount to losing business. Often sales and profits are lost to more unscrupulous companies, with the consequence that both the ethical company and the ethical individual are penalized. (Of course, companies help employees caught in the bribery trap by having clear policies, and giving support to employees who follow them.) The answer, then, lies not at the level where individuals face bribery, but at the level of the host country's background institutions. A solution involves a broadly based combination of business pressure, legal enforcement, and political will. Companies, in turn, should make a point not only of speaking out against bribery, but of doing so in cooperation with other companies.

Practical Implications of ISCT for Global Companies

The principles of moral free space and adherence to hypernorms imply a balanced approach for companies attempting to navigate global international waters. The presence of hypernorms means that companies must never simply adopt a "do in Rome as the Romans do" philosophy. They must be alert to the transcultural value implications of their actions. Moral free space, in turn, implies the need to precede judgment with an attempt to understand.

Hypernorms

Hypernorms are more than abstractions. As we saw in chapter 3, the research over the last fifteen years shows that in business ethics we're more alike than we think. Practically speaking, hypernorms mean that sometimes there is no compromising in business ethics. In 1992 Levi-Strauss cited its "Business Partners Terms of Engagement" when it broke off business with the Tan family in the Mariana Islands, a U.S. Territory. The Tan family reportedly "held twelve hundred Chinese and Philippine women in guarded compounds, working them seventy-four hours a week" (Franklin Research and Development Corporation, 1992). Strauss's "Business Partners Terms of Engagement" deals with the selection of contractors and requires practices compatible with the company's values on issues such as working hours, child labor, prison labor, discrimination, and disciplinary practices. Yet hypernorms should be applied carefully in the international arena and without rigidity. Even when it comes to ethics, facts make a difference. Consider the issue of price gouging in controlled economies. Price gouging is more unethical in a closed market than an open one because free markets automatically restrain arbitrary pricing (if one seller gouges, then another will grab his customers). In a controlled market, however, sellers can exploit customers by manipulating prices. When polled, Soviet Enterprise Executives in the former Soviet Union once ranked price gouging as the worst ethical problem they confronted in business (Ivancevich et al., 1992). This is not because the Soviet executives were confused; rather, it was because the rules of the Soviet game were different. When the rules of the game are different, so are the ethics of playing it.

Complying with hypernorms often demands considerable managerial creativity. Consider another situation confronted by Levi-Strauss, this time involving the hypernorms connected with child labor. The company discovered in the early 1990s that two of its suppliers in Bangladesh were employing children under the age of fourteen—a practice that violated the company's principles but was tolerated in Bangladesh. Forcing the suppliers to fire the children would not have insured that the children received an education, and it would have caused serious hardship for the families depending on the children's wages. In a creative arrangement, the suppliers agreed to pay the children's regular wages while they attended school and to offer each child a job at age fourteen. Levi-Strauss, in turn, agreed to pay the children's tuition and provide books and uniforms. This approach allowed Levi-Strauss to uphold its principles and provide long-term benefits to its host country (Kline, 1994).

Moral Free Space

Despite the importance of hypernorms, it is well to remember that ISCT implies the need for moral free space in global transactions. Here too, managerial creativity is often required. The most tempting and popular answer available for global companies is the "photocopy approach." Its simple advice is, "Do the same thing abroad you do at home." Falling into this trap, CEOs are often heard boasting that their companies act the same way ethically around the globe. Such claims are well-meaning, but eventually subvert the very ethics they intend to support. Saying "we pride ourselves on doing the same thing around the globe" is a bit like saying "I pride myself on saying the same thing to every one of my friends." Friends are different; cultures are different. And the demonstration of a company's ethics must be different as it recognizes cultural differences abroad.

Being true to one's own ethics often means not only sticking by one's own sense of right and wrong, but respecting the right of other cultures to shape their own cultural and economic values. Forgetting this can be a disaster. Consider the mess one well-intentioned effort created. In 1993 a large U.S. computer-products company insisted on using exactly the same sexual harassment exercises and lessons with Muslim managers halfway around the globe that they used with American employees in California. It did so in the name of "ethical consistency." The result was ludicrous. The managers were baffled by the instructors' presentation, and the instructors were oblivious of the intricate connections between Muslim religion and sexual manners.

The U.S. trainers needed to know that Muslim ethics are especially strict about male/female social interaction. By explaining sexual harassment in the same way to Muslims as to Westerners, the trainers offended the Muslim managers. To the Muslim managers, their remarks seemed odd and disrespectful. In turn, the underlying ethical message about avoiding coercion and sexual discrimination was lost. Clearly sexual discrimination does occur in Muslim countries. But helping to eliminate it there means respecting—and understanding—Muslim differences.

Such cultural conflicts suggest that we should revise a common litmus test for ethics, the one that asks, "How would you react if your action were described on the front page of the *Wall Street Journal?*" Instead we should sometimes ask the additional question: "How would you react if your action were described on the front page of Bangkok's *Daily News*, Rome's *Corriere Della Serra,* or the Buenos Aires *Herald?*" For example, in Africa, a businessperson may be invited to a family banquet following business dealings—and in order to attend he is expected to pay. This invitation is likely not to be a bribe, but a genuine sign of friendship and a commitment to good-faith business dealings in the future.

As we saw in earlier chapters, companies in India sometimes promise employees a job for one of their children when the child reaches the age of majority. Yet while such a policy may be in tension with Western notions of egalitarianism and antinepotism, it is clearly more in step with India's traditional values of clan and extended family. The ISCT framework we propose acknowledges that the Indian company's policy is in tension with the norms of other economic communities around the globe (hence placing it in the "moral free space" ring of the ISCT circle) while stopping short of declaring it ethically impermissible (a conclusion that would place it outside the circle). This third ring of the circle of the ISCT framework depicts an inevitable tension in values that any global manager must confront, and accept.

In short, ISCT suggests that international business ethics seldom come in black and white. On the one hand, managers must respect moral free space and cultural diversity. On the other, they must reject any form of relativism. Common humanity and market efficiency are part of the equation, but so too is a certain amount of moral tension. The lesson? Any manager unprepared to live with moral tension abroad should pack her bags and come home. Because ISCT is designed to help managers navigate the gray zones between ethical worlds, it pictures reality in more than black and white.

9

Social Contracts
and Stakeholder Obligations

What goes under the name of capitalism varies a lot from country to country,
even among rich economies. . . . In America and Britain, a public company
has traditionally had one overriding goal: to maximize returns to shareholders.
In Japan and much of continental Europe, in contrast, firms often accept
broader obligations that balance the interests of shareholders against those
of other *stakeholders* [emphasis added], notably employees, but including
also suppliers, customers and the wider community.

—*Economist* (1996: 23)

The concept of corporate obligations to stakeholders has been a
major theme in Western business ethics for several decades. The
essence of the stakeholder idea is that those who may be significantly
affected by an organization's action, or who are potentially at risk as
a result, have an obligation-generating "stake" in that decision. Typical listings of stakeholders include, among others: shareholders, consumers, users, neighbors, governments, suppliers, creditors, and distributors. The nature and scope of corporate obligations to
stakeholders is one of the most important and extensive components
of the modern literature on business ethics.

In this chapter we consider the relationship between ISCT and the
many theoretical approaches to corporate stakeholder obligations.
One might assume, on first impression, that ISCT and stakeholder
theories are either outright competitors or are inconsistent in the ethical guidance they provide for managers. These assumptions are mistaken; the two concepts are complementary—or, to be more precise,
one serves as the normative foundation for the other. ISCT serves as a
normative foundation for stakeholder theories and is capable of clarifying and strengthening their impact. In this chapter we will present
the core ideas of the main stakeholder theories, identify the more
stubborn problems and criticisms they have faced, discuss issues

involved with applying the stakeholder idea in a global context, and
then trace the interconnections between the two approaches. By iso-
lating certain weaknesses of the stakeholder theories as presently conceived, we will demonstrate the advantages of conceiving stakeholder
theory from the vantage point of ISCT. The final sections analyze the
implications of an ISCT-based approach to stakeholder management
and its ramifications for management practice and public policy.

Stakeholder Theories

An important task for business ethicists is to define when firms
should consider the interests of stakeholders in their decisions. The
extant conventional wisdom requires managers to act as follows: (1)
identify the full range of stakeholders for a given firm and decision,
(2) identify the stakes at issue in the decision, (3) assess the legitimacy
of the stakes, (4) allocate priority among conflicting stakeholder
claims, (5) identify strategic options for responding to the legitimate
stakes having priority, (6) assess the viability of the options within the
framework of corporate governance, including any special consideration to be given to the interests of stockholders, and (7) make a final
decision. Implicit in these steps are a number of difficult judgments,
including the ultimate question of why a firm should even bother with
stakeholder management.

Two primary types of justifications have been offered by scholars
advocating that firms adopt a strategy of stakeholder management.
The most prevalent justification is based on the assumption that business firms will become more profitable by catering to the interests of
stakeholders. The negative version of this justification stresses that
firms ignore stakeholders at their peril and that antagonizing important stakeholders may endanger the very viability of the business. A
second justification has been to argue that, regardless of the consequences to the firm, there is an ethical obligation to respond appropriately to stakeholder claims. The first approach can be described
as "instrumental" and the second as "normative" (Donaldson &
Preston, 1995).[1]

The instrumental approach (Jones, 1995) has been defined as one
concerned with "the connections, or lack of connections, between
stakeholder management and the achievement of traditional corporate objectives (e.g., profitability, growth)" (Donaldson & Preston,

1995: 71). An instrumental approach can be managed in the following way. First, management should consider the extent to which particular stakeholders might pose a threat to the organization or prove to be supportive allies to help the firm obtain its goals. In the case of a plant relocation decision, potential supportive stakeholder actions might include government agencies relaxing zoning laws or providing tax rebates, unions agreeing to more flexible work rules, and suppliers promising more favorable terms. Second, the firm should consider the costs that stakeholders are capable of imposing if they are antagonized by the decision. Unions might strike, community groups might boycott, existing suppliers might sue for breach of contract, and so on. The instrumentalist approach would require netting the costs and benefits that stakeholders are capable of generating, with that figure then being balanced against the net costs/benefits of all other financial consequences to the firm. This instrumental approach has been characterized as "strategic stakeholder analysis" by Goodpaster (1991).

In contrast, the normative approach emphasizes doing "the right thing," which may extend beyond a simple analysis of net costs to the firm. A classic example is a firm considering the legitimate interests in physical safety of consumer/user stakeholders as it decides how safe to make consumer goods. Thus, a firm might recall a dangerous product from the market even though the firm's lawyers advise that doing so might increase their liability exposure. Johnson & Johnson lawyers opposed the recall of Tylenol on such grounds. Goodpaster (1991) characterizes this normative approach as "multi-fiduciary" stakeholder analysis.

Many stakeholder theorists take the normative position that business firms do have fiduciary-type obligations to stakeholders. Their writings comprise what may be thought of as normative stakeholder theory—a conceptual framework defining right behavior for dealing with stakeholders (see Clarkson, 1994, 1995; Evan & Freeman, 1988/1993; Freeman, 1984; Mitchell, Agle, & Wood, 1997). Every attempt at developing a plausible, realistic stakeholder theory must grapple with a readily apparent set of foundational questions. Perhaps the most basic of these is, who should be considered a stakeholder? Does, for example, the concept extend to all who would claim such status for themselves, including terrorists or even parties opposed to the firm's very existence? Without clarity on the question of who counts as a stakeholder, doing "the right thing" for stakeholders becomes highly problematic.

Who Is a Stakeholder?

Mitchell, Agle, and Wood (1997) comprehensively survey existing definitions of stakeholders, noting that "theorists differ considerably on whether they take a broad or narrow view of a firm's stakeholder universe" (856). Freeman's early definition that a stakeholder is "any group or individual who can affect or is affected by the achievement of the firm's objectives" is one of the broadest in scope. Clarkson is among those who have offered both narrow and broad definitions in different contexts. In 1995 he provided a broad, summary definition that "[s]takeholders are persons or groups that have, or claim, ownership, rights, or interests in a corporation and its activities, past, present, or future" (106). Broad definitions raise many practical questions. Should, for example, anyone who claims an interest in an organization be considered a stakeholder? Should stakeholder status be limited to "persons," or could the environment generally, or even animals, particularly those treated as commodities (in pet shops) or used in medical research, be considered stakeholders? Controversial issues include whether the media, or even more abstract interests— e.g., freedom of the press or free speech—can rise to the status of stakeholders. A recent and surprisingly relevant issue after the Unabomber case has been whether terrorists can be considered stakeholders. An even more extreme example would involve whether the Ku Klux Klan or some similar organization can claim stakeholder status on the basis of their preferences for discrimination. Note that under a broad-based instrumental approach using either Freeman's or Clarkson's broad definition, the answer would be clearly yes.[2] The Ku Klux Klan or the Unabomber is fully capable of having an impact on the ability of an organization to achieve its goals.

Listing everyone who might qualify as a stakeholder for a large firm tends to produce messy combinations of overlapping groups with exceedingly diverse claims and interests. In order to provide some order, stakeholders have been variously classified according to set criteria.[3] For example, a relatively simple approach is to group stakeholders into primary and secondary classifications on the basis of the formality of their connection with the firm. Stakeholders who can assert direct claims due to contractual or other legally recognized interests are characterized as "primary" stakeholders. These would include consumers, suppliers, distributors, creditors, employees, and so on. All other more remote groups are classified as "secondary" stakeholders, whose claims are subordinate to those of primary stakeholders. Examples would involve consumer groups, the media, local communities, and even the environment. One implication of this classification scheme is that when conflicts arise, the claims of primary stakeholders are to be given greater weight than those of secondary stakeholders. Other creative groupings have been based upon the potential for threat or cooperation, which classifies stakeholders as supportive (high cooperation potential), marginal (low on both measures), nonsupportive (high threat potential) or mixed-blessing (high on both) (Savage et al., 1991). Mitchell, Agle, and Wood (1997) develop an elaborate analysis of stakeholder identification and stakeholder salience by emphasizing combinations of power, legitimacy, and urgency.

The issue of how to define a stakeholder remains open within the business ethics literature. There is no single definition supported by a widespread consensus. Instead there are competing approaches, which reflect, to some extent, the political and social controversies that run through stakeholder claims and disputes. They extend from Freeman's classic (1984) definition described earlier to those "in a relationship with an organization" (Thompson et al., 1991), to those who "bear some form of risk as a result of having invested some form of capital, human or financial, something of value, in a firm" (Clarkson, 1994). Later in this chapter, we will suggest how ISCT may help decision makers resolve the difficult question of whom they should recognize as legitimate stakeholders.

Assessing Stakeholder Claims

Managers attempting to respond to stakeholders face many difficult decisions. Once legitimate stakeholders have been identified, the next challenge is to somehow assess the legitimacy of the claims asserted. Some claims may be morally problematic. A terrorist's demand for ransom (as has happened with U.S. firms in Central America) or for a publication outlet (the Unabomber demanding that the *Washington Post* publish his tract) may be viewed instrumentally as a stakeholder claim, but that does not give it ipso facto normative validation as an obligation of an organization. Under ISCT, stakeholder theory cannot justify an obligation to respond, unless the claim satisfies a minimal threshold of normative merit as determined by legitimate ethical norms.

Stakeholder claims that violate hypernorms cannot create stakeholder obligations. Clear-cut examples would be an animal rights group demanding that a drug company give electrical shocks to medical researchers in order to sensitize them to the pain and fear of lab animals; or a terrorist group demanding that a utility give them enriched uranium in order to enable them to threaten urban communities. Most decisions involve less obviously problematic claims and therefore pose more difficult judgments for managers. Consider the examples of employees who wish to smoke in an environment in which secondhand smoke may be a problem for coworkers; or the HIV-infected nurse who applies for a job at an elementary school. The writings on normative stakeholder theory provide little guidance on these issues, yet their resolution is vitally important.

The manager who successfully judges the normative value of a particular stakeholder claim must also consider the possibility of additional stakes. Few difficult cases of business judgment involve a single stakeholder. In the commonplace multiple stakeholder situations, stakeholders' interests will often diverge. When this occurs, supporting the claims of one group of stakeholders may result in defeating the interests of competing groups.

Various strategies for resolving such conflicts have been proposed. As noted earlier, some have suggested that stakeholders be broadly grouped and ranked according to specific criteria, e.g., their legal status or their ability to have an impact on firm goals. More formal methodologies have also been proposed, including, for example, Hosseini and Brenner's (1992) instrumental application of Saaty's Analytic Hierarchy Process to competing stakeholder claims. The process works by asking managers and then stakeholders to make a series of pairwise comparisons of stakeholder interests, e.g., the relative importance of job security versus maintaining the dividend, or the relative importance of product safety versus job security. The AHP is applied to translate these judgments into a hierarchy and ultimately to produce a composite value matrix weight incorporating the views of managers and stakeholders. Their approach brings a useful discipline to the weighing process and helps clarify the identity of stakeholders; but their focus originates *from* the perspective of the firm and is not obviously anchored by a normative theory. At the very least, Hosseini and Brenner's approach is useful from an instrumental perspective.

The final, and for many the most difficult, issue for stakeholder theory is assessing the validity of legitimate stakeholder claims or interests in the context of the corporate governance framework. Goodpaster has argued that the conflicts between the strategic and multi-fiduciary approaches create a management "paradox" of mutually exclusive duties to stakeholders and shareholders. In his words, "the former (strategic approach) appears to yield business without ethics and the latter (multi-fiduciary approach) appears to yield ethics without business" (1991: 53). In its most extreme form, this debate inquires whether it is either legal or moral for managers to consider the interests of stakeholders, except as they contribute to the interests of shareholders. As Elaine Sternberg notes: "The stakeholder approach to corporate governance is based on a fundamental confusion. Starting from the fact that business is affected by and affects certain groups, stakeholder theory concludes that business should be accountable to them. In doing so, it undermines not only business, but property rights and the duty that agents owe to principals" (Sternberg, 1995: 10).

The claim that shareholders' interests are predominant is based upon several different arguments. Some assert that existing corporate law strictly limits the recognition of stakeholders by establishing fiduciary responsibilities for senior managers and board members that eliminate, or at least minimize, their discretion to respond directly to the interests of stakeholders. On a more theoretical level, the claim has been made that an implicit contract exists between stakeholders and shareholders to have the shareholders bear the risk and, as a consequence, monitor management. Under this view, stakeholders agree that shareholders will serve as their agents in making sure that management appropriately balances shareholder and stakeholder claims.

A popular argument of stakeholder skeptics claims that shareholders own the corporation and therefore should have unlimited discretion to control the disposition of their own property. Under this absolute shareholder dominance approach, instrumental stakeholder management would still be permissible so long as the actions taken did in fact contribute to shareholder wealth. Thus, paying attention to product liability issues and the possibility that a union might strike would satisfy the standard of shareholder dominance. In contrast, considering any stakeholder interest solely on its own merits would be inappropriate.

The view that all noninstrumental stakeholder considerations are inappropriate is extreme, and appears to be inconsistent with modern practice and opinion. Instead, the prevailing view appears to be that management has a primary, not exclusive, obligation to shareholders—a view that translates into a strong presumption in favor of shareholder claims. Once one moves away from the absolutist position, the issue then becomes how management should go about balancing shareholder and stakeholder claims. What, for example, would constitute an appropriate cost to shareholders in recognition of stakeholder claims that a firm should reduce airborne emissions, which, though legal, are having a detrimental impact on the local community?

Under the prevailing view, management has room to recognize truly important stakeholder claims in clearly defined circumstances. The problem then becomes how to distinguish between an appropriate and an inappropriate consideration of stakeholder interests. Later in this chapter we will describe how an ISCT-based stakeholder approach helps to make these important distinctions.

Global Stakeholder Obligations?

Application of normative stakeholder theory to a global context produces an additional set of thorny questions. Does the scope of stakeholder obligations vary according to the locus of the decision or the home country of the corporate actor? For example, can there be different stakeholder expectations for business decisions made in India than in the United States, regardless of the firm involved? Or, instead, do Indian and U.S. firms, due to their differing home cultures, have different stakeholder obligations even when acting in the same location? If so, what factors influence or control the definition of stakeholder interests that might allow this to be possible?

Consider the important issue of plant safety. Might stakeholder interests in India be appropriately defined to allow lower levels of plant safety than would be the case for operations in France or the United States? If so, then *all* firms operating plants in India would have lower levels of stakeholder obligation to employees and local communities than would firms conducting comparable operations in France or the United States. This question contains important implications for global business practice. If it is legitimate to define stakeholder obligations in relation to the country in which the decision is made, one might conclude that Union Carbide is entitled to follow lower standards for plant safety in Bhopal, India, than in Kanawha, West Virginia. Because the focus is solely on the locus country, the same would be true for Tata Steel, an Indian company, which would have a higher level of stakeholder obligations for operations in the United States than for domestic operations within India.

Or, instead, might the nature of stakeholder obligations vary with the decision-making firm itself, regardless of where it is doing business? Both Richard DeGeorge (1993) and Thomas Donaldson (1989) have suggested specific stakeholder-type obligations for the special case of global corporations that are based in developed countries and do business in less-developed countries. The wealth, capabilities, expert knowledge concerning risks, home-country values, and other advantages of these global firms serve to justify imposition of extensive stakeholder obligations. Under their approaches, a firm such as Union Carbide must satisfy a minimum core of stakeholder obligations wherever it does business, regardless of any local definitions of stakeholder obligation.

The universalist approach recognizing stakeholder obligations applicable to all organizations everywhere, regardless of circumstance, contrasts significantly with a focus limited to locally determined obligations or special categories of firms. Such fundamental, universal standards stand superior to local customs, norms, or laws; all firms, independent of the expectations of host and home countries alike, are required to honor universal obligations. Before suggesting how ISCT connects to these three options for a global application of the stakeholder idea, we must first consider additional objections to the stakeholder concept.

Criticisms of the Stakeholder Concept

The injection of "stakeholder" terminology into political debates in the late 1990s highlighted the broader social and political contexts in which the stakeholder concept is framed. A prime example was a speech entitled "The Stakeholder Economy" (given in Singapore on January 7, 1996), in which Tony Blair, the then leader of the Labour Party in the U.K., stated it was time to "shift the emphasis in corporate ethics—from the company being a mere vehicle for the capital market—to be traded, bought and sold as a commodity; towards a vision of the company as a community of partnership in which each employee has a stake, and where a company's responsibilities are more clearly delineated."[4]

Blair's view of stakeholders is narrow. His primary emphasis is on employees, whose interests he assumes would presumably trump other stakeholder claims. As might be expected, there was a considerable political reaction to the theme. Some pundits called stakeholders the New Socialist Persons. They argued that left-wing politicians were trying to place social obligations concerning the environment and health and day care on business firms after failing to win political battles toward the same goals.[5] An extension of this argument is that managers lack the political legitimacy to make what are essentially social or political choices by favoring certain groups of stakeholders. Instead, exacting such social or political obligations from them is considered a form of taxation without representation. Why, so the argument goes, should shareholders have their dividends or profits taxed so that firms can make contributions to charities the shareholders disfavor, or even worse, as in the case of contributions supporting Planned Parenthood, Right to Life, or other agencies connected to highly controversial issues, to positions that certain shareholders passionately abhor. In some cases, a shareholder may personally give money to support one position and find his or her dividends being taxed to support the opposite view.

Other critics have relied on an economic argument based on the empirical claim that the most efficient form of economic organization is one in which managers of for-profit organizations act solely on behalf of the interests of their owners. Under this view, managers are most successful when they focus on their primary objective of making profits. Since they are not particularly adept at making social decisions, managers will be both distracted and less efficient if they are considered to have obligations to respond to some broader social, stakeholder interest (Friedman, 1970).

Earlier, we discussed the argument that the law prohibits consideration of the interests of stakeholders and that shareholders, as owners of the corporation, have the right to deal with their property as they see fit. We believe that ISCT provides a solid basis for rejecting these attacks on the idea of normative stakeholder obligations.

ISCT and Stakeholder Theories

ISCT constitutes a systemic approach to economic ethics. Rather than being limited to a discrete set of principles or presenting a particular form of logic, it provides definitions and recognizes a process by which legitimate ethical rules or norms may be identified. ISCT has numerous implications for stakeholder theories. Authentic ethical norms, grounded in specific communities, define stakeholder status and provide criteria for sorting out conflicting stakeholder interests. Hypernorms place limits on authentic norms and may mandate the recognition of certain fundamental stakeholder claims. Relevant political, social, or economic communities may act to define the primary boundaries of stakeholder obligation for organizations operating within their boundaries and also for organizations established under their legal authority. For a given decision, candidate relevant communities would include those that have a significant interest in either the organization or the stakeholders significantly affected by the decision, or both. Relevant communities as sources of norms defining stakeholder obligations include interdependent global firms (the major oil companies), nation-states (Germany, the United States) or political subdivisions (Arizona), regional economic communities (the European Community), and industry associations (Chemical Manufacturers Association), among others.

The manner in which norms delineating stakeholder obligation will be established and evolve will vary among communities in reflection of local customs, legal systems, and economic goals. As should be expected in a culturally and economically diverse world, various nations can be expected to place different emphasis on the relative importance of shareholder profits versus stakeholder obligations for organizations established within their jurisdiction. Organizations within China are subject to different expectations than organizations in the United Kingdom. Even among capitalist countries, there is substantial variance in expectations (Steadman & Garrison, 1993).

Citizens in developing countries may want their fledgling industries to survive at all costs and may reasonably prefer that the management of organizations within those industries focus solely on profits and ignore any stakeholder interests that might endanger their survival (while, of course, paying close attention to those essential to their survival). In contrast, developed countries may prefer that certain of their national business organizations, particularly those sheltered from global competition, perform other roles within society beyond maximizing returns for shareholders/owners. This, however, is a matter of local choice. Believing that it will maximize national wealth, some nations may evolve norms reflecting a Friedmanesque approach in which shareholder interests are given predominance, thereby

requiring their home corporations to give consideration to stakeholder interests only when doing so would lead to enhanced shareholder wealth. Other developed, capitalist countries may evolve
norms reflecting a preference that their home corporations reject the
Milton Friedman approach and recognize obligations to stakeholders
that may, within certain clearly specified limits, conflict with shareholder interests. We surmise, based on evidence concerning the nature
of existing legitimate norms, that the latter describes the United
States.

As a means of implementing cultural preferences and economic
goals, communities create authentic ethical norms identifying who
should count as stakeholders and specifying legitimate stakeholder
obligations. Stakeholder-relevant authentic norms vary among communities, evolve over time, and reflect the economic, social, and
moral preferences of the local population.

Consistent with the standard method for applying ISCT, community norms relevant to the particular stakeholder decision would have
to be tested against universal hypernorms and, in certain circumstances, prioritized against competing norms from other communities
having a significant interest in the decision. For example, a claim by
Muslim banks in Bangladesh that women are not stakeholders to be
considered in their formulation of lending policies could be challenged by conflicting norms from broader commercial communities,
and also by hypernorms prohibiting invidious gender-based discrimination.

Although sociopolitical communities have the normative authority
to prescribe the range and nature of stakeholder obligations for organizations operating within their borders, it is unlikely that norms
resolving the full set of stakeholder issues would emerge. The current
debates about stakeholder obligations often involve hotly contested
political issues and/or competing empirical claims. It should not be
surprising, then, that communities may have areas in which there is
little consensus about certain types of stakeholder obligations. In
response to the natural "gaps" in norms, business organizations and
other communities have substantial moral free space in which to exercise their own ethical discretion. This firm-based moral free space in
turn is strictly bounded by universal hypernorms and the constraints
of consent, voice, and exit established in the macrosocial contract.

All organizations, wherever situated, and whatever their characteristics, must recognize the interests of stakeholders whenever failing to

do so may violate a hypernorm. Taking DeGeorge's (1993) first principle—multinationals should do no intentional direct harm (unless there is a cardinal overriding justification)—as a hypernorm,[6] it then becomes the obligation of all organizations to recognize this principle in regard to stakeholders. Thus, as DeGeorge suggests, an organization that sells carcinogen-contaminated pajamas in the Third World, knowing that they are prohibited for sale in the United States and Europe and are unacceptably dangerous to their intended users, fails to recognize a mandatory stakeholder duty. This obligation cannot be overridden by norms of either the organization itself, or the norms of the sociopolitical community in which it is organized or operates. Neither H. B. Fuller (a organization that sells glue in Honduras), nor Honduras, nor Minnesota (where H. B. Fuller is incorporated and has its headquarters), nor the United States, nor organizations doing business within Honduran borders may morally sanction the direct marketing of glue to young children as a means of getting high.[7]

Beyond hypernorms, an organization has an obligation under ISCT to follow legitimate norms defining stakeholder obligations in the relevant communities in which it is formed and in which it operates, subject to the operation of the priority rules. As a general rule, an organization must act consistently with such legitimate norms when applicable, and must do so even though no hypernorm compels such action. In the context of business organizations, there will be one legal community that sanctions or establishes its form and places restrictions on how it may operate. In the case of corporations, this will be the community under whose legal authority the organization is established. In the United States, this is the state of incorporation, which for many of the largest firms is Delaware. This relationship can be viewed as a form of contractual licensing of business organizations by the political community, an express detailing of powers, rights, limitations, and expectations, including stakeholder obligations.

Other communities may have interests in the decisions of the organization equivalent to or exceeding those of the licensing community, particularly within the United States. Some corporations incorporated in Delaware have far greater economic presence and impact in other states, particularly when their headquarters or major operations are located elsewhere. When within a given community, organizations provide significant employment for community members, have a direct effect on the natural environment, and pay taxes for and use government services, such activities help justify significant priority for that community's ethical norms. Thus, in most, although certainly not all, situations, the norms of either the community in which the organization's headquarters or major operations are located, or the sanctioning legal community, should be given priority. For example, German or Japanese organizations have an obligation to follow any clearly established mandatory norms of their nation-states concerning employee rights within their home countries, even though these obligations are not mandated by hypernorms. As is always the case under ISCT, the issue of priority rules comes into play only when there are conflicting *legitimate* norms. If the application of the priority rules fails to give a clear signal, then the decision makers may act within their moral free space and follow their own values in determining which of the competing norms to follow.

The implications of this ISCT-based approach to stakeholder theory can therefore be summarized as follows:

1. Relevant sociopolitical communities are a primary source of guidance concerning the stakeholder obligations of organizations formed or operating within their boundaries.

2. Where norms pertaining to stakeholder obligations are not firmly established in the relevant sociopolitical communities, organizations have substantial discretion in deciding how to respond to stakeholder claims and interests.

3. All decisions affecting stakeholders undertaken by organizations must be consistent with hypernorms.

4. Where there are conflicting legitimate norms concerning stakeholder obligations among relevant sociopolitical communities, the norms of the community having the most significant interests in the decision should be candidates for priority. Otherwise, where there are conflicting norms with no clear basis for prioritization, organizations have substantial discretion in choosing among competing legitimate norms.

Implications for Management Practice and Public Policy

The effect of these four principles is to establish two types of stakeholder standards for organizations: mandatory and permissible. Mandatory obligations exist whenever hypernorms and/or applicable legitimate norms establish nonoptional standards for organizations. For example, norms may require that consumers be warned about side effects of nonprescription drugs; or that organizations incorporate known, feasible safety equipment into the design of a plant. Permissive standards allow organizations discretion to respond to particular nonshareholder stakeholder interests without fear of being considered to have violated an obligation to shareholders or even to other community constituencies with competing interests.

The relationship between the types of norms and the resulting standards is demonstrated in Table 9-1.

A stakeholder strategy implemented by a global business organization must often balance, under an overarching framework of universal principles, stakeholder obligations resulting from a variety of organizational and economic communities. In certain limited though important circumstances, universal principles will require a response to stakeholder interests regardless of the locus of the transaction, or the nationality of the organization, or the existence of permissive local (nonlegitimate) norms. Thus, all global organizations should comply with the hypernorm to do no direct harm to humans by developing and maintaining a set of global stakeholder standards sufficient to insure that employees, consumers, and third parties are not subjected to reasonably avoidable physical risk. At the same time, global organizations should remain open to local preferences and expectations as an important dimension of their stakeholder management. For example, a Japanese vehicle manufacturer might impose a uniform test for ventilation to prevent carbon monoxide poisoning in all plants worldwide, regardless of the existence of more permissible

Table 9-1   Categories of Stakeholder Norms

Types of Standards/Norms	Examples of Hypernorms	Examples of Community Norms
Mandatory standards	Organizations may not use nonconsenting, uniformed human subjects for new drug development	Organizations are expected to lower salaries of senior managers before laying off general employees
Permissive standards	Organizations may exceed local plant-safety standards to protect employees from death or injury	For-profit, public organizations may give up to 5 percent of profits to charity without its being considered a violation of shareholder interests

local standards. On the other hand, the parent organization, which gives little to charity in Japan, might have its U.S. subsidiary engage actively in philanthropic activities in response to local norms within the relevant sociopolitical community of the United States.

General Implications of the Four Core Principles of Generic Stakeholder Theory

The implications of each of the specific principles of the generic stakeholder theory are briefly discussed in the sections that follow.

A. Relevant sociopolitical communities are a primary source of guidance concerning the stakeholder obligations of organizations formed or operating within their boundaries.

The key implication of principle A is that a decision maker should look to the norms of relevant sociopolitical communities in seeking answers to the questions of (1) who should be recognized as a stakeholder, (2) how to resolve conflicting interests between shareholders and stakeholders, and (3) how to resolve other competing stakeholder claims. Stakeholder-related norms can be identified using the processes described in chapters 4 and 7.

It may turn out that for very controversial issues, mandatory norms will not have evolved within the relevant communities. For example, there may not be clear-cut norms providing answers to questions such as the permissibility of firing workers for smoking off the job, or whether to allow HIV-positive employees to supervise young children in day care. In such circumstances, organizational managers have a broader range of choice and may freely turn to their own organization's values, or lacking guidance there, to their own values in resolving such issues.

Much of the existing business ethics literature on stakeholder theory, written primarily by scholars based in the United States, is consistent with the ISCT approach. The writers often focus on the choices sociopolitical communities within the United States have made on this issue. A prime recent example is the debate among Boatright (1994), Goodpaster and Holloran (1994), and others concerning the existence of a management "paradox" of mutually exclusive duties to stakeholders and shareholders. Implicit in their debate are disagreements over how to interpret the authentic norms of the fifty state governments (with special emphasis on Delaware) and, in some contexts, the national government (e.g., federal corporate governance issues). Their differing perspectives derive in part from the fact that some states appear to give greater relative preference to investor interests than others. This should not be surprising. The extent of any paradox is substantially mitigated when one looks more closely to identify relevant community norms indicating how the line should be drawn between shareholder and stakeholder interests. Under a contractarian approach the question is transformed into an empirical one of identifying dominant legitimate norms.

Suppose that the search turns up dry, indicating that the relevant communities have not evolved norms pertaining to the stakeholder claim in question. Is that a shortcoming of a contractarian approach? No. If there are no mandatory duties, then a paradox cannot exist since no established duty is being breached. In this circumstance, it becomes a matter of organizational free choice as provided in principle B.

Consider also Boatright's (1994) recent distinction between the fiduciary and nonfiduciary obligations of managers, intended to resolve the alleged paradox between stakeholder and shareholder interests. Boatright reasons that managers may not go beyond strategic stakeholder synthesis (considering only the ability of the stakeholders to have a direct impact on the firm's goals) when their fiduciary obligations are at issue, but that they may engage in multi-fiduciary stakeholder synthesis (consideration of the moral claims of stakeholders) when they are free from direct fiduciary obligations. Boatright's analysis is clearly limited to the presumed legitimate norms establishing fiduciary duties within U.S. states. Assuming that he is correct concerning the nature of those norms, his argument is entirely consistent with an ISCT-based stakeholder approach applicable to U.S. firms and transactions.[8]

Maitland (1994) has argued that agency theory justifies giving substantial preference to the interests of shareholders over stakeholder claims. Under his agency theory model, stakeholders are considered to implicitly contract to have the shareholders bear the risk and monitor the operation of the organization. Stakeholders agree to grant stockholders this special status because monitoring by a single group is more efficient and should result in reduced agency costs and lower costs of production. Under principle A, these claims reduce to an empirical question of whether Maitland's view is reflected in the norms and preferences of the relevant communities. That is, do the relevant business, social, and legal communities within the United States recognize agency obligations as a mandatory principle to be followed by all corporations? If they do, then organizations acting within those communities have an obligation to recognize the strong shareholder preference embodied in the theory. There is good reason to believe that agency theory, at least in that form, is not accepted by relevant U.S. communities, and that as Quinn and Jones (1995) argue, managers have an obligation to do what is morally right in a manner transcending the narrowly defined view of agency obligation. Under this more broadly defined approach "[t]he agency morality view of business policy has much in common with two other normative approaches . . . , the stakeholder approach and the social contract approach" (1995: 38).

Through this process of reference to community authentic ethical norms, organizational managers can obtain useful guidance concerning the resolution of difficult stakeholder questions. Consider, for example, an organization deciding whether to close a particular plant and transfer its operations to another location within the same sociopolitical (e.g., nation-state) community. The organization is faced with a number of competing stakeholder claims. Citizens of the present locale, the union, certain employees, certain suppliers, and local government organizations stake claims in support of a decision to keep the plant open in its present location. Potential employees and suppliers, citizens, and local government organizations at the new location as well as creditors and stockholders all stake claims in support of a move. Whatever decision the organization makes, some stakeholder interests will be defeated while others will be realized.

Under principle A, the organization must give consideration to the norms and expectations of the relevant communities, particularly those of the national community, in deciding among the competing claims. Presumably, many of the communities involved in the plant relocation decision will have competing norms concerning the relative weights that should be given to staying put versus relocating. However, in this case it will probably be the national community that has the most significant interests because it encompasses the claims of all the groups supporting or opposing the move. The norms of this over-arching sociopolitical community should be identified and should play a prominent role in the decision. Obviously, there are many alternatives concerning the norms relating to relocation that might be identified in a given community. For example, the national community may have norms reflected in laws requiring notice to terminated employees and setting the parameters of severance packages. Surveys of citizens of the national community may reveal a general, though not universal, acceptance of the need for labor mobility and a recognition of the need to control costs so as to compete globally. Tax laws may be identified that encourage other locales to bid for the relocation of plants into their areas. The predominant thrust of these laws, regulations, and attitudes may represent a preference within the overall national community that no special status be given to claims in favor of a location status quo whenever there is a significant economic advantage in relocation. Or, the national community may be found to have the opposite preference—for the maintenance of employment and local communities even at a substantial cost in economic output. Whichever way they cut, the norms of the relevant communities will provide a rough measure of the full expectations concerning how such a move should be handled—for example, the notice and severance packages to be given to discontinued employees, the extent of cost savings required to justify moving, and so on.

B. Where norms pertaining to stakeholder obligations are not firmly established in the relevant sociopolitical communities, organizations have substantial discretion in deciding how to respond to stakeholder claims and interests.

Principle B is based upon the reality that sociopolitical communities often fail to develop a consensus concerning the extent and nature of the social obligations of organizations, particularly in cases where significant tradeoffs may be involved. As Salbu (1994) suggests, a divergence of consensus within the moral free space of a community may in fact be a healthy process encouraging colloquy. By that process a consensus may emerge providing societal guidance concerning right behavior. Organizations are part of the process when they act within their own moral free space in deciding how to respond to stakeholder claims. In Carroll's words, "[d]iscretionary . . . responsibilities are those about which society has no clear-cut message for business" (1979: 500).

Orts (1992) discusses at length the mixed signals that U.S. states have sent through their corporate constituency statutes. It is often unclear whether a given state legislature intended to extend legal protection to some limited form of Goodpaster's stakeholder synthesis, or instead merely intended to ratify preexisting law allowing stakeholder analysis only when it benefits shareholders. Communities are not likely to evolve bright-line norms pertaining to mandatory stakeholder obligations when important groups of constituents hold conflicting views. Thus, organizations typically have substantial moral free space in choosing how to respond to stakeholder interests. Unless and until directing or constraining norms evolve in relevant communities, organizations in such an environment may respond to stakeholders on the basis of their own internal values. Their range of choice is always subject to the constraint of hypernorms, but otherwise they are free to be responsive to the interests of significant stakeholders so long as doing so does not directly violate relevant legitimate norms. For example, corporate philanthropy has long been considered to fall within a discretionary domain for management (Carroll, 1979). Philanthropy is not mandatory, and firms may decide to give nothing at all to charity. Tax laws and tradition demarcate the outer boundary: firms may give up to 5 percent of net earnings. Giving more would breach norms protecting shareholders' interests.

An illuminating example of discretionary action was Merck's decision to expend substantial resources in an attempt to develop an effective treatment for onchocerciasis (river blindness). There was little reason for Merck to believe that it would be able to generate investment returns comparable to its typical marketplace drugs, since the areas in which the condition was found were severely impoverished. Merck's decision to commit resources was not compelled by hypernorms, nor was it mandated by the legitimate norms of any relevant community, not even Merck's home community. On the other hand, the decision was not prohibited by either source. This brings the decision squarely within the framework of principle B. Merck was entitled to act within its moral free space and expend resources to develop an effective drug. In so doing Merck acted consistently with its own organizational (community) values. On the other hand, it seems clear that the norms of the relevant communities would not allow for Merck to invert its organizational objectives and decide, suddenly, that it was solely in business to cure diseases endemic to the developing nations, eschewing all opportunity for long-term profit.

Such a decision would have exceeded the boundaries of Merck's moral free space and would be impermissible under principle B.

Organizations can be expected to develop their own sets of values concerning stakeholder interests within the realm of moral free space. Realistically, this should be a primary source of stakeholder management. Generally, an activist approach to stakeholder management should be readily transparent, thereby allowing capital markets to value the strategies. In addition, an organization can signal future stakeholder policies by statements in annual reports, disclosures in required financial filings, discussions with security analysts, and so on.

The fact that there is a significant range of permissibility for organizations in responding to stakeholder claims and interests should not be taken as justifying ignoring all stakeholder claims that extend beyond mandatory obligations established by community norms and hypernorms (principles A and C). Nor will successful organizations be likely to adopt such a stance. Instrumental factors may be dominant in guiding an organization to consider whether to engage in discretionary stakeholder management. In this context, the relationship between "good ethics" and successful business becomes critical. The academic literature has yet to produce a definitive answer to this important question (Wood & Jones, forthcoming). Managers who believe that stakeholder-oriented organizations are more likely to accomplish their goals or, contrariwise, that failing to respond adequately may cause significant stakeholders to "withdraw," possibly even leading to bankruptcy (Clarkson, 1995), should be most likely to engage in discretionary stakeholder activities. The financial position of an organization may also be a critical variable in determining its approach in the discretionary domain, with more successful and secure organizations believing that they have more leeway in affirmatively responding to stakeholder claims and publicly disclosing their activities (Roberts, 1992; Ullman, 1985). Merck's profitability may be viewed as a condition precedent to its ability to continue research on river blindness.

C. All decisions concerning stakeholder interests must be consistent with widely accepted hypernorms.

In ISCT, hypernorms trump all other ethical norms. Hypernorms may affirmatively require that organizations act in a particular way toward stakeholders, e.g., take steps to insure a specific minimal level of workplace or product safety. Or they may prohibit certain actions, such as dumping toxic wastes in a manner likely to result in human physical harm.

It should be noted that stakeholders themselves may conceivably raise claims that, if recognized, would result in organizational actions violating fundamental and universal principles of human behavior. Consider the earlier hypothetical example of an animal rights group demanding that a drug company give electrical shocks to medical researchers in order to sensitize them to the pain and fear of lab animals. Such a group may claim status as either an independent stakeholder, in and of its own right, or as a vocal advocate of the interests of the research animals, who as mute stakeholders cannot speak for themselves. Or a terrorist group might demand that a utility give them enriched uranium in order to enable them to threaten urban communities. Yielding to the demands of either group would require violation of virtually any list of core hypernorms.

As we have stressed, it is neither necessary nor desirable to have a formal list of hypernorms for the concept to be valuable to organizational decision makers. On many occasions, just asking the question of whether a given action would be consistent with hypernorms may lead to a meaningful intuitive response. Surely a high percentage of decision makers would concur that giving electrical shocks to employees or distributing carcinogen-contaminated children's pajamas in Central America violates a hypernorm.

> *D. Where there are conflicting legitimate norms concerning stakeholder obligations among relevant sociopolitical communities, the norms of the community having the most significant interests in the decision should be candidates for priority. Otherwise, where there are conflicting norms with no clear basis for prioritization, organizations have substantial discretion in choosing among competing legitimate norms.*

Some of the most difficult questions in stakeholder theory pertain to situations in which transactions cross the boundaries of communities that have quite different norms concerning how much weight should be given to particular stakeholder interests. The issue then becomes how to prioritize the conflicting community stakeholder norms. As always, this is one of the most difficult steps in applying ISCT. But it is also vital to realizing the ability of the theory to provide a middle ground between extreme particularist and universalist claims.

Consider the classic question in business ethics of the extent to which claims from putative stakeholders outside a nation-state carry equivalent weight with claims of national stakeholders. The issue arises, for example, when a U.S. firm is thinking of closing a plant in New England and moving it to Mexico, where it will provide much-needed employment. In some ways, the need of the Mexicans is greater since they lack the background institutions to provide social services equivalent to those in the United States. It may even be that the survival and well-being of the potential Mexican workers is at issue in a manner not true for the U.S. workers who would be displaced. Yet, political and employee stakeholders are heard to make the claim that it is "unethical" to close a U.S. plant in order to obtain cheaper wage costs in Mexico. When AT&T Consumer Products considered moving a manufacturing facility from the United States to Singapore or Mexico, stakeholder claims were advanced that AT&T had an obligation to its home community to maintain employment and honor the loyalty of long-standing employees.[9]

Recall Merck's evaluation of whether to invest in a drug to treat the river blindness infestation afflicting millions around the globe, but virtually no one in the United States. Other health threats, including heart disease and cancer, are widespread in Merck's primary market areas. People afflicted with those illnesses may claim as stakeholders that Merck should invest all of its research efforts toward resolving the widespread health problems found at home. How then are these competing stakeholder interests to be resolved? Is it appropriate for Merck to give greater weight to the stakeholders in its home country? Assuming in both cases that legitimate norms in the different communities support each of the competing viewpoints, which norms should be followed?

Under ISCT, priority rules have been identified that may serve as general guidelines for choosing among competing legitimate norms. These rules admittedly provide only a rough screening device for resolving such difficult and ambivalent questions. We have suggested that in the context of corporate stakeholder obligations, special weight should be given to the community in which the organization has its primary economic presence, or the legal community by whose concession the organization exists.

In the river blindness decision, it is unlikely that there were significant community norms that would take the judgment call out of Merck's moral free space. The claims of anyone who would want all of Merck's research to be spent on domestic cases would probably not be supported by broader community norms. If they were, the priority rules would need to be applied to determine which set of norms should prevail. If the answer to this question appears ambiguous, then the decision is within the organization's moral free space. Merck's long-standing and well-recognized corporate values of serving humanity and commitment to medical research would become the critical factor in the decision. The horrors of river blindness coupled with the fact that Merck was the best positioned of all possible parties to find and produce a remedy were sufficient, within the strong culture of Merck's moral free space, to justify taking action.

The issue of transferring jobs from one national community to another directly involves the application of the priority rules. Here, it should be possible to identify a number of stakeholder communities having mutually exclusive norms on this issue. The universalizability of a norm would enhance its status as a desirable candidate for priority as implied by the priority rules emphasizing the scope of the communities involved and patterns of consistency among legitimate norms. For example, a norm providing that an ethical organization should give severance pay for a period roughly the length of time that it takes, on average, to find a new job would be generally applicable to all jobs and would not arbitrarily prefer the members of one community over other communities. Such a norm could be expected to be found in many communities and might also be buttressed by the "rules of thumb" discussed in chapter 7, which support the transaction environment and recognize specificity and precision. If, indeed, the norm supporting a decision to relocate a plant were to be sustained by this many rules of thumb, it should surely be given priority.

Again, it must be kept in mind that the rules of thumb are only to be applied to norms found to be legitimate and therefore consistent with all of the terms of the macrosocial contract. When the rules of thumb yield conflicting signs, their divergence should be assessed to determine if the signal in one direction is noticeably superior. For example, a preference should be given if a clear preponderance of the number of signals is in a given direction, or if the signals in one direction are noticeably stronger and clearer. If the rules of thumb fail to give clear-cut guidance in a given conflict, then the decision maker may act within his/her moral free space in choosing which norms to follow, remembering that, after all, the choice is among competing *legitimate* norms.

Implications of ISCT for Stakeholder Management

As a starting point, an organization should identify its own core values concerning stakeholders. There are an increasing number of valuable external benchmarks, although ultimately the values chosen must reflect the organization's own culture, history, and shared beliefs. A useful benchmark is the "Principles for Business" offered by the Caux Round Table as "a world standard against which business behavior can be measured" (Caux Round Table, 1994). As discussed in chapter 3, the Caux Principles stress stakeholder obligations throughout by emphasizing responsibilities toward customers, employees, suppliers, sociopolitical communities, and even competitors. An organization's core values will be particularly critical in guiding decision making about stakeholder obligations within the substantial arena of moral free space. Evolutionary change of the core values is to be expected as an organization learns from outcomes in specific cases and as the external environment changes.

In the context of a specific decision (what level of plant safety should be followed by a chemical company in constructing a new plant in Bhopal?), the organization must initially determine the scope of its mandatory stakeholder obligations. These may be found in hypernorms or in the applicable norms of relevant communities (e.g., political, social, and business communities within India and the United States). Hypernorms would require that an organization incorporate existing knowledge concerning safety techniques and devices into its decision. A failure to consider and carefully evaluate the use of common safety measures would surely violate a moral minimum standard for plant safety.

Assume that the norms followed for plants built in the United States and/or other developed countries involve a higher standard of safety than is true for plants in the host country. Further assume that, beyond the moral minimum for safety, the developed countries' norms aren't considered mandatory for less-developed countries. In that circumstance, the organization would confront the issue of how to act within its moral free space. This decision would be driven by the organization's core values (if any).

Many organizations have taken a position on this issue. As noted in chapter 7, DuPont Chemical has taken the position concerning overseas plant safety standards that "[if] our safety policies are higher, we use ours. If the other country's are higher, we use theirs" (Hofmann, 1988: 12). Union Carbide, at least at the time of the Bhopal incident, was operating a U.S. plant and had a significant ownership interest in a comparable Indian plant with significantly lower safety standards. Firms may face different competitive and technical constraints and in response to those may rationally choose disparate approaches to plant safety beyond the required moral minimum. Presumably, firms may also differ in their approach to stakeholder claims for safety, some choosing to sacrifice other important interests, including competing claims of other stakeholder groups (e.g., employees' claims for job security), in order to maximize safety.

Finally, an organization may determine that certain actions are prohibited either by hypernorms or by the applicable norms of relevant communities. A global organization operating coal mines in a developing country may not use locals as human sensors to determine whether poisonous gases are escaping inside the mine. The division of stakeholder obligations into required, permissive, and prohibited dimensions is indicated in Table 9-2.

Consistent with many of the virtue theories popular today, ISCT allows considerable room for positive actions on the part of the firms in the context of stakeholder relationships. There is a recognition that firms vary significantly in their orientation and circumstances and that this is a highly desirable attribute of a diverse marketplace. Firms may take different positions regarding their relationships with others so long as they act consistently with mandatory legitimate norms and hypernorms. Presumably, some firms will actively manage their relationships with stakeholders, and others will take a more passive approach. As the success of the different stakeholder strategies is demonstrated, some firms will become exemplars to others, while others may become notorious for inappropriate or failed policies. Stakeholder-related actions are typically transparent, contributing to this phenomenon. If firms take actions that are inconsistent with the norms and preferences of significant communities with which they interact or in which they transact, those communities may send stronger signals concerning the existence of mandatory norms. Or, instead, the communities may, in effect, withdraw the norms upon finding that significant constituencies tend to act inconsistently with the norms.

Thus, it is good for firms to have substantial discretion, since by their actions, firms and communities align and harden their ethical norms. The dynamics of this process are likely to lead toward more positive corporate behavior in relation to significant stakeholder interests.

An ISCT-grounded stakeholder theory avoids the problem of imposing upon a community a particular ethical theory as the foundation for organizational obligations within the society. There is no requirement that all communities accept a particular (e.g., Kantian, as implied by Evan and Freeman's proposal) justification for a stakeholder theory. Instead, all communities may develop stakeholder norms reflecting the aggregate preferences of their membership. If a majority apply utilitarian or Confucian reasoning in the process of resolving ethical issues, then that rationale will serve as the basis for the authentic norms. So a non- or even anti-Kantian society would still come within the ecumenical parameters of this far more open-ended stakeholder approach.

Table 9-2 Categories of Stakeholder Obligation

	Required	Permissive	Prohibited
Definition	Action required by hypernorms or by dominant legitimate norms	Action not prohibited by hypernorms or by dominant legitimate norms	Contemplated action prohibited by hypernorms or by dominant legitimate norms
Examples involving dominant legitimate norms	Must provide nutritional information on food products when selling into a community with norms requiring same	For-profit organization may give up to 5 percent of net earnings to charity, to whom and as it wishes	Merck may not spend most or all of its research and development budget for drugs for diseases for which there is no reasonable expectation of profit
Examples involving hypernorms	Must test drugs for potential fatal or serious side effects before mass distribution	Merck may commit research and development funds toward finding a cure for river blindness	Cannot sell carcinogen-contaminated pajamas to developing world consumers

As should be clear from the discussion above, an ISCT-based stake-holder theory will not provide concrete external guidance for resolving every difficult question found in stakeholder management. No theory or approach can, or even should, do that. An internal revenue code level of detail in defining who is a stakeholder is neither possible nor desirable. Similarly, there needs to be play in the weighing of competing stakeholder interests. The primary advantage of this approach is that it does provide important additional reference points by looking to the norms of the affected communities. In many cases, these norms will serve as lighthouses showing the way to safe harbors of consensus.

Notes

Chapter 1   Why Contracts?

1. The seriousness of these events also has to do with their impact on future business. Bad publicity could bog down future, critical projects in sticky governmental and public debate. For example, in 1997 Shell entered the Peruvian rain forest, one of the earth's last virgin territories. There it hoped to develop South America's largest gas field near the banks of Camisea River, three hundred miles east of Lima. Good public relations would be crucial for keeping projects like this one alive (*Fortune,* 1997).

2. Another attempt at reconciliation is Reidenbach and Robin (1990), whose multidimensional scale for evaluating perceptions of ethical content incorporates two contractarian factors recognizing unspoken promises and unwritten agreements.

3. The thesis could be used to analyze tensions and suggest remedies for many of the problems that bedevil business and society. In providing a general template to use in analyzing broad conflicts in business ethics, Frederick's work dovetails nicely with attempts at analyzing "levels" of value thinking in business by Henk van Luijk (1992) of the Netherlands.

4. I can know the physical, causal forces that made Bertrand Russell's hand write ~(A --~ A), i.e., the logical principle of noncontradiction, without understanding a whit about the significance of the noncontradiction axiom in logic. Similarly, I may know well that a childhood of poverty, abuse, and neglect was the causal antecedent to a criminal's aberrant behavior, without knowing a thing about how to construe it morally.

5. In the domain of professional ethics, Dunfee and Maurer (1992) have employed an explicit consequential framework in analyzing the ethical dimensions of corporate attorney whistle-blowing.

6. The phrase "view from nowhere" is adapted from Thomas Nagel, *The View from Nowhere* (New York: Oxford University Press, 1986). We use it with a somewhat different meaning here.

7. In turn, without making reference in a significant way to the institution of private property, the ethical analysis of corporate behavior becomes a sham. For example, if one applies utilitarianism to the corporation, the immediate conclusion one will reach is that the corporation and its managers should do "whatever maximizes the greatest happiness for the greatest number." But this is the same conclusion one immediately reaches when applying utilitarianism to the Red

Cross, the United Nations, and the German government—organizations that are strikingly different and that possess different sets of obligations. It would be silly to evaluate the ethical correctness of CEO X's action by asking simply whether it maximized the sum total of happiness, because the ethical correctness of CEO X's actions cannot be separated from the fact that he is an agent working on behalf of share owners, i.e., people who have detailed property interests in the corporation. Perhaps CEO X could maximize happiness by giving away all of the corporation's assets to a fund to alleviate world hunger. Yet, it certainly does not follow that doing so is the right thing for CEO X to do. As Allen Buchanan notes, the distinctive ethical principles of any bureaucratic organization, including for-profit corporations, often derive from the distinctive agency-risks that arise from that organization's complex web of principal/agent relationships (Buchanan, 1996: 419–440).

8. In 1992, the journal *Ethics* devoted a special edition (vol. 102) to this very issue.

Chapter 2   *The Social Contract for Business*

1. See Conlisk (1996) for a comprehensive and excellent survey.

2. In this context, we view ethical behavior quite broadly to include all decisions that may have an impact upon the interests of other human beings. Our definition is quite similar to that used by Gert (1988: 6), who conceives of "morality as a public system applying to all rational persons governing behavior which affects others."

3. In later chapters the word "authentic" will be described in greater detail.

4. Even so, organizers of an economic community may often be responding to formal requirements for organization set by a broader social or political community, as in the case of promoters organizing a corporation.

5. One may initially consent in a manner that constrains the right to revoke consent during a given time period, as in the case of employment for a term, or for an unspecified time, as in the case of a group who mutually pledge to work toward the resolution of a particular problem (e.g., certain joint-venture arrangements). An agreement constraining the right to revoke consent should be explicit in order to be effective and, even so, should not be binding if the circumstances in which it is given violate any hypernorms.

6. There may be circumstances in which one exits a community but still remains a member of a broader community that recognizes a moral obligation concerning the first community. Consider the case of a product design engineer who signs a confidentiality agreement with her employer and then exits the employer's community and takes a job with a competing firm. The engineer remains a member of the broader political community that recognizes the validity of confidentiality agreements. Merely exiting the community of the former employer does not break all moral obligations to honor the agreement. As a member of the broader political community, the engineer remains obligated to

follow its norms. This cone of ever broader communities is an important dimension of ISCT-derived obligations.

7. This example is given as a hypothetical. It is not clear that there is an authentic norm within the American Bar Association to the effect that all members have an obligation to support choice on abortion, or even that the organization itself supports choice.

8. Assuming that such an authentic norm can be recognized for Iraq.

9. Assuming that a principle of totally unvarnished equal opportunity does not have hypernorm status.

Chapter 3   Hypernorms: Universal Limits on Community Consent

1. "Universalists" are not to be confused with the defenders of "universalism," who are opposed to ethical relativism (discussed in chapter 1).

2. This is true of all of what we will later call "substantive" hypernorms.

3. Walzer also notes that from a still different perspective, Habermas's rules of engagement contain more morality than they should. He writes, "[T]he rules of engagement constitute in fact a way of life. How could they not? Men and women who acknowledge each other's equality, claim the rights of free speech, and practice the virtues of tolerance and mutual respect, don't leap from the philosopher's mind like Athena from the head of Zeus. They are creatures of history; they have been worked on, so to speak, for many generations; and they inhabit a society that 'fits' their qualities . . ." (Walzer, 1994: 12).

4. See the lengthy discussion in the section "Views about Hypernorms," below.

5. Thomas Donaldson has argued against the possibility of a thoroughgoing naturalism in business ethics.

6. It is not clear how Mayer concludes that there would not be a hypernorm against slavery in 1600.

Chapter 4   Ethical Norms and Moral Free Space

1. An example of an overtly Christian firm is the highly successful Servicemaster Corporation, which provides cleaning and maintenance services.

2. Noting variations in practices concerning ethics codes of Japanese corporations.

3. For an expanded discussion of workplace attitudes, see Dunfee (1987).

4. The appendix for this chapter contains a more formal statement of the definition and process of generation of authentic norms.

5. In fact, we believe that dominant antibribery norms will generally meet the requirements of an authentic norm under ISCT and will prevail over any pro-bribery norms. The antibribery norms will be found in broader sociopolitical communities that bear the detrimental consequences of the bribers' actions. In these communities the vast majority of people do not participate in the practice.

These communities' norms should dominate probribery norms of smaller business communities.

6. It is hard to imagine an example of physical coercion that would not also represent a violation of a hypernorm (see discussion in chapters 3 and 5), so that a putative norm may fail under that test.

7. An Education Department audit found that $176 million in undeserved Pell grants were awarded during the 1995–96 academic year (Stecklow, 1997).

8. The term "community" will be used as inclusive of "group" in this section. The word "group," which refers to people or things being classified together, is used to signify the flexibility in the requirement. It also is intended to make the business context clear, in that some people may tend to think of community as connoting a social combination rather than a business entity.

9. In a somewhat bizarre extension of this phenomenon, social psychologists have found people believing they are part of a group because of a nonrational factor, such as an alleged tendency to get heads more than half of the time when they flip a coin (Kramer & Brewer, 1986).

10. Note that we are using a different definition than the one typically used in the marketing literature or in antitrust jurisprudence.

11. An exception to the behavioral requirement is coerced behavior that is not representative of how the individual members would have behaved in the absence of the coercion. In that circumstance, norms will be based on attitudes alone. If genuine attitudes of community members cannot be identified, then it may not be possible to ascertain authentic norms for the community.

12. Business school faculty regularly hear naive comments concerning the nature of ethics in the business world. Many students have an extreme Hobbesian view of the world that awaits them.

Chapter 5   Hypernorms Revealed: The Hypernorm of Necessary Social Efficiency

1. The same basic notion of aggregative welfare functions in Rawls's concept of the "difference principle," which relies on the notion that some goods (called "primary goods") are the sort that we all want more of, not less of.

2. Note that all hypernorms need not be generic. Some traditional candidates, such as "Treat other people as having value in themselves and not merely as means to ends (Kant's famous Categorical Imperative) *are* generic in this sense—that is, they apply in all contexts. Others, however, are context specific, and some, indeed, have meaning only within particular social institutions. For example, the maxim from the Ten Commandments against coveting thy neighbor's wife (or, in a more modern formulation, against coveting thy neighbor's "spouse") and the cultural proscription against incest, apply directly to the *family.* Similarly, the Aristotelian dictum to fulfill one's duty within one's society (or *Polis*) gains its special meaning in the context of *political* activity (Allen, 1968).

3. It is often noted that voting is irrational from an exclusively self-interested perspective. Taking the time and energy to cast one's ballot in an election in

which one's own vote is practically speaking never decisive cannot be justified in terms of its potential self-interested consequences. For a broader discussion of the importance of altruism in maintaining systems, see Frank (1988).

4. The presence of a market in society reflects the existence of one sort of N-Strategy for achieving aggregate welfare. Free-market theory emphasizes how most, if not all, market participants can benefit, at least when certain free-market assumptions are met. When these assumptions prevail, Pareto Optimality, a condition in which no one can be made better off without someone being made worse off, necessarily follows (Sen, 1985).

5. Especially difficult problems arise when the two classes of goods discussed earlier (fairness and aggregative goods) come into conflict. When this happens, efficiency considerations become extremely complex because they concern the concurrent pursuit of both aggregative and fairness consideration. Consider, for example, the ongoing debate in advanced Western societies about the role of social welfare systems. On the one hand, fairness considerations dictate that the unemployed, the poor, and the handicapped be given help by society. Clearly, efficiency becomes an issue in the design of systems for delivering such help. But the problem is more complex than that. It is also argued that doles from the government destroy incentive in those that receive them and that this negatively impacts the aggregative good of *overall economic welfare*. Hence, to the extent society rewards those with no gainful employment, an incentive exists to refuse gainful employment and to refuse to engage in productive labor. Confronted with such complexity, society often throws up its hands and fails to notice the subtle efficiency gains that can be made regarding both sets of goods. For example, Sen has noted that the incentive argument does not apply in its direct form when what is at issue is not differences in decisions but human diversities of particular types. "For example," he observes, "since it is impossible to change one's age rapidly, and particularly hard to change one's sex, the special treatments may not generate incentive problems of the standard kind" (Sen, 1992: 142).

Chapter 6   Moral Free Space Revealed

1. For example, whether advertising hard liquor on television or directly attacking a competitor's product is appropriate.

2. For an excellent discussion of the empirical research on these topics, see Fritzsche (1997).

3. And, if all else fails, one may try to be a utilitarian.

4. A norm-based approach contrasts with an approach based upon a broad conception of "truth," a necessarily exclusive ethical theory. After all, one could not allow a competing theory, which by definition is not true, to be the source of ethical judgment. The result is an authoritarian approach, under which the rightness of all actions are to be judged by the true theory. Thus, if utilitarianism is seen as the exclusive source of truth (which appears to be the position of some of our colleagues in economics and finance) then those who would refuse to trade off particular human lives or states of health against the greater welfare of a

broader community will be found to be ethically wanting (or at least foolish and weak-minded).

5. Jean-Jacques Rousseau wrote *The Social Contract* in 1762.

6. Frederick assumes that ISCT rests upon assumptions that reject a scientific basis for values. He points to the discussion of artifactual economic institutions (1995: 257–258) underpinning the debate over strongly bounded rationality, which he describes as "confident, vainglorious assertions, delivered *ex cathedra*" (244). We meant to emphasize the range of choice available in designing systems, reflected in the great diversity of results. In fact, as will be discussed below, we believe that ISCT is quite compatible with evolutionary economics. We don't believe, however, that it is essential that one identify with precision, and in detail, the specific components of the evolutionary process, so that one could, for example, predict what the process of evolution is likely to produce in the future. Evolution just happens. Social Darwinism is rightly feared, in politics and in literature. It is not something to be forced upon humans by "Eternals" (the masters of time travel in Asimov, 1955) who, by developing an understanding of the core processes of evolution, attempt to bring about a society compatible with their particular conception of the Good and the Right. Ultimately, we agree with Wax (1996), who after considering the critiques of sociobiology, concludes that "although an outright denial of the influence of genetic evolution on human psychology is incoherent, it is a mistake to view that influence as decisively foreclosing the possibility of quite significant variety in social arrangements or patterns of behavior" (311).

7. The common law is judge-made law, deriving from the doctrine of precedent. The common law has produced many principles of tort and contract law.

8. E.g., The Great Adventure case, where the operator of an amusement park was tried for reckless manslaughter after a fire causing loss of life in a Haunted Castle attraction. See Caiazza v. Bally Mfg., Inc., 509 A.2d 187 (N.J. App. Div., 1986), a subsequent civil action, for a brief summary. See also, "'Wrong People Were on Trial' Says Haunted Castle Juror," *Philadelphia Inquirer*, July 22, 1985: 1-A, 6-A, in which the forewoman of the jury is quoted as saying that testimony about whether the defendants' actions were in line with accepted standards of corporate ethics "did help in narrowing [the jurors'] doubts" about whether to vote for acquittal.

9. State v. Richard Knutson, Inc., 537 N.W.2d 420 (Wisc. App., 1993), relying on Walt and Laufer (1991). See also Laufer (1994).

10. Much of this section is based, sometimes literally, on Dunfee (1997).

11. See Hirschman (1970) for the seminal discussion of voice and exit in the context of markets.

12. Incarceration for violation of the criminal laws is a restriction on exit. As long as the criminal laws meet universal standards both as to procedures and substantive scope, then being in jail for having committed a crime should not be considered an impermissible restriction on exit.

13. Assuming that the entire staff is the relevant community, see the discussion in chapter 4.

14. Whether or not each of these alleged social contract terms represents an authentic norm is an empirical question. Certainly it seems plausible that her suggested terms would be agreed to by a substantial majority of employees in a given organization. But there might be special circumstances—where, for example, the retired executives are popular and appear to be providing real value to the firm—in which the fourth of her suggested contract terms might not meet the test of an authentic norm. The main point, though, is her use of the concept of ethical norms supported by an implicit social contract found in a broader political sphere.

Chapter 7 ISCT and Ethical Decision Making: *Priorities, Proxies, and Patterns*

1. Reproduced with the permission of Sikorsky Aircraft Corporation. This example is taken from the *Corporate Counsel's Guide to Business Ethics Policies*, an excellent reference for practical information and examples concerning corporate ethics programs and policies.

2. This is offered as a plausible hypothetical rather than as an actual description of the organization of SmithKline Beecham.

3. Assuming, of course, that no hypernorms are implicated.

4. We would expect some to object to this characterization.

5. The complex model was developed jointly by Mark Hanna, a doctoral student at Wharton, and Tom Dunfee.

Chapter 9 Social Contracts and Stakeholder Obligations

1. Donaldson and Preston describe three, not two, versions of stakeholder theory: the normative, the descriptive, and the instrumental. We mention only two here (the instrumental and the normative) because they are the only candidates for *strategic* corporate adoption. The third, the descriptive stakeholder theories, merely describe or explain corporate activities with no implications for what they should *do*.

2. Note that an instrumental approach can be based on a much narrower conception, that an orientation toward consideration of the interests of closely related stakeholders may make a firm more profitable. The broadest statement, which we are using here, is that a firm will maximize its goals by considering the potential impact of everyone who has any power to affect, positively or negatively, the firm's ability to achieve its goals.

3. See Carroll (1996, chap. 3) for an excellent summary of the concept of stakeholder management.

4. The *Guardian's* Website on The Guardian Stakeholder Debate at http://www.guardian.co.uk/stakeholder/.

5. William Safire, *New York Times*, February 26, 1996.

6. DeGeorge describes this principle both as "widely recognized" and as prohibiting something that is "generally immoral" (1993: 46).

7. There is no evidence that any such thing has occurred, and the example is used here as a hypothetical. See the case "H. B. Fuller in Honduras: Street Children and Substance Abuse" by Norman E. Bowie and Stefanie Ann Lenway in Boatright (1995).

8. The test for an authentic legitimate norm is broader than merely analyzing existing legal rules. Instead, there may be a generally accepted practice inconsistent with the formal legal rules, which has become established as a norm. Even so, one might reasonably expect a high correlation between legal rules and authentic norms for this type of issue.

9. For a description of this issue, see White and Badaracco (1994).

References

Ades, A., & Di Tella, A. 1997. *National champions and corruption: Some unpleasant interventionist arithmetic.* Paper presented at the University of Pennsylvania, Philadelphia.

Akaah, I. P., & Riordan, E. A. 1989. Judgments of marketing professionals about ethical issues in marketing research: A replication and extension. *Journal of Marketing Research,* 26: 112–120.

Akaah, I. P., & Riordan, E. A. 1990. The incidence of unethical practices in marketing research: An empirical investigation. *Journal of the Academy of Marketing Science,* 18(2): 143–152.

Allen, D. J. 1968. *The philosophy of Aristotle.* Oxford, England: Oxford University Press.

Allinson, R. E. 1985. The Confucian golden rule: A negative formulation. *Journal of Chinese Philosophy,* 12: 305–315.

Allinson, R. E. 1990. *Understanding the Chinese mind.* Oxford, England: Oxford University Press.

Aristotle. 1962. *Nicomachean ethics.* New York: Macmillan Publishing Company.

Aristotle. 1975. *The politics of Aristotle.* (E. Barker, Ed. and Trans.) Oxford, England: Oxford University Press.

Aristotle. 1976. *Ethica: The ethics of Aristotle.* (J. A. K. Thompson, Trans.) New York: Penguin.

Arrow, K. J. 1973. Social responsibility and economic efficiency. *Public Policy,* 3(21): 300–317.

Asimov, I. 1955. *The end of eternity.* Greenwich, CT: Fawcett Publications.

Aupperle, K. E., Carroll, A. B., et al. 1985. An empirical examination of the relationship between corporate social responsibility and profitability. *Academy of Management Journal* 28(2): 446–463.

Axelrod, R. 1986. An evolutionary approach to norms. *American Political Science Review,* 80(4): 1095–1111.

Barney, G. O. 1993. *Global 2000 revisited: What shall we do?* Arlington, VA: The Millennium Institute.

Baron, J. 1990. Thinking about consequences. *Journal of Moral Education,* 19(2): 77–87.

Barry, B. 1982. The case for a new international economic order. In J. R. Pennock & J. W. Chapman (Eds.), *Ethics, economics, and the law: Nomos,* vol. 24. New York: New York University Press.

Becker, L. C. 1992. Places for pluralism. *Ethics,* 102: 707–719.

Benchmark corporate environmental survey. 1991. United Nations Centre on Transnational Corporations: 1–37.

Bentham, J. 1789. *An introduction to the principles of morals and legislation.*

Bigoness, W. J. & Blakely, G. L. 1996. A cross-national study of managerial values. *Journal of International Business Studies,* 27(4): 739–752.

Blackstone, W. T. 1974. The right to a livable environment as a human right. In W. T. Blackstone (Ed.), *Philosophy and environmental crisis.* Athens, GA: University of Georgia Press.

Blagov, Y. 1996. *Ethical aspects of privatization in Russia.* Paper presented at the Ninth Annual European Business Ethics Network Conference, Seeheim, Germany.

Blair, M. M. 1995. *Ownership and control: Rethinking corporate governance of the twenty-first century.* Washington, DC: Brookings Institution.

Bliss, C., & Di Tella, R. 1997. *Does competition kill corruption?* Paper presented at the University of Pennsylvania, Philadelphia.

Boatright, J. R. 1994. What's so special about shareholders? *Business Ethics Quarterly,* 4(4): 393–407.

Boatright, J. R. 1995. *Cases in ethics and the conduct of business.* Englewood Cliffs, NJ: Prentice Hall.

Boddewyn, J. J. 1986. *International political strategy: A fourth "generic" strategy.* Paper presented at the Annual Meeting of the American Academy of Management, and at the Annual Meeting of the International Academy of Business.

Boddewyn, J. J., & Brewer, T. L. 1994. International-business political behavior: New theoretical directions. *The Academy of Management Review,* 19(1): 119–143.

Bok, S. 1992. The search for shared ethics. *Common Knowledge,* Winter: 12–24.

Bond, M. H. 1988. Finding universal dimensions of individual variation in multicultural studies of values: The Rokeach and Chinese value surveys. *Journal of Personality and Social Psychology,* 55(6): 1009–1015.

Bowie, N. 1988. The moral obligations of multinational corporations. In S. Luper-Foy (Ed.), *Problems of international justice:* 97–113. Boulder, CO: Westview Press.

Bowie, N. E. 1982. *Business ethics.* Englewood Cliffs, NJ: Prentice Hall.

Brenner, S. N., & Molander, E. A. 1977. Is the ethics of business changing? *Harvard Business Review,* 55(1): 57–71.

Brummer, J. J. 1991. *Corporate responsibility and legitimacy: An interdisciplinary analysis.* New York: Greenwood Press.

Buchanan, A. 1996. Toward a theory of the ethics of bureaucratic organizations. *Business Ethics Quarterly,* 6(4): 419–440.

Buchholz, R. 1989. *Fundamental concepts and problems in business ethics.* Englewood Cliffs, NJ: Prentice Hall.

Buchholz, R. A., and Rosenthal, S. B. 1998. *Business ethics: The pragmatic path beyond principles to process.* Upper Saddle River, NJ: Prentice Hall.

Butterfield, K. D., Trevino, L. K., & Ball, G. A. 1996. Punishment from the manager's perspective: A grounded investigation and inductive model. *Academy of Management Journal,* 39(6): 1479–1512.

Cameron, R. 1989. *A concise economic history of the world.* Oxford, England: Oxford University Press.

Carroll, A. B. 1979. A three-dimensional conceptual model of corporate social performance. *Academy of Management Review,* 4: 497–505.

Carroll, A. B. 1996. *Ethics and stakeholder management* (3rd ed.). Cincinnati: SouthWestern.

Carroll, S. J., & Gannon, M. J. 1997. *Ethical dimensions of international management.* Thousand Oaks, CA: Sage.

Carter, S. L. 1992. Custom, adjudication, and Petrushevsky's watch: Some notes from the intellectual property front. *Virginia Law Review,* 78: 129–140.

Caux round table principles for business. 1994. Washington, DC: Caux Round Table Secretariat.

Cavanaugh G. F., Moberg, D. J., & Velasquez, M. G. 1981. The ethics of organizational politics. *Academy of Management Review,* 6(3): 363–374.

Clarkson, M. B. E. 1994. *A risk-based model of stakeholder theory.* Proceedings of the Toronto Conference on Stakeholder Theory. Centre for Corporate Social Performance and Ethics, University of Toronto, Toronto, Canada.

Clarkson, M. B. E. 1995. A stakeholder framework for analyzing and evaluating corporate social performance. *Academy of Management Review,* 20(1): 92–117.

Clifford, M. 1991. Counting the cost: South Korea tackles appalling work-safety record. *Far Eastern Economic Review,* 154(47): 64–65.

Coase, R. H. 1991. The nature of the firm. In O. E. Williamson and S. G. Winter (Eds.), *The nature of the firm: Origins, evolution, and development:* 18–33. New York: Oxford University Press.

Cochran, P. L., & Wood, R. A. 1984. Corporate social responsibility and financial performance. *Academy of Management Journal,* 27: 42–56.

Cohen, W., & Czepiec, H. 1988. The role of ethics in gathering corporate intelligence. *Journal of Business Ethics,* 7(3): 199–203.

Confucius. 1948. *The four books.* (J. Legge, Trans.) Shanghai: International Publication Society.

Conlisk, J. 1996. Why bounded rationality? *Journal of Economic Literature,* 34: 669–700.

Conry, E. J. 1995. A critique of social contracts. *Business Ethics Quarterly,* 5(2): 187–212.

Corporate Counsel's Guide to Business Ethics Policies. Current service. Chesterland, OH: Business Laws, Inc.

D'Amato, A. 1990. Its a bird, it's a plane, it's jus cogens! *Connecticut Journal of International Law,* 6(1): 1–6.

DeGeorge, R. T. 1993. *Competing with integrity in international business.* Oxford, England: Oxford University Press.

DePaulo, B. M., Zuckerman, M., & Rosenthal, R. 1980. *Journal of Communication,* 30(4): 129–139.

Dern, D. P. 1994. *The Internet guide for new users.* New York: McGraw-Hill.

Dienhart, J. W. 1995. *Moral imagination and the foundations of business ethics: Implications for stakeholder and integrative social contracts theories.* Paper presented at the annual meeting of the Society for Business Ethics, Vancouver, Canada.

Donaldson, T. 1982. *Corporations and morality.* Englewood Cliffs, NJ: Prentice Hall.

Donaldson, T. 1989. *The ethics of international business.* New York: Oxford University Press.

Donaldson, T. 1990. Morally privileged relationships. *Journal of Value Inquiry,* 24: 1–15.

Donaldson, T. 1994. When integration fails: The logic of prescription and description in business ethics. *Business Ethics Quarterly,* 4: 157–169.

Donaldson, T. 1996. Values in tension: Ethics away from home. *Harvard Business Review,* 74(5): 48–56.

Donaldson, T., & Dunfee, T. W. 1994. Toward a unified conception of business ethics: Integrative social contracts theory. *Academy of Management Review,* 19(2): 252-284.

Donaldson, T., & Dunfee, T. W. 1995. Integrative social contracts theory: A communitarian conception of economic ethics. *Economics and Philosophy,* 11(1): 85–112.

Donaldson, T., & Preston, L. E. 1995. The stakeholder theory for the corporation: Concepts, evidence, implications. *Academy of Management Review,* 20(1): 65–91.

Dubinksy, A. J., & Loken, B. 1989. Analyzing ethical decision making in marketing. *Journal of Business Research,* 19: 83–107.

Dunfee, T. W. 1987. Work-related ethical attitudes: A key to profitability? In S. P. Sethi & C. M. Falbe (Eds.), *Business and society: Dimensions of conflict and cooperation.* Lexington, MA: Lexington Books.

Dunfee, T. W. 1991. Business ethics and extant social contracts. *Business Ethics Quarterly,* 1(1): 23–51.

Dunfee, T. W. 1996. *Ethical challenges of managing across cultures.* Invited plenary paper presented at the Ninth Annual European Business Ethics Network Conference, Seeheim, Germany.

Dunfee, T. W. 1997. On the synergistic, interdependent relationship of business ethics and law. *American Business Law Journal,* 34(2): 317–328.

Dunfee, T. W., & Donaldson, T. 1995. Contractarian business ethics: Current status and next steps. *Business Ethics Quarterly,* 5(2): 173–186.

Dunfee, T. W., Gibson, F. F., Blackburn, J. D., Whitman, D., McCarty, F. W., Brennan, B. A., & Cohen, D. B. 1996. *Modern business law.* New York: McGraw-Hill.

Dunfee, T. W., & Maurer, V. C. 1992. Corporate attorney whistle-blowing: Devising a proper standard. *Business and Professional Ethics Journal,* 11(3&4): 3–39.

Dunlap, A. J. 1996. *Mean business.* New York: Times Business.

Dutch/Shell, R. 1998. *The Royal Dutch/Shell Group commitment to health, safety, and environment (Hse)*. Royal Dutch/Shell.

Economist. 1995a. Multinationals and their morals. 337: 18–20; UK 20–22.

Economist. 1995b. Oil platforms: Hollow shell. 335: 76–77; UK 110–111.

Economist. 1996. The fun of being a multinational. 340 (7975): 51–52.

Economist. 1997. Shellman says sorry. 343: 65; UK 95.

Edmond, M. 1997. Berkeley's boycotts hit all seven major oil companies in area. *Npn: National Petroleum News,* 89: 28.

Enderle, G. 1995. *What is international? A topology of international spheres and its relevance for business ethics.* Paper presented at the annual meeting of the International Association of Business and Society, Vienna, Austria.

Epstein, R. A. 1992. International News Service v. Associated Press: Custom and law as sources of property rights in news. *Virginia Law Review,* 78: 85.

Esposito, J. L., 1988. *Islam: The straight path.* New York: Oxford University Press.

Etzioni, A. 1988. *The moral dimension: Toward a new economics.* New York: The Free Press.

Evan, W. M., and Freeman, R. E. 1988. A stakeholder theory of the modern corporation: Kantian capitalism. In T. L. Beauchamp & N. E. Bowie (Eds.), *Ethical theory and business* (3rd ed.). Englewood Cliffs, NJ: Prentice Hall.

Ferrell, O. C., & Gresham, L. G. 1985. A contingency framework for understanding ethical decision making in marketing. *Journal of Marketing,* 49(3): 87–96.

Financial Times. 1997. Europe's most respected companies: BP steals the limelight from Shell. London, September 24: I–II.

Fishbein, M., & Ajzen, I. 1975. *Belief, attitude, intention and behavior: An introduction to theory and research.* Reading, MA: Addison Wesley.

Fisher, D. 1996. A comment on bribery. E-mail communication, April 16, in IABS Listserver.

Fortune. 1997. It's not easy being green. 136: 124; European 56.

Frank, R. H. 1988. *Passions within reason: The strategic role of the emotions.* New York: W. W. Norton & Company.

Frank, R. H. 1993. A new contractarian view of tax and regulatory policy in the emerging market economies. *Social Philosophy and Policy,* 258–281.

Frank, R. 1996. Can socially responsible firms survive in a competitive environment? In D. M. Messick & A. E. Tenbrunsel (Eds.), *Behavioral research and business ethics:* 86–103. New York: Russell Sage Foundation.

Franklin Research and Development Corporation. 1992. Human rights: Investing for a better world. Boston, MA.

Frederick, W. C. 1991. The moral authority of transnational corporate codes. *Journal of Business Ethics,* 10(3): 165–177.

Frederick, W. C. 1995. *Values, nature and culture in the American corporation.* New York: Oxford University Press.

Freeman, R. E. 1984. *Strategic management: A stakeholder approach.* Boston, MA: Pitman.

Freeman, R. E., & Gilbert, Jr., D. R. 1988. *Corporate strategy and the search for ethics*. Englewood Cliffs, NJ: Prentice Hall.

French, P. 1979. The corporation as a moral person. *American Philosophical Quarterly*, 16: 207–215.

Fritzsche, D. J. 1997. *Business ethics: A global and managerial perspective*. New York: McGraw-Hill.

Fritzsche, D. J., & Becker, H. 1983. Ethical behavior of marketing managers. *Journal of Business Ethics*, 2(4): 291–299.

Fritzsche, D. J., & Becker, H. 1984. Linking management behavior to ethical philosophy—An empirical investigation. *Academy of Management Journal*, 27(1): 166–175.

Fritzsche, D. J., Huo, P. Y., Sugai, S., & Dun-Hou, S. 1995. Exploring the ethical behavior of managers: A comparative study of four countries. *Asia Pacific Journal of Management*, 12(2): 37–61.

Fukuyama, F. 1995. *Trust: The social virtues and the creation of prosperity*. The Free Press.

Gauthier, D. 1986. *Morals by agreement*. Oxford: Oxford University Press.

Gert, B. 1988. *Morality: A new justification of the moral rules*. New York: Oxford University Press.

Gilligan, C. 1982. *In a different voice*. Cambridge, MA: Harvard University Press.

Goldberg, L. A., & Greenberg, M. R. 1993. Ethical issues for industrial hygienists: Survey results and suggestions. *American Industrial Hygiene Association Journal*, 54(3): 127–134.

Goodpaster, K. E. 1991. Business ethics and stakeholder analysis. *Business Ethics Quarterly*, 1(1): 53–74.

Goodpaster, K. E., & Holloran, T. E. 1994. In defense of a paradox. *Business Ethics Quarterly*, 4(4): 423–29.

Greenberg, J. 1990. Employee theft as a reaction to underpayment inequity: The hidden cost of pay cuts. *Journal of Applied Psychology*, 75: 561–568.

Habermas, J. 1990. *Moral consciousness and communicative action*. (Lenhardt, C., & Nicholsen, S. W., Trans.) Cambridge, MA: MIT Press.

Hadari, S. A. 1988. Value trade-off. *The Journal of Politics*, 50: 655–676.

Haidt, J., Koller, S. H., & Dias, M. G. 1993. Affect, culture, and morality, or is it wrong to eat your dog? *Journal of Personality and Social Psychology*, 65(4): 613–628.

Hampden-Turner, C., &, Trompenaars, F. 1993. *The seven cultures of capitalism*. New York: Doubleday.

Hardin, R. 1988. *Morality within the limits of reason*. Chicago: University of Chicago Press.

Hargreaves Heap, S. 1989. *Rationality in economics*. Oxford: Basil Blackwell.

Hartman, E. M. 1996a. *Organizational ethics and the good life*. New York: Oxford University Press.

Hartman, E. M. 1996b. Personal letter to Thomas Dunfee, August 23.

Harveson, P. & Corzine, R. 1997. In defense of international reputations. *Financial Times*. London, October 31: 16.

Hegel, G. W. F. 1807 (trans. 1977). *Phenomenology of spirit.* Oxford: Clarendon Press.

Hegarty, W. H., & Sims, H. P. 1978. Some determinants of unethical decision behavior: An experiment. *Journal of Applied Psychology,* 63(4): 451–457.

Heimann, F. F. 1994. Should foreign bribery be a crime? Cited in Nichols, P. M. 1997. Outlawing transnational bribery through the World Trade Organization. *Law and Policy in International Business,* 28(2): 305–386 (footnote 73).

Hillman, A., & Keim, G. 1995. International variation in the business-government interface: Institutional and organizational considerations. *Academy of Management Review,* 20(1): 193.

Hirschman, A. O. 1970. *Exit, voice, and loyalty.* Cambridge, MA: Harvard University Press.

Hofmann, M. A. 1988. Loss control can be lost in translation. *Business Insurance* (November 21): 11.

Hofstede, G. 1980. *Culture's consequences.* Beverly Hills, CA: Sage.

Hosmer, L. T. 1994. Strategic planning as if ethics mattered. *Strategic Management Journal,* 15: 17–34.

Hosmer, L. T. 1995. Trust: The connecting link between organizational theory and philosophical ethic. *Academy of Management Review,* 20(2): 379–403.

Hosseini, J. C., & Brenner, S. N. 1992. The stakeholder theory of the firm: A methodology to generate business ethics. *Business Ethics Quarterly,* 2(2): 99–119.

HR Magazine. 1995. Do corporate executives think ethics matter? 40(10): 90.

Hunt, S. D., Chonko, L. B., & Wilcox, J. B. 1984. Ethical problems of marketing researchers. *Journal of Marketing Research,* 21(3): 309–324.

Hunt, S. D., & Vitell, S. 1986. A general theory of marketing ethics. *Journal of Macromarketing,* 6(1): 5–16.

Hunt, S. D., Wood, V. R., & Chonko, L. B. 1989. Corporate ethical values and organizational commitment in marketing. *Journal of Marketing,* 53(3): 79–90.

Husted, B. W. 1996. *An empirical critique of integrative social contracts theory.* Paper presented at the annual meeting of the Society for Business Ethics, Quebec City, Canada.

Institute of Moralogy. 1987. *An outline of moralogy: A new approach to moral science.* Kashiwa-Shi, Japan: The Institute of Moralogy.

Ivancevich, J. M., DeFrank, R. S., & Gregory, P. R. 1992. The Soviet enterprise director: An important resource before and after the coup. *Academy of Management Executive,* 6(1): 42–55.

Jones, T. M. 1991. Ethical decision making by individuals in organizations: An issue-contingent model. *Academy of Management Review,* 16(2): 366–395.

Jones, T. 1995. Instrumental stakeholder theory: Synthesis of ethics and economics. *Academy of Management Review,* 20(2): 404–437.

Jones, W. K. 1994. A theory of social norms. *University of Illinois Law Review*, 3: 545–596.

Kabanoff, B., Waldersee, R., & Cohen. 1995. Espoused values and organizational change themes. *Academy of Management Journal*, 38(4): 1075–1104.

Kahneman, D., Knetsch, J. L., & Thaler R. 1986. Fairness as a constraint on profit seeking: Entitlements in the market. *American Economic Review*, 76(4): 728–741.

Kant, I. 1785/1959. *Foundations of the metaphysics of morals*. (L. W. Beck, Trans.) New York: Liberal Arts Press.

Kant, I. 1788/1956. *Critique of practical reason*. (L. W. Beck, Trans.) New York: Library of Liberal Arts.

Kanter, R. M. 1991. Transcending business boundaries: 12,000 world managers view change. *Harvard Business Review*, 69(3):151–166.

Keeley, M. 1988. *A social contract theory of organizations*. Notre Dame, IN: University of Notre Dame Press.

Keeley, M. 1995. Continuing the social contract tradition. *Business Ethics Quarterly*, 5(2): 241–255.

Kline, J. 1994. *Corporate social responsibility and transnational corporations*. World Investment Report 1994: Transnational Corporations, Employment and the Workplace: 313–324. United Nations: New York and Geneva.

Kluckhorn, C. 1955. Ethical relativity: Sic et non. *Journal of Philosophy*, 52: 663–677.

Knott, D. 1997. Now God also is against Shell. *Oil and Gas Journal*, 95: 26.

Kohlberg, L. 1968. The child as a moral philosopher. *Psychology Today*, 9(2): 25–30.

Kohlberg, L. 1981. *Essays in moral development, volume I: The philosophy of moral development*. New York: Harper & Row.

Kohlberg, L. 1984. *Essays in moral development, volume II: The psychology of moral development*. New York: Harper & Row.

Kollack, P. 1992. *The emergence of markets and networks: An experimental study of uncertainty, commitment, and trust*. Paper presented at the SASE Conference, Irvine, CA.

Kramer, R. M., & Brewer, M. B. 1986. Social group identity and the emergence of cooperation in resource conservation dilemmas. In Wilke, H., Messick, D., & Rutte, C. (Eds.), *Experimental Social Dilemmas*: 205–234. Frankfurt: Verlag Peter Lang.

Kung, H. 1991. *Global responsibility: In search of a new world ethic*. New York: Crossroad, 63–69.

Kurland, N. 1996. Sales agents and clients: Ethics, incentives, and a modified theory of planned behavior. *Human Relations*, 49(1): 51–74.

Laczniak, G. R. 1990. International marketing ethics. *Bridges*, 155–177.

Ladd, J. 1970. Morality and the ideal of rationality in corporate organizations. The monist. 1970. In T. Donaldson & P. Werhane (Eds.), *Ethical issues in business* (2d ed.): 110–122. Englewood Cliffs, NJ: Prentice Hall.

Laufer, W. 1994. Corporate bodies and guilty minds. *Emory Law Journal*, 43(2): 648–730.

Laufer, W. S. 1996. Integrity, diligence, and the limits of good corporate citizenship. *American Business Law Journal,* 34(2): 157–181.

Limited, S. I. 1996. *Society's changing expectations: Report of roundtable participants.* The Hague, The Netherlands, Royal Dutch Shell.

Locke, J. 1690/1948. *The second treatise of civil government and a letter concerning toleration.* Oxford: Basil Blackwell.

Los Angeles Times. 1987. Talks with Texaco dragging, Pennzoil claims. (July 20): 2.

Lydenberg, S. 1996. Presentation at the 1996 Stakeholder Conference at the University of Toronto, sponsored by the Sloan Foundation, May 15.

MacDonald, G. M. 1988. Ethical perceptions of Hong Kong/Chinese business managers. *Journal of Business Ethics,* 7: 835–845.

MacIntyre, A. C. 1981. *After virtue: A study in moral theory.* Notre Dame, IN: University of Notre Dame Press.

Maitland, I. 1994. The morality of the corporation: An empirical or normative disagreement. *Business Ethics Quarterly,* 4(4): 445–458.

May, L. 1987. *The morality of groups: Collective responsibility, group-based harm, and corporate rights.* Notre Dame, IN: University of Notre Dame Press.

Mayer, A. E. 1991. *Images of women and the eclipse of Islamic personal status law.* Working Paper 91-155, Department of Legal Studies, The Wharton School, University of Pennsylvania, PA.

Mayer, D. 1994. Hypernorms and integrative social contracts theory. *Proceedings: International Association for Business and Society.* Annual conference, Hilton Head, SC.

Mayer, D. & Cava, A. 1995. Social contract theory and gender discrimination. *Business Ethics Quarterly,* 5(2): 257–270.

McCabe, D. L., Dukerich, J. M., & Dutton, J. E. 1991. Context, values and moral dilemmas: Comparing the choices of business and law school students. *Journal of Business Ethics,* 10: 951–960.

Messick, D. M. 1991. On the evolution of group-based altruism. In R. Selten (Ed.), *Game equilibrium models.* Berlin: Springer-Verlag.

Messick, D., & Bazerman, M. H. 1996. Ethical leadership and the psychology of decision-making. *Sloan Management Review,* 37(2): 9–22.

Mill, J. S. 1965. *Mill's ethical writings.* (J. B. Schneewind, Ed.) New York: Collier.

Mitchell, R. K., Agle, B. R., & Wood, D. J. 1997. Toward a theory of stakeholder identification and salience: Defining the principle of who and what really counts. *Academy of Management Review,* 22(4): 853–886.

Moore, G. E. 1903/1951. *Principia ethica.* Cambridge: Cambridge University Press.

More, Sir Thomas, Saint. 1516/1753. *The Common-wealth of Utopia.* (J. Chattin, Trans.) Philadelphia: Robinson.

Morton, S. W. 1984. *Japan: Its history and culture* (3rd ed.). New York: McGraw-Hill.

Nadelmann, E. A. 1990. Global prohibition regimes: The evolution of norms in international society. *International Organization,* 44: 479–526.

Nagel, I. H., & Swenson, W. M. 1993. The Federal Sentencing Guidelines for Corporations: Their development, theoretical underpinnings, and some thoughts about their future. *Washington University Law Quarterly*, 71: 205–258.

Nardin, T. 1983. *Law, morality and the relations of states*. Princeton, NJ: Princeton University Press.

Nash, L. L. 1981. Ethics without the sermon. *Harvard Business Review*, 59: 78–90.

Nelson, J. 1994. Business ethics in a competitive market. *Journal of Business Ethics*, 13(9): 663–667.

Nelson, J. 1996. *A communitarian contract for business: Conditions necessary and sufficient*. Revision of paper presented at Society for the Advancement of Socio-Economics Meeting, HEC School of Management, Jouy-en-Josas, France.

Newman, K. L. 1996. *Good apples need good barrels: The role of person-situation congruence in ethical decision-making*. Paper presented at the 1996 meeting of the Academy of Management, Cincinnati.

Nichols, P. M. 1997. Outlawing transnational bribery through the World Trade Organization. *Law and Policy in International Business*, 28(2): 305–386.

Nickel, J. W. 1974. Classification by race in compensatory programs. *Ethics*, 84(2): 146–150.

Note. 1990. Constructing the state extraterritorially: Jurisdiction discourse, the national interest, and transnational norms. *Harvard Law Review*, 103: 1273.

Noonan, J. T. 1984. *Bribes*. New York: Macmillan Publishing Company.

Oil and Gas Journal. 1997. Shell reveals Brent spar safety analysis. 95: 34–35.

Orts, E. W. 1992. Beyond shareholders: Interpreting corporate constituency statutes. *George Washington Law Review*, 61(1): 14–135.

Paine, L. S. 1994. Law, ethics, and managerial judgment. *Journal of Legal Studies Education*, 12(2): 153–169.

Parker, K., & Neylon, L. B. 1989. Compelling the law of human rights. *Hastings International & Comparative Law Review*, 12: 411.

Pastin, M., & Hooker, M. 1980. Ethics and the Foreign Corrupt Practices Act. *Business Horizons*: 43–47.

Pava, M. L. 1998. Developing a religiously grounded business ethics: A Jewish perspective. *Business Ethics Quarterly*, 8(1): 65–83.

Peterson, R. B. (Ed.). 1993. *Managers and national culture: A global perspective*. Westport, CT: Quorum Books.

Phillips, R.A. 1997. Stakeholder theory and a principle of fairness. *Business Ethics Quarterly*, 7(1): 51–66.

Piderit, J. J. 1993. *The ethical foundations of economics*. Washington, DC: Georgetown University Press.

Plato. 1968. *The republic*. (A. Bloom, Trans.) New York: Basic Books.

Poindexter, G. C. 1995. Addressing morality in urban Brownfield redevelopment: Using stakeholder theory to craft legal process. *Virginia Environmental Law Journal*, 15(1): 37–76.

Polonsky, M. J. 1996. The importance of internal stakeholders to Japanese management practices: Rejoinder to Steadman, Green and Zimmerer. *International Journal of Management,* 13(2): 193–197.

Posner, B. Z., & Schmidt, W. H. 1996. The values of business and federal government executives: More different than alike. *Public Personnel Management,* 25(3): 277–289.

Posner, E. A. 1996. The regulation of groups: The influence of legal and nonlegal sanctions on collective action. *University of Chicago Law Review,* 63: 133–197.

Post, R. J., & Goodpaster, K. E. 1981. *H. J. Heinz Company: The administration of policy (A).* Harvard Business School Case 9-382-034.

Preston, L. E. & Windsor, D. 1991. *The rules of the game in the global economy: Policy regimes for international business.* Norwell, MA: Kluwer Academic Publishers.

Prevost, R. 1997. *Integrated [sic] social contracts theory and business ethics.* (Working draft.) Copy of unpublished manuscript available from authors.

Puffer, S. & McCarthy, D. J. 1995. Finding the common ground in Russian and American business ethics. *California Management Review,* 37(2).

Puffer, S. M., & McCarthy, D. J. 1997. Business ethics in a transforming economy: Applying the integrative social contracts theory to Russia. *University of Pennsylvania Journal of International Economic Law,* 18(4): 1281–1304.

Quinn, D. P., & Jones, T. 1995. An agent morality view of business policy. *Academy of Management Review,* 20(1): 22–42.

Randall, D. M. 1989. Taking stock: Can the theory of reasoned action explain unethical conduct? *Journal of Business Ethics,* 8: 873-882.

Randall, D. M., & Gibson, A. M. 1990. Methodology in business ethics research: A review and critical assessment. *Journal of Business Ethics,* 9(6): 457–471.

Rawls, J. 1971. *A theory of justice.* Cambridge, MA: Harvard University Press.

Rawls, J. 1993. *Political liberalism.* New York: Columbia University Press.

Reidenbach, R. E. &, Robin, D. 1990. Toward the development of a multidimensional scale for improving evaluations of business ethics. *Journal of Business Ethics,* 9(8): 639–653.

Rest, J. R. 1979. *Development in judging moral issues.* Minneapolis: University of Minnesota Press.

Richardson, H. S. 1990. Specifying norms as a way to resolve concrete ethical problems. *Philosophy and Public Affairs,* 19(4): 279–310.

Roberts, R. W. 1992. Determinants of corporate social responsibility disclosure: An application of stakeholder theory. *Accounting, Organizations and Society,* 17(6): 595–612.

Robertson, D. C., & Nicholson, N. 1996. Expressions of corporate social responsibility in U.K. firms. *Journal of Business Ethics,* 15(10): 1095–1106.

Robertson, D. C. & Ross, W. T., Jr. 1995. Decision-making processes on ethical issues: the impact of a social contract perspective. *Business Ethics Quarterly,* 5(2): 213–240.

Robertson, D. C., & Schlegelmilch, B. 1992. *Corporate ethics initiatives: An empirical comparison of the United States and Great Britain.* Paper presented at the European Business Ethics Network Conference, Paris. Published in *EBEN '92 International Conference—Shaping Cities: The Role and Responsibilities of Business.*

Ross, W. D. 1930. *The right and the good.* Oxford, England: Oxford University Press.

Rousseau, D. M. 1995. *Psychological contracts in organizations.* Thousand Oaks, CA: Sage Publications.

Rowan, J. R. 1997. Grounding hypernorms: Toward a contractarian theory of business ethics. *Economics and Philosophy,* 13(1): 107–112.

Rynning, H. 1996. Political liberalism and integrative social contracts theory. In J. Logdson & K. Rehbein (Eds.), *Proceedings of the Seventh Annual Meeting of the International Association for Business and Society:* 113–118. Santa Fe, NM.

Salbu, S. R. 1994. True codes versus voluntary codes of ethics in international markets: Towards the preservation of colloquy in emerging global communications. *University of Pennsylvania Journal of International Business Law,* 15: 327.

San, Z. F., 1987. Traditional western value from Asian perspective. *Dialectics and Humanism,* 14(3/4): 57–64.

Satchell, M. J. 1994. Deadly trade in toxics. *U.S. News & World Report,* March 7: 64, 66, 68.

Savage, G. T., Nix, T. W., Whitehead, C. J., & Blair, J. D. 1991. Strategies for assessing and managing organizational stakeholders. *Academy of Management Executive,* 5(2): 61–75.

Scheppele, K. L. 1993. It's just not right: The ethics of insider trading. *Law and Contemporary Problems,* 56(3): 123–173.

Scheppele, K. L., & Waldron, J. 1991. Contractarian methods in political and legal evaluation. *Yale Journal of Law and the Humanities,* 3: 195–230.

Schwartz, S. H., & Bilsky, W. 1987. Toward a psychological structure of human values. *Journal of Personality and Social Psychology,* 53: 550–562.

Sen, A. K. 1977. Rational fools: A critique of the behavioural foundations of economic theory. *Philosophy and Public Affairs,* 6: 317–344.

Sen, A. K. 1985. The moral standing of the market. *Social Philosophy & Policy,* 3: 1–19.

Sen, A. K. 1992. *Inequality reexamined.* New York; Cambridge, MA: Russell Sage Foundation; Harvard University Press.

Shea, V. 1994. *The core rules of netiquette.* San Francisco: Albion Books.

Shell, G. R. 1988. Substituting ethical standards for common law rules in commercial cases: An emerging statutory trend. *Northwestern Law Review,* 82(4): 1198–1254.

Shell, G. 1991a. Opportunism and trust in the negotiation of commercial contracts: Toward a new cause of action. *Vanderbilt Law Review,* 44: 221–282.

Shell, G. 1991b. When is it legal to lie in negotiations? *Sloan Management Review*, 32(3): 93–101.

Sheppard, B. H., Hartwick, J., & Warshaw, P. R. 1988. The theory of reasoned action: A meta-analysis of past research with recommendations for modifications and future research. *Journal of Consumer Research*, 15(3) 325–343.

Shue, H. 1980. *Basic rights: Subsistence, affluence, and U.S. foreign policy*. Princeton, NJ: Princeton University Press.

Shue, H. 1981. Exporting hazards. *Ethics*, 91: 579–580.

Simmons, A. J. 1979. *Moral principles and political obligations*. Princeton, NJ: Princeton University Press.

Simmons, A. J. 1988. Consent and fairness in planning land use. *Business & Professional Ethics Journal*, 6(2): 5–20.

Solomon, R. C. 1992. *Ethics and excellence: Cooperation and integrity in business*. New York: Oxford University Press.

Sorley, W. R. 1904/1969. *The ethics of naturalism* (2d ed.). Freeport, NY: Books for Libraries Press.

Steadman, M. E., & Garrison, S. H. 1993. The impact of stakeholder theory on the international firm: A United States v. Japanese comparison. *International Journal of Management*, 10(3): 325–331.

Stecklow, S. 1997. Student applications for financial aid give lots of false answers. *Wall Street Journal*, March 11: 1.

Steidlmeier, P. 1990. Hazardous wastes: Ethical dilemmas of ends and means, heroes and villains. In Hoffman, W. M., Frederick, R., & Petry, E. S. (Eds.), *The corporation, ethics and the environment*. Greenwich, CT: Quorum Books.

Steinmann, H., & Scherer, A. G. 1997. Intercultural management between universalism and relativism: Fundamental problems in international business ethics and the contribution of recent German philosophical approaches. In S. Urban (Ed.), *Europe in the global economy*. Wiesbaden, Germany: Gabler.

Sternberg, Elaine. 1995. Letter to the editor. *Financial Times*, August 29: 10.

Stewart, S., & Donleavy, G. 1995. *Whose business values? Some Asian and cross-cultural perspectives*. Hong Kong: Hong Kong University Press.

Strandell, B. 1991. A question of ethics. *Executive Excellence*, 8(1): 15.

Strong, K. C., & Ringer, R. C. 1997. *An empirical test of integrative social contracts theory: Social hypernorms and authentic community norms in corporate drug testing programs*. Proceedings of the International Association for Business and Society, annual meeting.

Strudler, A. 1995. On the ethics of deception in negotiation. *Business Ethics Quarterly*, 5(4): 805–822.

Swinyard, W. R., Rinne, H., & Kau, A. K, 1990. The morality of software piracy: A cross-cultural analysis. *Journal of Business Ethics*, 9: 655–664.

Symposium on Impartiality and Ethical Theory. 1991. *Ethics* (Special Ed.), 101: 698–864.

Symposium on Law, Economics, and Norms. 1996. *University of Pennsylvania Law Review*, 144(5).

Taka, I. 1996a. Integrative social contracts theory and business ethics: Possibility of transparency test. *Organizational Science,* 29(3): 69–78. (Japanese journal, in Japanese.)

Taka, I. 1996b. A new direction of integrative social contracts theory. *Journal of Japan Society for Business Ethics,* 3: 3–15. (In Japanese.)

Taka, I., & Dunfee, T. W. 1997. Japanese moralogy as business ethics. *Journal of Business Ethics,* 16(5): 507–519.

Tarantino, D. 1997. *The legacy of the twin cities region: Lessons for the global frontier.* Minneapolis: Minnesota Center for Corporate Responsibility.

Taylor, C. 1989. *Sources of the self.* Cambridge, MA: Harvard University Press.

Taylor, C. 1992. *Multiculturalism and the politics of recognition: An essay by Charles Taylor.* Princeton, NJ: Princeton University Press.

Thaler, R. H. 1992. *The winner's curse.* New York: The Free Press.

Thompson, J. K., Wartick, S. L., & Smith, H. L. 1991. Integrating corporate social performance and stakeholder management: Implications for a research agenda in small business. *Research in Corporate Social Performance and Policy,* 12: 207–230.

Towards a global ethic. 1993. Council for a Parliament of the World's Religions, Chicago, IL.

Trevino, L. K. 1986. Ethical decision making in organizations: A person-situation interactionist model. *Academy of Management Review,* 11: 601–617.

Trevino, L. K. 1992. The social effects of punishment in organizations: A justice perspective. *Academy of Management Review,* 17(4): 647–76.

Trevino, L. K., & Weaver, G. R. 1994. Business ethics/business ethics: One field or two? *Business Ethics Quarterly,* 4: 13–128.

Trevino, L. K., & Youngblood, S. A. 1990. Bad apples in bad barrels: A causal analysis of ethical decision-making behavior. *Journal of Applied Psychology,* 75(4): 378–385.

Tsalikis, J., & Wachukwu, O. 1991. A comparison of Nigerian to American views of bribery and extortion in international commerce. *Journal of Business Ethics,* 10 (2): 85–98.

Tsalikis, J., & LaTour, M. S. 1995. Bribery and extortion in international business: Ethical perceptions of Greeks compared to Americans. *Journal of Business Ethics,* 4: 249–265.

Turner, C. H., & Trompenaars, A. 1993. *The seven cultures of capitalism.* New York: Doubleday.

Tyler, T. R. 1998. *Procedural strategies for gaining deference: Increasing social harmony or creating false consciousness?* Paper presented at the Conference on Ethics and Social Influence, Northwestern University, January. Copy available from Dunfee.

Ullmann, A. 1985. Data in search of a theory: A critical examination of the relationships among social performance, social disclosure, and economic performance of U.S. firms. *Academy of Management Review,* 10(3): 540–557.

Umezu, M. 1995. International communitarianism and moral consensus building procedure. *Journal of Japan Society for Business Ethics,* 2: 21–32. (In Japanese.)

Universal declaration of human rights. 1948. Reprinted in T. Donaldson & P. Werhane (Eds.). 1979. *Ethical issues in business:* 252–255. Englewood Cliffs, NJ: Prentice Hall.

Van Luijk, H. 1992. *Rights and interests in a participatory market society:* 1–31. Paper presented at INSEAD.

Velasquez, M. 1998. *Business ethics: Concepts and cases.* (4th ed.). Upper Saddle River, NJ: Prentice Hall.

Vidaver-Cohen, D. 1993. Creating and maintaining ethical work climates: Anomie in the workplace and implications for managing change. *Business Ethics Quarterly,* 3(4): 343–358.

Vidaver-Cohen, D. 1995. Creating ethical work climates: A socioeconomic perspective. *The Journal of Socio-Economics,* 24(2): 317–343.

Vidaver-Cohen, D. Forthcoming. Moral climate in business firms: A conceptual framework for analysis and change. *Journal of Business Ethics.*

Velasquez, M. 1992. International business, morality, and the common good. *Business Ethics Quarterly,* 2: 27–40.

Vogel, D. 1992. The globalization of business ethics: Why America remains distinctive. *The California Management Review,* 35(1): 30–49.

Wagstyl, S., & Corzine, R. 1997. Rights and wrongs: Stefan Wagstyl and Robert Corzine on Shell's new stance on business practices. *Financial Times,* London, March 18: 24.

Wall Street Journal. 1996. Ads for liquor on TV worry FCC chairman. November 7: B10.

Walt, S. and Laufer, W. S. 1991. Why personhood doesn't matter: Corporate criminal liability and sanctions. *American Journal of Criminal Law,* 18(3): 263–287.

Walzer, M. 1992. Moral minimalism. In W. R. Shea & G. A. Spadafora (Eds.), *The twilight of probability: Ethics and politics.* Canton, MA: Science History Publications.

Walzer, M. 1994. *Thick and thin: Moral argument at home and abroad.* Notre Dame, IN: University of Notre Dame Press.

Wartick, S. L. 1995. *Organizational cultures in transnational companies: An empirical analysis of shared managerial values.* Paper presented at the Academy of Management Meeting, Vancouver, Canada.

Wax, A. L. 1996. Against nature—On Robert Wright's The moral animal. *University of Chicago Law Review,* 63: 307–359.

Weber, J. 1991. Adapting Kohlberg to enhance the assessment of managers' moral reasoning. *Business Ethics Quarterly,* 1(3): 293–318.

White, W., & Badaracco, J. 1994. *AT&T consumer products.* Harvard Business School Case 9-392-108.

Williams, B. 1985. *Ethics and the limits of philosophy.* Cambridge, MA: Harvard University Press.

Wilson, E. O. 1978. *Sociobiology*. Cambridge, MA: Harvard University Press.

Wilson, J. Q. 1993. *The moral sense*. New York: The Free Press.

Wolf, S. 1992. Two levels of pluralism. *Ethics* 102: 785–798.

Wood, D. J. 1991. Social issues in management: Theory and research in corporate social performance. *Journal of Management,* 17(2): 383–384.

Wood, D. J., & Jones, R. E. Forthcoming. Research in corporate social performance: What have we learned? In D. Burlingame and D. R. Youngs (Eds.), *Corporate philanthropy at the crossroads.* Bloomington, IN: Indiana University Press.

Worrell, D., Walters, B. & Coalter, T. 1995. Moral judgment and values in a developed and a developing nation: A comparative analysis. *Academy of Management Best Paper Proceedings:* 401–405.

Wright, R. 1994. *The moral animal: Evolutionary psychology and everyday life.* New York: Pantheon Books.

Wu, X. 1996. *Business ethical perceptions of business people in East China.* Paper presented at the Colloquium on Chinese and American Economic Ethics, Chinese Academy of Social Sciences, Institute of Philosophy, Beijing, July–August. Copy available from Dunfee.

Yannaca-Small, C. 1995. Battling international bribery: The globalization of the economy. *OECD Observer:* 16–18.

Yezer, A. M., Goldfarb, R. S., & Poppen, P. J. 1996. Does studying economics discourage cooperation? Watch what we do, not what we say or how we play. *Journal of Economic Perspectives,* 10(1): 177–186.

Index

absolutism, 21, 22, 54, 242
accountability, 9, 127, 221
accounting practices, 118, 136, 137, 204, 225
actions, 12, 86–88, 119
   discretionary, 254, 258
   future, 198, 199, 200, 202, 204
   stakeholder-related, 254–261
   See also behavior; cooperation/coopera-tive action; reasoned action theory
advertising and marketing, 88–89, 90, 102, 135
   authentic ethical norms and, 112–113, 141–142
   See also media
affirmative action, 104, 163, 181
agency theory, 251–252
Agle, B. R., 238, 239
agreements
   collective, 68–69
   economic, 66
   formal, 180–181
   hypothetical, 17, 18, 19, 26–27, 37
   implicit, 127, 146, 147, 148, 161, 187, 224, 241
   See also social contract for business ethics; social contracts/social contracts theory
Ajzen, I., 142
alcohol. *See* liquor industry
Alexy, R., 51
alternative concepts, 57, 221, 253
altruism, 26
   business practices and, 90–91, 94, 100, 173, 254–255, 257, 258
Analytic Hierarchy Process, 240
animal rights, 8, 163, 240, 256
anti-Semitism, 57, 58
arbitration. *See* principles for conflict resolution
Aristotle, 13, 25, 59, 129, 132–133, 195
Arrow, Kenneth, 228
Arthur Anderson accounting firm, 225
AT&T, 257

attitudes, 156, 165, 253
   aggregate/communal/majority, 104, 153, 160, 162, 163, 168
   as basis for identification of norms, 90–94
   behavior and, 142, 158
   changing nature (evolution) of, 6, 148, 158
   context-specific, 107, 109, 189–191
   within corporations, 99, 158, 160–165, 166
   development of, 139, 150
   ethical, 86–87, 160, 166
   ethical norms and, 153, 158, 160–165
   influence on generation of norms, 98, 102–103
   influences on, 99, 166–167
   research on, 105, 106–108, 109, 139, 142, 152, 156
   See also behavior; global business ethics; misinformation/misunder-standing of attitudes; personal precepts and standards
auctions, 41, 45, 96, 101, 163, 187–188
auditing functions, 225
authentic norms. *See* norms, authentic; norms, authentic ethical; norms, authentic global
autonomy, 25, 26, 35, 36, 37, 38, 166
Axelrod, R., 96–97

Baron, J., 31
Baumhart, R., 7
Becker, L. C., 144–145, 147
behavior, 156, 165
   appropriate, 151, 167–168
   attitudes and, 142, 156, 160
   business/organizational, 118, 124, 141, 144, 156, 160–165, 216–217
   codes of, 65, 99, 102, 144, 146, 147
   communal/majority, 162, 202–203
   influences on, 95, 97–98, 104, 108, 128, 139, 140, 141–142, 146, 147, 148–150, 160, 161

behavior (*continued*)
  justification for, 13, 16, 142, 158
  normative judgments about, 166
  rational, 35–36, 144–148
  research on, 105, 106–108, 109, 139,
    142, 152, 156
  unethical, 34, 84, 87–88, 104,
    108–109, 112, 124, 140, 141,
    154, 172, 216–217, 223, 225,
    256, 257
  See also actions; attitudes; coercion;
    cooperation/cooperative action;
    norms: behavioral; personal
    precepts and standards
benefits systems, 122, 125
Bentham, Jeremy, 12
bias, 91–92, 93, 104
  in decision making, 28, 194
  See also fairness
bidding for contracts, 213, 223
Bilsky, W., 65
biology, 11, 54, 153, 195
Blackstone, William, 79
Blagov, Y., 199
Blair, Tony, 244–245
Bliss, C., 228
Boatright, J. R., 250, 251
Boddewyn, J. J., 220, 221
Bok, Sissela, 52
Bond, M. H., 64–65
bounded economic rationality, 28–33, 36,
    37
bounded moral rationality, 28–33, 36, 37,
    38, 83, 84, 86, 100
  conflict of norms and, 44–46, 187–188,
    191
  stakeholder obligations and, 246
Bowie, Norman, 18
Branson, Richard, 77, 191
Brenner, S. N., 7, 240
Brent Spar oil facility, North Sea, 2, 3–4,
    5–6, 90, 94, 114–115, 188–189
Brewer, T. L., 220
bribery, 58, 61, 65, 78, 90, 92, 93, 112,
    135–137, 185, 187, 217, 220
  business ethics and, 151–152, 223–230
  economic efficiency of, 137, 138,
    228–229
  See also gift-giving and entertainment
Brickner, Balfour, 134
Buchholz, R., 13
business communities. *See* economic
    communities
business ethics, 1, 3, 4, 12–14, 17, 22, 31,
    47, 63–64, 83, 88, 98, 135, 144,
    147, 149, 163, 255, 257
  artifactual problem in, 14, 16, 31–32

  authentic norms and, 86–90, 166–167
  behavioral norms and, 90, 92, 94–98,
    144, 156–158, 160, 166, 173
  business-specific, 34–35, 128, 156
  codes of behavior and, 106–107, 108,
    139, 156–158
  context-specific, 107, 189–191
  cooperative action and, 128, 129
  core values in, 154–155, 161
  cultural influences on, 16, 32
  decision making and, 142, 173
  empirical/behavioral approach to, 9,
    10–12, 13, 24, 156
  extant agreements and, 20, 24
  hypernorms and, 135, 215–220,
    231–232
  implicit, 127–128, 187
  Integrative Social Contracts Theory
    (ISCT) and, 90, 139, 149,
    165–170
  integrative theory of, 10, 12, 24, 156
  management and, 7, 98, 139, 156–158
  moral free space and, 139–140
  normative approach to, 9, 10–12, 16,
    24
  political beliefs and activities and,
    165–168
  research, 9–12, 24, 47, 106–107, 108,
    156
  stakeholder obligations and, 235, 236,
    239, 243–244, 250, 257
  standards for, 105, 149, 161
  See also decision making; global busi-
    ness ethics; social contract for
    business ethics; social
    contracts/social contracts theory:
    business ethics and; stakeholder
    obligations
Business Ethics (Bowie), 18
business-government interface, 24, 63
business organizations, 60
business-political relationships, 167
business practices, 13, 134, 166
  authentic ethical norms for, 172
  competitive, 8, 102, 128, 135, 166,
    213, 225, 228, 245
  employment policies, 7, 24, 29–30, 33,
    128, 149, 253, 258
  global, 242–243, 245
  international, 66–67
  mergers and acquisitions, 180–181
  principles and standards for, 66–67,
    83–84, 168, 187, 259
  See also downsizing and layoffs; gift
    giving and entertainment;
    transactions
Business Roundtable, 109

Cameron, Rondo, 132
capitalism, 31, 123, 128–129, 246
Carroll, A. B., 253
Carter, Stephen, 15
Categorical Imperative, 14, 33
Caux Round Table (CRT), 60, 61, 66–67, 109, 259
Cava, A., 74–75, 192
Cavanaugh, G. F., 142
ceteris paribus. *See* economics/economic activity
child labor, 8, 42, 44, 56, 102, 229, 231–232
child psychology, 150
Chinese Value Survey, 64
choice, right of, 21, 25–26, 37, 38, 42, 81, 150, 166, 251. *See also* social choice analysis
choice-of-law, 183, 184
citizenship/citizenry, 79, 125, 199, 218
civil disobedience, 42
civil rights, 2, 80
Clarkson, M. B. E., 238
class distinctions, 129
coercion, 42, 43, 51, 90–92, 93, 103, 141, 161, 201
    cultural beliefs and principles and, 233
    in economic systems, 119
    of employees, 90–91, 94, 104
cognitive processes, 64, 67, 104
collective ownership systems, 129
common sense convictions. *See* conventional wisdom
communication, 55–56, 63
    within corporations, 99, 148–149
    voice as, 51, 163–164
communitarianism, 76, 80, 81
    moral free space and, 83–86
communities
    consent issues and, 162–163
    constituent, 186–187
    definition of, 39, 40, 98, 101
    divided opinions in, 168, 252–253
    ethical judgments and, 107, 160, 252–253
    microsocial, 44, 51
    national, 252, 253
    political will of, 157
    professional, 100–101
    relationships among, 179–181
    relevant, 114, 200, 201, 245, 252, 253, 254, 259, 260
    as source of authentic ethical norms, 98–102
    standards for, 8, 80, 84, 88
    structure of, 100–102, 180–181
    subcommunities, 199–200, 201

    See also economic communities; sociopolitical communities
compensation, principles of, 32
competition. *See* business practices: competitive
conduct. *See* actions; behavior; cooperation/cooperative action
confidentiality, 42, 86, 91, 100, 101, 172, 187, 202, 204. *See also* privacy issues
conflict, 135, 158, 190. *See also* norms: conflicting/competing; principles for conflict resolution
consensus, 253
    authentic ethical norms as, 166
    communal, 27, 60, 77, 86, 88, 90, 169, 189, 196, 262
    moral, 7, 77, 84, 158
    overlapping of doctrines, 56, 57
    social, 11
    in sociopolitical communities, 253–255
    for stakeholder obligations, 246
consent, 17, 18, 19, 21, 24–26, 41, 49–50, 140, 166, 246
    of accepting dissenters, 39, 43, 140, 141
    communal/majority, 12, 13, 38, 43, 44, 160–163, 167, 168, 169, 171
    implicit, 101, 161
    informed, 19, 68
    microsocial contracts and, 39, 41–43, 51
    in organizational moral free space, 160–165
    rights of exit and voice and, 41, 51
consequentialism, 12, 13, 20
consistency
    norms of, 60, 96, 140, 165, 172, 184, 188–189
    patterns of, 188–189
constituency statutes/actions, 186, 254, 261
consultants, 213, 223
contractarianism, 17, 137, 251
contracts. *See* agreements; macrosocial contracts; microsocial contracts; social contract for business ethics; social contracts/social contracts theory
conventional wisdom, 30–31, 95, 202, 236
convergence, 44, 63–64, 158
    of basic values, 57–59, 65, 66, 67
    of conflicting/competing norms, 89, 189
    hypernorms and, 50, 74–75, 76
    principle of, 50, 75, 76–77, 78, 153, 158

cooperation/cooperative action, 16,
        121–123, 125, 126, 127, 162
    in economic communities, 125–126,
        128
    ethical/moral, 18, 137
    among multinationals, 214
    support for, 123–124
    See also behavior
Coopers & Lybrand accounting firm, 225
corporate governance. See management
corporations, 11, 24, 31, 253
    codes of ethics and ethical behavior, 10,
        12–14, 45, 63, 86–88, 103–104,
        105, 106–107, 147, 156–158,
        167–168, 202, 214, 221, 261
    cooperative behavior in, 128, 129
    corporate culture/values, 35, 84, 85, 95,
        100, 141, 144, 169, 202, 217,
        254–255, 259
    disclosure policies, 255
    duties and obligations to shareholders,
        176, 250–251
    efficiency in, 30, 34
    environmental policies and concerns of,
        79, 86, 88, 135, 156–158,
        188–189, 256
    ethical responsibilities of, 7, 18–19, 113
    ethics programs, 63, 98–99, 144, 167,
        214, 230
    evolution of norms within moral free
        space of, 94–98, 156–158
    legal liability of, 159
    social responsibility of, 95, 159
    as source of authentic ethical norms,
        98–99, 100
    subcommunities within, 99
    subsidiaries, 102, 179–180, 183
    See also business ethics; business prac-
        tices; economic communities;
        global business ethics; manage-
        ment; multinationals; profit
        motive; stakeholder obligations;
        value(s): corporate
corruption, 119, 215, 218, 226, 228–229
    global business ethics and, 222–230
cosmopolitanism, 49, 218
cultural beliefs and principles, 34–36, 37,
        46, 80–81, 83, 125, 129, 148, 155
    codes of behavior and, 146, 231–233
    conflicts and overlaps among, 49, 56,
        57, 63, 64–65, 200
    core principles, 59
    diversity among, 49, 63, 85–86
    economy-based, 221, 222
    generation and evolution of norms and,
        246
    global business ethics and, 214–221
    stakeholder obligations and, 243

customers, 18, 34, 67, 85, 128, 134, 213
    social contracts with, 167
    See also stakeholder obligation

D'Amato, A., 50
Dawai Bank, 179
decision making, 6, 13, 95, 98, 147, 191
    bias in, 28, 194
    business ethics and, 142, 173, 229
    business-specific/economic, 29–30, 33,
        138, 152
    among conflicting/competing legitimate
        norms, 184–190, 193–207, 259
    context-specific, 32–33, 109, 189–191,
        193–194
    controversial judgments, 107
    effects of, 184, 185–186
    errors in, 4, 28
    ethical, 11–12, 30, 59, 87, 106–107,
        139–140, 141, 142, 144–147,
        169, 175, 178, 179, 183–184,
        193–194, 196
    evaluation scale for, 145–146
    hypernorms and, 54, 59–60, 169,
        181–182, 255–256
    information and, 6, 28, 30, 178, 188,
        191, 194, 195
    Integrative Social Contracts Theory
        (ISCT) and, 173, 175, 179,
        193–207
    models, 182, 195–196
    moral, 30–31, 33, 41–42, 59, 63, 95,
        152
    moral free space and, 38–39, 192
    by multinationals, 221
    norms for, 125, 175
    personal, 35, 182
    about stakeholder obligations, 259
    See also business ethics; problem solving
Defining Issues Test, 153
DeGeorge, Richard, 96, 220–221, 243, 247
democracy/democratic beliefs, 160, 166,
        167
deontology, 12, 13, 20, 23, 47, 145
Dern, D. P., 89
deterrence concept, 97
difference principle, 58–59
differential association theory, 141–142
disclosure, 8, 41, 83, 85, 124, 172, 173,
        180, 198, 205, 255
    incomplete, 124
    public opinion and, 112
    stakeholder obligations and, 255
    threat of, 91
discrimination, 61, 68, 75, 138, 149, 158,
        181, 238. See also bias; gender
        issues: discrimination; racism/racial
        issues

disinterested observer concept, 193–194
dissent, 47, 49, 140
    accepting dissenters, 39, 43, 140, 141
    against norms, 42–43, 115, 140
    in organizational moral free space,
        160–165
    within organizations, 160–165, 201
Di Tella, R., 228
divergence theory, 63, 64, 258
downsizing and layoffs, 24, 29–30, 33,
        128, 191, 253, 258. *See also* busi-
        ness practices: employment policies
drug testing of employees, 198, 199–200,
        207, 219
Duncan multiple range tests, 220
Dunlap, Al, 29, 33
DuPont Chemical, 175–176, 178, 260
duties and obligations, 118, 141, 151, 243
    of corporations, 18, 176, 250–251,
        253–255, 261
    derived from the efficiency hypernorm,
        119, 133–138
    of disclosure, 205
    ethical, 17, 100, 115, 138, 144, 158,
        163
    exclusion from, 163
    hypernorms and, 179, 248
    mandatory, 254, 259–260
    of necessary social efficiency, 118–121,
        130, 132
    public/social, 5, 159
    to shareholders/stakeholders, 144, 176,
        250–251
    See also management: ethical duties and
        obligations of; norms: legitimate
        (obligatory); stakeholder obliga-
        tions

economic communities, 8, 26, 28, 33, 36,
        83, 170, 172, 245
    choice of/membership in, 37, 38, 41, 119
    conflicting/competing norms in, 44–46,
        185
    diversity in, 47, 49
    efficiency in, 127
    ethical behavior in, 21, 37, 42, 46–47,
        123–124
    exit from, 41–43
    generation and evolution of norms in,
        21, 38–40, 43, 44, 45, 46, 47,
        89, 160
    microsocial, 39–40, 224
    moral free space and, 41, 46, 51, 246
    social good and, 118–121
    stakeholder obligations and, 249
    transaction-based, 101, 187–188
    See also economic institutions and
        systems

economic institutions and systems, 16,
        31–34, 47, 117–118, 133, 135, 136,
        137–138
    opportunity in, 68, 75, 80–81, 84, 117
    production, 127, 133
    rationality in, 18, 27, 28
    See also economic communities; Third
        World economies
economics/economic activity, 12, 17, 30,
        40, 45, 125, 132, 134–137
    bounded rationality and, 28–33, 36, 37,
        46
    cooperative, 125–126
    democratic, 136
    efficiency/efficiency concept of, 28, 30,
        33–34, 36, 37, 83, 85, 120, 128,
        129, 131, 136
    efficiency hypernorms and, 117–118
    ethical, 25–36, 37
    free-entry equilibrium, 228
    mechanisms of, 125, 228
    moral free space and, 43
    welfare issues, 117–118, 121, 125–126,
        228
    See also market economics; welfare,
        social and economic
economic theory, 26, 33, 125, 141, 171,
        195
    Marxist, 51, 136
    See also bounded economic rationality
efficiency/efficiency concept
    cultural independence of, 131–132
    economic, 38, 117–118, 122, 127–128,
        134, 138, 187, 228–229, 233
    economizing parameters of, 129, 131,
        132, 133, 136, 138
    measurement of, 135
    in microsocial contracts, 133, 137
    strategies for, 126–130, 131, 132–133,
        137
    See also hypernorms: efficiency/effi-
        ciency concept of; necessary
        social efficiency concept; social
        good concept: necessary and
        efficient components of
efficient breach concept, 157
egoism, 145
Elkington, John, 4
embezzlement, 225
empirical research. *See* research
empiricism, 59
employees, 186, 200, 260
    bribery and, 227–228, 230
    coercion of, 90–91, 94, 104
    discrimination against, 61
    displaced, 253, 257, 258
    ethical/unethical behavior of, 34, 172,
        223

employees (*continued*)
    protest of norms of business practices,
        42–43, 46, 87, 176
    rights of, 41, 121, 201, 247, 248
    social contracts with, 24, 167
    stakeholder obligations and, 238, 242,
        244, 252, 259
    voice of, 163, 164
    whistle-blowing by, 87–88, 164, 172
    See also business practices; downsizing
        and layoffs; drug testing of
        employees
Enderle, George, 217, 219
enforcement mechanisms, 123
environmental policies and concerns, 1–7,
        8, 67, 78–79, 135, 136, 137, 204,
        259
    authentic ethical norms and, 114–115,
        156–158
    influence on behavior, 150
    norms for, 139, 188–189
    stakeholder obligations and, 242, 247
    See also corporations: environmental
        policies and concerns of
epistemology, 59, 74, 76
Epstein, Richard, 16
equality principle, 74, 121, 166–167, 192
ethical theory, 8–9, 12–16, 19, 20, 24, 29,
        39, 55, 60, 65, 80–81, 146–148,
        155, 195
    alternative, 23
    analysis of, 24, 159
    as basis for hypernorms, 76
    business ethics and, 9–10, 24, 144, 169
    conflicting conceptions of, 6–7, 55
    formal, 150, 152
    liberal, 76
    universalist perspective of, 79–80
    See also hypernorms
ethics/ethical behavior, 6, 10, 37, 58–59,
        83, 85, 86, 103, 106, 196
    attitudes and, 86–87
    in business and economic communities,
        123–124, 136
    codes of, 38, 63, 84–85, 167, 202, 245
    community-based, 4, 15, 17, 24, 79–80,
        88, 217
    cultural beliefs and principles and,
        231–233
    discrimination and, 14, 75
    economic, 9, 13, 80, 244–245
    global, 15, 57, 66, 204
    influences on, 144, 147, 152, 159, 160
    law and, 9, 18, 140, 158, 159, 160
    of management, 153–156
    mandatory, 156, 254, 261
    norms of, 140–144, 156–158

    private *vs.* public responsibility, 5–6
    rational, 74–75, 144–148
    technology and, 168–169
    universal, 14, 16
ethnicity, 79, 80, 129, 149
ethnocentrism, 81
Etzioni, Amatai, 80, 134
European Community, 60, 245
European Union, 217
Evan, W. M., 13
exit
    from communities/organizations,
        41–43, 162–163, 164–165
    restricted, 196, 201
exit and voice
    in microsocial contracts, 41–43, 46, 51
    persecution and, 58
    protection of, by hypernorms, 54, 117
    relativism and, 170
    stakeholder obligations and, 246
ex post judgments, 60, 104, 105

fairness, 7, 14, 17, 32, 104, 120, 121, 134,
        146
    in business practices, 187
    through cooperative action, 121, 126,
        134
    under the law, 52, 68, 117
    in moral obligations, 162
    in society, 125, 127
    of treatment, 167–168
    See also bias; decision making; discrimi-
        nation; justice/justice theory;
        law(s)
false signaling of attitudes. *See* misinforma-
        tion/misunderstanding of attitudes:
        false signaling as cause of
family, 7, 14, 80, 129
    duties and obligations to, 137, 151
    freeholding, 131–132
    moral principles and, 27, 31, 146
favoritism, 137. *See also* nepotism
Federal Corporate Sentencing Guidelines,
        158
Ferrell, O. C., 142
Film Recovery Company case, 201
Fishbein, M., 142
Fisher, David, 230
Foreign Corrupt Practices Act, 13, 159,
        184, 225, 229
for-profit organizations, 5, 7, 8, 15, 107,
        121, 244. *See also* corporations;
        multinationals; organizations/orga-
        nizational structures; profit motive
forums, 183, 184
Frank, Robert, 19, 128, 154

fraud, 33, 123
Frederick, William, 10–11, 64, 74, 76, 154–155
free inquiry, 100
Freeman, R. E., 13, 170, 238, 239
free market concept, 119, 135, 138, 229, 231. *See also* market economics
free-riders, 133–134, 162
Friedman, Milton, 107, 245
Fritzsche, D. J., 142–145, 147, 148
Fukuyama, Francis, 129

game theory, 31, 32, 133, 231
Gauthier, David, 18
gender issues, 7, 74–75, 79
  discrimination, 34, 61, 64–65, 80–81, 90, 95, 147, 192, 233, 246
  equality, 74, 192
  research, 151
  See also sexual harassment
General Motors, 113–114
Getty Oil, 85
gift-giving and entertainment, 39, 83, 87, 90, 127, 141
  authentic ethical norms and, 113–114
  conflicting/competing norms and, 176–178, 182, 185
  cultural differences and, 178
  decision making about, 175
  implicit misunderstandings about, 137
  See also bribery; business ethics; business practices
Gilbert, D. R., Jr., 170
Gilligan, C., 151
global business ethics, 213–215, 233–234
  academic views of, 220–221
  cultural beliefs and principles and, 214–221
  Empire Type approach to, 217, 218
  Foreign Country Type approach to, 217, 218
  Global Type approach to, 217, 218, 219, 221–222
  hypernorms and, 215–220, 231–232
  Integrative Social Contracts Theory (ISCT) and, 215, 218, 222–230, 231–234
  Interconnection Type approach to, 217–218, 219
  management and, 233–234
  microsocial contracts and, 215–220
  moral free space and, 214, 215–220, 222, 223, 231, 232–234
  rights-based theories and, 216–217, 218, 227
  See also business ethics; multinationals

global contractors, 37, 39, 45–47
good, concept of, 44, 47, 76, 80
  individual, 118
  universal/communal, 129–130, 171
  See also social good concept
Goodpaster, K. E., 237, 241, 250, 254
goods and services, 25, 28, 117–118, 119, 121, 125, 130, 196, 204, 228–229. *See also* product liability issues
Green, Ronald, 13
Greenpeace organization, 2, 189
Gresham, L. G., 142
groups. *See* communities; corporations

H. B. Fuller organization, 247
H. J. Heinz, 103–104
Habermas, Jurgens, 51, 55, 56, 77
Haifu, Shen, 225
handshake. *See* social contracts/social contracts theory: implicit/informal
Hardin, R., 31
Hartman, E. M., 55, 76
Harvard Business Review, 7, 63
Heap, Hargreaves, 125
Hegarty, W. H., 147
Hegel, Georg, 59
Heimann, Fritz, 225
Helsinki Final Act, 64
Herkstroter, Cor, 1–2, 4, 15
Hewlett-Packard, 35
Hillman, A., 63
Hiroike, Chikuro, 65
Hitler, Adolf, 57, 58
Hobbes, 26, 27
Holloran, T. E., 250
honesty/integrity, 6, 33, 139, 154, 166, 189, 218. *See also* promise keeping; trustworthiness
Hooker, M., 12–13
Hosseini, J. C., 240
household, concept of, 131–132
human nature
  ethical behavior and, 80, 139–140, 153–156, 158–159
  value systems and, 10–11
human rights, 4, 6, 15, 61, 66, 67, 68, 227
  individual, 79
  See also rights-based theories
Husted, B. W., 75
Hutton, E. F., 159
hypernorms, 27, 41–43, 46, 68, 144, 149, 192, 214
  categories, 53
  community-based, 89, 255
  conflicting/competing norms and, 43–46, 163, 182, 185, 193, 204

hypernorms (*continued*)
  core, 59, 152, 256
  decision making and, 59–61, 169, 182, 193, 255–256, 259
  definition/nature of, 44, 54–61, 74, 76, 130, 131, 246
  duties and obligations under, 179, 248
  efficiency/efficiency concept of, 51, 117–118, 119, 130–132, 133–138, 172, 187, 188, 204, 226–230, 228
  global, 221, 249
  global business ethics and, 215–220, 231–232
  governing actions, 254, 260
  identification and validation of, 44, 50–51, 59, 60, 61–67, 76, 77, 78, 204
  in Integrative Social Contracts Theory (ISCT), 49–53, 77, 78, 171, 218, 230, 255
  mandatory legitimate, 260
  moral free space and, 49, 50, 152, 187
  presumptive, 50, 60–62, 67, 78–79
  procedural, 51, 54, 55, 117, 119, 187, 204
  recognition and, 79–81
  relativism and, 170
  social contract for business and, 43–44
  for social justice, 52, 56, 187
  sources of, 27, 50, 54–61, 74, 76, 77, 152, 179–181
  stakeholder obligations and, 240, 245–248
  structural, 51–52, 54, 55, 74, 78, 117, 138, 187, 188, 204, 205
  substantive, 52, 54–61, 63, 67–69, 74, 78, 117, 119, 187, 189, 204
  testing of, 75, 76, 171
  views about, 74–79
  violation of, 162, 178, 223, 226–230, 240, 247, 256

IBM, 35
identity, 79–80, 99
  national, 218, 219, 220
impact statements, 225
imperialism, ethical/moral, 176, 177, 182, 218, 230
incentive systems, 95, 104, 129, 164
individualism, 64, 79, 118, 166, 216, 217
industrial policies, 228
information
  availability of, 14, 123, 124, 135, 178
  decision making and, 6, 28, 30, 178, 188, 191, 194, 195
  false/misleading, 139, 165, 166
  informed consent and, 19, 68
  technology and, 169
  See also inside information/insider trading; misinformation/misunderstanding of attitudes
inside information/insider trading, 7, 16, 18, 95, 168, 179, 217
Integrative Social Contracts Theory (ISCT), 3, 12, 20, 38, 74, 92, 144, 162, 173
  analysis of, 192, 193–207
  application of, 54, 59, 76, 100, 112–116, 175, 191–193, 221
  authentic ethical norms in, 152, 155–156, 160, 168–170
  authentic norms in, 96, 114, 146, 170, 171, 226
  business ethics and, 90, 139, 149, 165–170
  communitarianism and, 81, 100, 101, 180
  consistency of norms with, 140, 168, 184, 257
  corporations and, 98–99
  decision making and, 173, 175, 193–207
  economic ethics and, 46–47
  ethical norms in, 43, 96, 160
  foundations of, 25–36
  global business ethics and, 215, 218, 222–234
  hypernorms and, 49–53, 77, 78, 171, 218, 230, 255
  law and, 160, 182–184
  legitimate norms, 44, 46–47
  moral free space and, 83–86, 140, 148, 170, 171, 175, 184, 218, 222
  moral psychology and, 152
  norm evaluation process, 175, 182–190
  pluralism *vs.* relativism in, 19–24, 170–172
  political dimensions of, 165–168
  priority rules, 184–193
  right of choice and, 21, 22, 81
  stakeholder obligations and, 235–236, 239, 242, 244–248, 250, 256, 259–262
  See also norms, legitimate ethical; norms, legitimate (obligatory); priority rules
intellectual property, 16, 33, 118, 135, 136, 137, 169, 187, 215
intermediaries, 96
international business and relations. *See* multinationals
International Chamber of Commerce, 60
International Labour Organization (ILO), 60, 62, 64

International News Service v. *Associated Press,* 16, 17
Internet, 88–89
intuition, 18, 166, 168
investments, 238, 251
    ethics of, 7–8, 134, 163, 172
    opportunism and, 123, 187

Jefferson, Thomas, 133, 227
Johnson & Johnson, 128, 237
Jones, T., 252
Jones, Thomas, 10, 11, 123, 128
Jones, William, 122–123, 127
J. P. Morgan & Co., 96
judgments. *See* decision making
jus cogens, 50
justice/justice theory, 10, 14, 19, 21, 51,
    57, 117, 126, 142, 145, 146, 153
    under the law, 149
    as necessary social good, 119, 120–121
    norms based on, 161
    social and political, 52, 56, 125
    See also fairness; law(s)

Kant, Immanuel, 12, 13, 14, 16, 27, 33,
    47, 59, 65, 76, 79, 146, 151, 155,
    227, 230, 261
Keeley, Michael, 18, 90
Keim, G., 63
Keynes, John Maynard, 125
kinship, 129
Kohlberg, Lawrence, 150–151, 152, 157,
    230
KPMG accounting firm, 225
Kung, Hans, 69
Kurland, N., 142

Lamott Core Drilling, 198, 200, 202, 205,
    206–207
language, 54–57, 89
law(s), 50, 60, 98, 118, 149, 150, 159,
    165, 183, 184, 214, 253
    anti-bribery, 225
    conflicting/competing standards and,
        182–184
    contract, 15, 85
    corporate, 241, 244, 254–255
    ethics and, 9, 18, 33, 86, 138, 140,
        156–159, 160
    fair treatment under, 52, 68, 117
    forum courts, 183
    influence of, on behavior, 95, 97–98,
        156–158, 160
    intellectual property, 136
    international, 50
    jurisdictions for, 183
    liability under, 133, 156–158

in moral free space, 156–160
procedural, 183
substantive, 182–183
systems and institutions of, 15, 52,
    120–121, 159, 160
theory of, 15–16
See also justice/justice theory; legal
    communities; product liability
    issues
lawyers, 99, 157, 158, 172, 202, 205
leadership, 8, 49, 94, 95, 120, 170
legal communities, 204–205, 247, 248,
    252. *See also* law(s)
legitimate norms, 44, 46–47. *See also*
    norms, legitimate ethical; norms,
    legitimate (obligatory)
Levi Strauss, 38–39
Levi-Strauss company, 186, 231–232
licensing of businesses, 247
liquor industry, 42, 88, 97, 102, 169
lobbying, 180
Locke, John, 17, 19, 20, 26, 227
Lockheed Corporation, 112, 227
loyalty, 128, 137, 147

MacIntyre, A. C., 80
macrosocial contracts, 6, 12, 19–20, 24,
    36–37, 43, 46–47, 51, 52, 152, 246
    conflicting/competing norms and,
        44–46, 161, 189
    consent issues and, 162
    generation and evolution of ethical
        norms and, 38–41, 84, 162
    hypernorms and, 51, 78
    legitimate norms and, 258
    priority rules and, 45–46, 188
    terms of, 41–46, 50
Maitland, I., 251–252
majoritarianism, 105, 161, 166, 167, 201.
    See also norms: majoritarian foun-
    dation of
management, 24, 63, 128, 236, 241, 244,
    251
    business ethics and, 7, 98, 139,
        146–147, 152, 166
    creativity in problem solving, 231–232
    ethical behavior of, 148, 152, 153–158,
        169, 172, 230
    ethical duties and obligations of, 17–18,
        141, 144–145, 158, 251, 252
    global business ethics and, 233–234
    Integrative Social Contracts Theory
        (ISCT) and, 259–262
    international, 66, 213–215, 219
    paradox, 250–251
    stakeholder obligations and, 248–250,
        255, 262

management (*continued*)
  values, 63, 219–220
  workplace safety standards and,
    178–179
  See also corporations
Mao Tse Tung, 226
market economics, 18–19, 28, 31, 51, 119,
    126, 128–129, 131
  capital, 255
  consumer, 123
  efficiency in, 233
  research, 62
  See also free market concept
Marx, Karl/Marxism, 51, 65, 84, 171, 226
Mayer, D., 74–75, 76, 77, 192
McCarthy, D. J., 191
McKee Corporation, 94, 95
media, 60, 102, 105, 112, 167, 202, 238,
    239. *See also* advertising and mar-
    keting
medical ethics, 9, 163, 172
membership, 26, 27, 41, 97, 98
  aggregate preferences of, 261
  in communities, 129–130, 165, 199
  consent issues and, 17, 140, 162–163,
    165
  dual or multi, 101, 102
  influence on generation of norms, 102,
    104
  limited duration of, 101
  represented in surveys, 107, 162
  See also psychological contracts
Merck, 100, 254–255, 257, 258
mergers and acquisitions, 180–181
Messick, David, 30, 91–92
metanorms, 96, 98
microsocial contracts, 6, 19–20, 24, 50, 78,
    126
  bribery and, 224
  community-specific, 36, 37
  consent to, 39
  in economic communities, 224
  efficiency strategies and, 133, 137
  global business ethics and, 215–220
  hypernorms and, 44, 46
  illegitimate, 6, 20, 21
  in Integrative Social Contracts Theory
    (ISCT), 20
  right to exit and voice in, 41–43, 46
  See also communities: microsocial
Microsoft, 100
Mill, John Stuart, 12, 79, 227, 230
minimalism, 56–57
misinformation/misunderstanding of atti-
    tudes, 104, 124
  false signaling as cause of, 90–94, 139,
    165, 166, 187, 190, 192, 193,
    253–254, 258–259

  norms and, 105, 113, 114
  See also information
Mitchell, R. K., 238, 239
mobility, restricted, 165
Molander, E. A., 7
monitoring mechanisms, 123, 128, 241,
    251
monopolies, 126, 128, 220
moral free space, 36, 38–41, 54, 169
  authentic ethical norms in, 140,
    158–160
  business ethics and, 139–140
  community/communitarian, 81, 86,
    181, 184
  conflicting/competing norms in, 175,
    179, 182, 259–260
  decision making and, 192
  in economic communities, 43, 46, 51,
    246
  ethical implications of, 112–116
  evolutionary psychology and, 152,
    153–156
  global business ethics and, 214,
    215–220, 222, 223, 231,
    232–234
  hypernorms and, 44, 49, 50, 152, 187
  instrumental value of, 172–173
  in Integrative Social Contracts Theory
    (ISCT), 83–86, 140, 148, 175,
    184
  moral psychology and, 150–153
  norms in, 94–98, 139–140, 190–191
  organizational, 160–165
  political dimensions of, 165–168
  psychological contracts and, 148–150
  role of law in, 156–160
  self-determination concept and, 68
  stakeholder obligations and, 253–254
  universalism and, 170–172
  validity of, 79, 140
morality/moral principles, 22, 27, 28,
    30–31, 33, 54, 55, 56, 57, 65, 76,
    80, 230
  business, 83
  collective, 18, 20–21, 27
  of communities, 64, 172
  of conflicting/competing norms, 179
  economic, 37
  extralegal, 158
  in global business ethics, 218–219
  law and, 160
  minimal, 55–57
  personal, 34–36
  rational, 58, 59
  rules of, 37, 38, 45
  thick/thin structure of, 14, 17, 37,
    43–44, 55, 56
  See also bounded moral rationality

Morals by Agreement (Gauthier), 18
More, Thomas, 129
Morning Baking Corporation, 198, 199,
    200, 202, 204, 205
multiculturalism. *See* cultural beliefs and
    principles
multinationals, 3, 5, 56, 65, 100, 245
    competition among, 166, 220
    cooperation among, 214
    environmental policies and concerns of,
        114–115, 215
    ethical duties and obligations of, 5–6,
        18, 96, 247
    guidelines for, 64, 220–221
    Integrative Social Contracts Theory
        (ISCT) and, 230–234
    political responsibility of, 15
    relations with host government, 96,
        215, 220, 221, 232, 243
    social responsibility of, 15
    stakeholder obligations and, 243
    See also corporations; global business
        ethics; profit motive

Nadelmann, E. A., 65
NAFTA, 217
national business organizations, 245
National Socialism, 171
nation-states, 40, 75, 89, 102, 136, 168,
    199, 217–219, 227, 228, 245, 248,
    257. *See also* social institutions and
    structures; sociopolitical communi-
    ties
necessary goal strategies, 126
necessary goods. *See* goods and services;
    social good concept
necessary social efficiency concept,
    117–121, 130, 132, 138
    cultural independence of the efficiency
        hypernorm, 131–132
    duties derived from the efficiency hyper-
        norm, 133–138
    limits on strategies, 132–133
    strategic implications of, 121–131
negotiation, 108, 123, 124
Nelson, Julienne, 77, 135, 191–192
nepotism, 232, 233. *See also* favoritism
Nichols, Philip, 65, 226
Nigeria, 2–4, 5–6, 15, 29
nihilism, normative, 56
nongovernmental organizations, 60, 225,
    228
Noonan, J. T., 65
normative theory, 54, 149, 166, 235, 236,
    237, 240, 242, 244, 252, 253
norms, 11, 144, 204
    alternative, 22, 192, 253
    ambiguity of, 77, 189–190, 196

authentic, 38–40, 41, 43–45, 49, 77,
    86–96, 102–116, 142, 144, 146,
    148, 149, 169, 192, 195,
    202–205, 226, 246, 261
authentic ethical, 95, 98–102, 112–116,
    139, 140, 149, 153, 155–156,
    159, 162, 165, 166, 168–170,
    245, 252
authentic global, 215, 221
behavioral, 88–89, 90–94, 146–147,
    158, 161, 172, 196
business-specific, 19, 83, 86–90, 97,
    133, 139–140, 156–158, 164,
    167–168
changing nature (evolution) of, 84, 85,
    92–93, 94–98, 99, 102–103,
    113, 139, 155–156, 163, 164,
    170, 246
community-based, 91, 92–93, 98–102,
    144, 161, 170, 185–186, 196,
    199–200, 206, 252, 255, 258,
    262
community-generated, 40, 44, 45, 50,
    84, 86, 88, 89, 94–98, 140, 155,
    163–166, 179, 180, 246
compliance with, 140, 141, 142,
    156–158, 164
conflicting/competing, 43–46, 47,
    83–84, 89, 99, 101, 114, 161,
    163, 170, 175, 179–181, 182,
    184–193, 195–198, 205–207,
    246, 248–249, 252, 256–259
conflicting/competing legitimate, 257,
    259
consistent/compatible, 22, 96, 140, 165,
    172, 184, 188–189, 192, 195,
    196, 221, 222, 247, 253, 258
decision making and, 184, 195–198
defined, 46–47
dominant, 192, 206, 251
economic, 39, 130
efficiency, 192, 196
ethical, 19, 21, 32, 36, 41, 45, 47, 77,
    83–90, 106, 107, 112–113, 133,
    139–144, 160, 166
extant, 163
false/corrupt, 57, 103–104, 106, 222
formal, 126, 133, 152, 196
formulation specifications, 115–116
generation and evolution of, 38,
    102–103, 155–156, 161,
    163–164, 170, 179, 180, 187,
    191, 201, 246
global, 65, 74, 186–187, 204
identification and validation of,
    102–112, 155, 161, 162, 166,
    189, 191, 196, 200, 202, 251
informal, 84, 126–127

norms (*continued*)
    justice-based, 161
    legitimate ethical, 239, 245
    legitimate (obligatory), 42, 44–47, 149,
        156, 161, 165, 178, 179, 182,
        195, 204–207, 221, 222, 226,
        248, 251, 254
    majoritarian foundation of, 41, 58,
        102, 103–104, 161, 172
    mandatory, 248–250, 252, 254, 255,
        260–261
    microsocial, 78, 133, 137, 138, 226
    moral, 12, 28, 32, 36, 38, 51, 57–58,
        66, 124, 146, 160
    moral free space and, 85–86, 94–98,
        112–116, 139–140, 191, 222
    multiple, 195, 200
    national, 146
    organizational, 148, 156–158, 160–165
    overlapping, 200
    permissive, 248, 249
    presumptive, 103, 105, 106, 182, 195,
        202–203
    priority rules for, 184–193
    procedural, 12, 68, 103, 114, 204
    protest of (voice), 42–43, 46
    published, 201, 202
    relevant, 199–200, 247–248, 250, 251,
        252
    replacement of, 169
    "second-order," 50, 78, 130
    social, 12, 90–94, 113, 127, 158
    social-contract-based, 142, 149
    sources of, 98–102, 200
    stakeholder obligations and, 239, 243,
        245, 246, 248, 249, 250–251,
        252–253, 256
    structural, 204
    subjective, 142
    subsidiary, 96
    testing of, 39, 42, 44, 102, 103,
        105–106, 153, 155, 165, 175,
        178, 182–190, 191, 195,
        196–198, 201, 202, 204, 205
    transcultural, 67, 68, 79, 227
    universal, 81, 126, 140, 258
    variations in, among corporations, 99,
        115
    violation of, 15–16, 43, 156–158, 165,
        196, 204, 207, 254
    voice and, 163–164
    See also standards

obligations. *See* duties and obligations
opportunism, 34, 91–92, 123, 134,
    187–188
opportunity
    economic, 68, 75, 80–81, 84, 117

    right to, 117–118, 127
organizational ethics. *See* business ethics
Organization of American States (OAS),
    60, 61
Organization of Economic Cooperation
    (OECD), 60, 61, 64, 187, 225, 229
organizations/organizational structures, 95,
    129
    consent and dissent within, 160–165,
        201
    cooperative action and, 18, 121–122,
        123
    fairness as goal in, 120
    global, 18, 40
    implicit social contracts in, 140, 156
    informal, 98
    moral development of employees and,
        152
    psychological contracts and, 149
    See also norms: organizational
outsourcing, 8, 38–39
overriding factors concept, 60, 144, 149,
    172, 224, 247

Paine, L. S., 158, 159
Pastin, M., 12–13
Pava, M. L., 171
Pell Grants, 98
Penzoil, 84–85
personal precepts and standards, 34–36,
    37, 38, 50, 64, 91, 142, 182, 217
    business-specific, 35
    codes of behavior and, 146, 147
    development of, 150
    ethical, 47, 80
    See also attitudes; behavior; preferences
philanthropy. *See* altruism
Phillips, R. A., 162, 168
philosophical beliefs and principles, 34–36,
    44, 46, 56, 57, 58, 60, 204
    core principles, 59
    ethical theory and, 65
    hypernorms and, 50, 68–69
    moral norms and, 51
Piderit, J. J., 120
Plato, 129
pluralism, 19, 22–24, 49, 147, 170
Poindexter, G. C., 192
policies (general discussion), 17, 95, 119,
    126, 135, 224, 248–250
political beliefs and activities, 3, 16, 227
    bribery and, 226–230
    coercion of, 43
    in communities, 204
    conflicting/competing norms and,
        184–185
    economic welfare and, 118, 125
    ethics and, 31

freedom of, 80, 117
hypernorms and, 50, 117
institutions of, 27–28, 40
moral free space and, 165–168
stakeholder obligations and, 243–244,
    247
Political Liberalism (Rawls), 125
political will, 157, 230
Politics (Aristotle), 132
Posner, Eric, 158
poverty, 118, 138, 229, 254
predictability, 137, 142, 228
pre-ecological economism, 135
preemption strategies, 50, 55
preferences, 26–27, 30, 147, 150, 193
    aggregate/communal, 260–261
    moral, 84, 86
    personal, 41–43, 47
    rules, 185
    See also attitudes; personal precepts and
        standards
prescriptive concepts, 9, 24
presumptions, 90, 92. *See also* norms: pre-
    sumptive
Prevost, R., 78
pricing policies, 228–229, 231
"Principles for Business" (Caux Round
    Table), 61, 66–67, 259
principles for conflict resolution, 15, 16,
    44, 55, 56, 179, 181–182, 185,
    191–193, 206–207, 258–259, 261
    application of, 184–191
    basic nature of, 182–184
    concerning stakeholder claims,
        238–239, 240, 245
    concerning stakeholder obligations,
        250, 252, 254–255, 256–259,
        261–262
    cultural differences and, 185
    global business ethics and, 214–215
    norms for, 83, 190
    See also problem solving
priority rules, 12, 45, 46, 47, 77, 102, 175
    for choosing among conflicting/compet-
        ing norms, 170, 184–193, 258
    in global business ethics, 215
    macrosocial contracts and, 45–46, 188
    in stakeholder obligation claims,
        247–248, 256–259
    See also rules (general discussion)
prisoners' dilemma. *See* cooperation/coop-
    erative action
privacy issues, 89, 139, 169, 172, 219. *See*
    also confidentiality
private property/property rights, 14,
    15–16, 17, 20, 25, 51, 52, 68, 118,
    125–126, 128–129
    stakeholder obligations and, 241, 244

privatization, 201
problem solving, 147–148, 164
    through cooperative action, 118, 121
    See also principles for conflict
        resolution
production economies, 135, 137
productivity, 121–122, 129, 133–134
product liability issues, 124, 128, 189–190,
    237, 241, 247, 256. *See also* law(s):
        liability under
profit motive, 77, 100, 115, 216–217, 228,
    244, 245, 253
    bribery and, 61, 230
    business ethics and, 255
    multinationals, 253
    stakeholder obligations and, 254–255
promise keeping, 25, 28, 33–34, 118, 127,
    139, 172. *See also* trustworthiness
proof, social, 97
property. *See* private property/property
    rights
propriety
    of actions, 86–88
    of norms, 166, 180
proxies, 90, 92, 103–104, 113, 202, 204
    for decision making, 193, 195
    for evidence of norms, 105, 106,
        109–112
psychological contracts, 148–150. *See also*
    membership
psychology, 148
    ethical decision making and, 30, 63,
        139–140
    evolutionary, 152, 153–156
    moral, 150–153
    social, 64–65
public policies, 113, 167–168, 248–250
public resources, 121–122, 127, 130–131,
    135, 137, 228, 229, 254
public will, 160
Puffer, S. M., 191
punishment systems, 44, 122, 161, 225

quality of life, 7, 38, 123
Quinn, D. P., 252

racism/racial issues, 7, 78, 79, 95, 149,
    158, 181, 214, 238. *See also* dis-
        crimination
Randall, D. M., 142
rational behavior. *See* behavior: rational
rationalism in ethics, 74–75
rationality
    authentic norms and, 114
    See also bounded moral rationality
rationalization, moral, 80
Rawls, John, 14, 17, 19, 26, 30, 56, 57,
    59, 69, 79, 120, 121, 125, 134, 227

reasonable doctrines theory, 56
reasoned action theory, 142–144
reason/reasoning, 74, 76
  behavior and, 144–148
  for decision making, 195–196
  development of, 150, 152–153
  errors in, 28
  ethical/moral, 144, 153
  moral, 230
recognition, 79–81, 83, 100
regulations, 34, 168, 179, 217
Reidenbach, R. E., 145–146
relativism, 19–24, 54, 57, 58, 77, 140, 145,
    214, 218, 233
  moral free space and, 170–172
religious beliefs and principles, 26, 27, 28,
    34–36, 37, 46, 56, 57, 60, 65, 83,
    125
  as basis for communities, 171
  bribery and, 226
  community-generated norms and, 94,
    171
  convergence of basic values, 65, 66
  core principles, 59
  differences in, 58–59
  discrimination and, 149
  economic norms and, 39, 103
  global business ethics and, 221
  hypernorms and, 50
  moral free space and, 171
Republic (Plato), 129
research, 54, 62, 63, 64, 96, 104, 108, 109,
    142, 144, 150
  on attitudes and behavior, 105,
    106–108, 109, 139, 142, 152,
    156
  on business ethics, 9–12, 24, 47,
    106–107, 108, 156
  on gender issues, 151
responsibility. See duties and obligations
restraint, duty of, 134, 163, 165
reward systems, 122, 133, 134
Ricardo, David, 226
Richardson, H. S., 190
rights-based theories, 10, 13, 65, 66, 75,
    78, 142
  ethical decision making and, 147
  exit and voice privileges, 41–43, 46,
    164
  global business ethics and, 216–217,
    218, 227
right/wrong behavior, 8, 146, 149, 150,
    166
  authentic norms and, 204
  in global business ethics, 218
  principles of, 27, 253

Ringer, R. C., 193
risk, 201, 241, 243, 249
  assessment, 178
  management, 159
  moral, 31
Robertson, D. C., 63, 147
Robin, D., 145–146
Rokeach, Milton, 219–220
Rokeach Value Survey, 64
Ross, W. D., 147
Rousseau, Denise M., 148, 149, 167
Rousseau, Jean-Jacques, 227
Rowan, J. R., 51, 54
Royal Dutch Shell, 1–7, 8, 15, 29, 90, 94,
    114–115, 188–189
rules (general discussion), 41, 91, 108, 126
  of argumentation, 51
  of engagement, 55, 56
  social, 44, 150
  See also principles for conflict resolu-
    tion; priority rules
Rynning, H., 76, 77

Saaty, T. L., 240
safety standards. See workplace: safety
    standards of
Salbu, S. R., 253
Salomon Brothers scandal, 159
sanctions, 133
Saro-Wiwa, Ken, 2, 29
Schepple, Kim, 17, 18
Scherer, A. G., 74, 78
Schlegelmilch, B., 63
Schwartz, S. H., 65
screening, 257
Seagram's, 88, 102
search mechanisms, 123
security issues, 199
self-determination concept, 68
self-interest, 124, 128, 133, 134, 135, 185
Sen, Amartya, 121
sensitive payments. See bribery
sexual harassment, 90, 92, 160–161, 163,
    232–233. See also gender issues
shareholders, 18, 34, 254
  duties and obligations to, 144, 176,
    250–251
  profits/wealth, 29, 30, 107, 156, 245
  social contracts with, 167
  See also stakeholder obligations;
    stakeholders
Shell, G., 159
Sidgwick, Henry, 79
Simon, Herbert, 30
Sims, H. P., 147
situational moderators, 152

slavery, 76, 78, 119, 132–133, 160, 165
smart cheater concept, 123, 154
Smith, Adam, 65, 134–135, 138, 226
smuggling, 220
social choice analysis, 191–192. *See also*
    choice, right of
social contract for business ethics, 18–19,
    24, 25, 36–38
    conflict among norms, 44–46
    exit and voice, 41–43, 46
    foundations of, 25–36
    hypernorms and, 43–44
    moral free space and, 38–41, 186
    See also business ethics
social contracts/social contracts theory,
    5–9, 18–19, 24, 93, 151, 152,
    155–156, 165, 252
    ambiguity in, 189–190
    breach of, 147, 167
    business ethics and, 8, 18–19, 24,
        127–128, 140, 144, 155–156,
        167–168
    changing nature of, 7, 15
    community-generated, 100, 149
    ethical norms for, 16–18, 142
    formal, extant, explicit ("micro"), 6,
        17, 19, 20
    hypothetical ("macro"), 19, 37
    implicit/informal, 1, 6, 11, 17, 19, 20,
        24, 37–38, 89, 126–128, 146
*Social Contract Theory of Organizations,
    A* (Keeley), 18
social good concept, 117–118, 121,
    129–130, 172
    necessary and efficient components of,
        117–121, 130, 132, 138
    See also good, concept of; welfare,
        social and economic
social institutions and structures, 14, 17,
    27–28, 108, 125, 126, 252
    defects in, 134
    economizing parameters of, 129, 131,
        132, 133
    mode of production and, 137
    organization of, 131–132
    organization and activities, 40, 51,
        85–86
socialization, 64–65
social status, 153
sociopolitical communities, 112, 246, 247,
    248, 250–255
    stakeholder obligations and, 256–259
    See also nation-states
Solomon, Robert, 13
specification techniques, 190
SS United States, 214

stakeholder obligations, 144, 235–236, 248
    claims, 236–237, 238–242, 248, 250,
        253–255, 260
    criticisms of, 235, 243–244
    to customers, 259
    definitions of stakeholders and, 237,
        238–239
    discretionary action of corporations
        and, 254, 255, 256–259
    divisions of, 260–261
    global, 236, 242–243
    hypernorms and, 240, 245–248
    implications of, 235, 250–259
    implications for management and
        public policy, 248–250
    Integrative Social Contracts Theory
        (ISCT) and, 235–236, 239, 242,
        244–248, 250, 256, 259–262
    justification for, 236, 239
    multi-fiduciary stakeholder analysis,
        237, 241, 251
    norms for, 239, 243, 245, 246, 248,
        249, 250, 256
    organizational response to, 253–255
    strategic stakeholder analysis, 237, 241,
        251, 254, 260
    theories of, 236–243, 244–248,
        250–259, 261
    See also business ethics; shareholders
stakeholder theory. *See* stakeholder obliga-
    tions
stakeholders, 11, 34, 67, 192, 199
    ethical norms of the corporation and,
        114, 237, 241, 244–245
    relations with organization, 260
    values of, 254
    See also customers; shareholders
standards
    of behavior, 51, 84, 259
    of business ethics, 8, 83–84, 113, 149,
        161
    community, 8, 175–176, 185, 219
    conflicting, 175–179
    cultural, 81, 146
    ethical, 55, 83–84, 86, 93, 105, 159,
        160, 214, 259
    formal organizational, 99
    formation of norms for, 16, 39
    global, 60, 204, 243, 249
    legal, 159
    living, 122–123
    minimal, 178
    moral, 158, 159, 219, 225
    nonoptional, 248–249
    peremptory, 50
    personal, 91

standards (*continued*)
    preemptory, 55
    traditional, 146
    violations of, 159, 161, 225, 259–260
    See also norms
Standell, Barbara, 167
Steidlmeier, Paul, 135
Steinmann, H., 74, 78
Sternberg, Elaine, 241
strangers, 80, 84, 124
Strong, K. C., 193
surveys, 105, 106, 107–109, 162, 202
SustaiNability, 4

Taka, I., 77, 191, 192
Tanaka, prime minister of Japan, 112, 227
taxation, 198, 200, 206–207, 225, 244, 247
Taylor, Charles, 44, 50, 79, 80–81
technology, 95, 96, 129, 135, 168–169
teleological theory, 13, 76
terrorism, 237, 238, 239, 240, 256
Texaco, 84–85
third-party contracts, 149, 185
Third World economies, 5, 137, 138, 201, 230
    mandatory norms and, 259–260
    stakeholder obligations and, 243, 245
    See also economic institutions and systems
thought experiments, 26, 96, 202, 204, 226
time sensitivity, 216
tipping practice, 136, 140–141, 213
tobacco industry, 7–8, 42, 90, 112–113, 169
totalitarianism, 172
Towards a Global Ethic, 66
transactions, 90, 101, 162
    cost of, 34, 42, 229
    decision making and, 184–185, 188–189
    economic, 154, 187–188
    efficiency in, 122, 134, 138, 187
    global, 154, 187, 225, 232
    mergers and acquisitions, 180–181
    rules governing, 187–188, 258
    See also business practice
transcultural concepts, 6, 14, 47, 130, 136, 178
Transparency International, 60, 61, 225
transparency test, 191
Trevino, Linda, 10, 11, 141, 142, 144, 152
trust, 33–34, 67, 89–90, 118, 123, 128, 129, 134, 154

trustworthiness, 25, 33, 128, 154. *See also* honesty/integrity; promise keeping
truth, 57, 58, 62, 187, 218

Ukrop's Super Markets, 94, 95
Umezu, M., 77
uncertainty, 31, 33, 36, 37
unemployment, 125–126
Union Carbide, 102, 243, 260
unions and strikes, 237, 241, 252
unique identity concept, 79–80
United Nations, 66, 69
United Technologies-Skorsky Aircraft, 176–177
Universal Declaration of Human Rights (United Nations), 66, 69
universalism, 21–22, 49, 57, 64, 79–80, 230, 243, 246, 257
    concept of good and, 129–130, 171
    ethical, 14, 16
    moral free space and, 170–172
    norms of, 81, 126, 140, 258
    principles of, 204, 249
    See also value(s): universal
user primacy, 168
utilitarianism, 10, 11, 16, 23, 27, 29, 65, 142, 144–145, 147, 151, 155
Utopia (More), 129

value-adding activities, 220–221
value(s), 164
    as basis for hypernorms, 27, 76, 152
    changing nature (evolution) of, 259
    community/group, 159, 160, 168
    conflicting/competing, 181
    core, 186, 259–260
    corporate, 154–155, 214, 219–220, 250, 258
    cultural, 10–12, 85, 86, 155
    efficiency and, 120
    ethical, 112, 147, 154–155, 159, 160
    individual/personal, 64, 86–88, 147–148, 217
    natural, 74, 76, 154
    preferences, 35
    social, 120
    systems, 57
    transcultural, 231
    universal, 60, 64–65, 67, 80, 87, 100, 123, 219–220, 221–222
Values, Nature and Culture in the American Corporation (Frederick), 10
Value Scale, 219–220
Velasquez, M., 159
Vidaver-Cohen, D., 95

virtue ethics, 12, 23, 47, 59, 76, 260
vision-value statements, 221
Vogel, David, 229
voice, 163, 164. *See also* exit and voice: in
  microsocial contracts
voluntarism, 24, 165

Walzer, Michael, 44, 56, 57, 68
Wartick, S. L., 64
Watchdog Incorporated, 198, 199–200,
  202, 205, 207
wealth
  distribution, 38, 229
  generation, 38
  personal, 26, 129, 132
  shareholder, 156, 245, 246

Weaver, Gary, 10, 11
Weber, J., 152
welfare, social and economic, 128, 137
  aggregative, 119, 121, 122–123,
    125–129, 131, 137
  hypernorms for, 51, 52, 56
whistle-blowing, 87–88, 164, 172
Williams, B., 80
Wolf, Susan, 79
Wood, D. J., 238, 239
workplace, 90, 91, 95, 148, 151
  safety standards of, 44, 62, 64, 68, 102,
    147, 164, 175–179, 201, 204,
    229, 242–243, 249–250, 256,
    259–260
Wright, Robert, 153

About the Authors

Thomas Donaldson is the Mark O. Winkelman Professor at The Wharton School of the University of Pennsylvania and the director of the Wharton Ethics Program. He is also a Senior Fellow of the Olsson Center for Ethics at the Darden School of the University of Virginia. He has lectured and consulted many corporations, including the American Medical Association, AT&T, Bankers Trust, EDS, IBM, the International Monetary Fund, Johnson & Johnson, J. P. Morgan, Motorola, NYNEX, Shell International, Walt Disney, Western Mining Company–Australia, and the World Bank.

Professor Donaldson has written broadly in the area of business values and professional ethics. Among his authored or edited books is *Ethics in International Business,* winner of the 1998 SIM Academy of Management Best Book Award. His articles have appeared in publications such as the *Academy of Management Review, Harvard Business Review, Ethics,* and *Economics and Philosophy.* Professor Donaldson is a founding member and past president of the Society for Business Ethics, and a member of the editorial boards of a number of journals, including the *Academy of Management Review* and *Business Ethics Quarterly.*

Thomas W. Dunfee is the Kolodny Professor of Social Responsibility and director of the Carol and Lawrence Zicklin Center for Business Ethics Research at The Wharton School of the University of Pennsylvania, where he chaired the Legal Studies Department for many years. He has consulted widely; served as an expert witness; and been a judge for several ethics awards, including the American Business Ethics Awards and those given by Better Business Bureaus and *Business Ethics Magazine.* He has also served as president of the Academy of Legal Studies in Business and president of the Society for Business Ethics. In 1991, Professor Dunfee received the Distinguished Senior Faculty Award for Excellence from the Academy of Legal Studies in Business.

He has written numerous books and has published articles in a variety of journals, including the *Academy of Management Review, American Business Law Journal, Business and Professional Ethics Journal, Business Ethics Quarterly, California Law Review, Economics and Philosophy, Journal of Business Ethics, Journal of Marketing,* and *Northwestern Law Review.* Professor Dunfee is on the editorial board of several journals, among them *Business Ethics Quarterly* and *Journal of Business Ethics,* and he served as editor-in-chief of the *American Business Law Journal.*